Challenge and Decision

CHALLENGE

Political Issues

◂ SECOND EDITION ▸

HARPER & ROW, PUBLISHERS

AND DECISION

of Our Time

REO M. CHRISTENSON
Miami University (Ohio)

NEW YORK, EVANSTON, AND LONDON

CHALLENGE AND DECISION: Political Issues of Our Time.
Second Edition.

Library of Congress Catalog Card Number: 67-11643

To

MAY DOOLING

Little known but much loved

CONTENTS

PREFACE

This second edition of *Challenge and Decision* was hastened by President Lyndon B. Johnson's regal indifference to the impact of his program on books about public policy! The massive legislative output of the Eighty-ninth Congress, in response to massive Presidential pressures, virtually compels revision of every book that seeks to keep the reader abreast of leading national problems and controversies. It is not that the President has solved so many problems but that his efforts to do so have been of a magnitude that demands attention.

Because *Challenge and Decision* seeks to focus on problems of enduring rather than transient importance, much of the material in this edition is drawn from its predecessor. The struggle for racial equality, "right-to-work" laws, the place of labor unions, the farm budget, the federal role in education (including parochial schools), the "welfare state," full employment, inflation and disarmament—these will concern the responsible citizen throughout the 1960s and probably well beyond.

This edition, however, gives special attention to the cultural factors that handicap the Negro's drive for full equality, the problem of housing discrimination, the development of the poverty program in general and Appalachia in particular. The British National Health Service is given extensive treatment, as is the shift in agricultural policy. The background of the welfare state is traced; more space is devoted to our historic efforts to grapple with full employment. New facets of old problems, as well as factual updating, are introduced throughout. A greater effort is made to demonstrate that broad-gauged political developments, rather than argumentative superiority, usually determine the outcome of policy struggles. (The democrat has faith, however, that rationality and the more decent human impulses are not unrelated to the changing expressions of political power.)

As before, the issues are discussed in terms of their roots, their growth, their dimensions, the choices we face, and the arguments that nourish or challenge those choices.

Who can claim objectivity in such a value-ridden field? I have opinions, and these opinions protrude from time to time. I have made a determined attempt, nonetheless, to present fairly the case for causes that least appeal to me.

An effort has been made to reproduce not only the arguments but the characteristic phraseology employed by contending camps. If this has led to occasional repetition, it is because the disputants involved frequently utter similar war cries in supporting or attacking various proposals having a common ideological core.

I would like to express my indebtedness to the editors and writers of leading contemporary periodicals that deal with national public policies, and which have contributed so much to this book. Long an enthusiastic addict of American magazines, I am particularly indebted to *The Atlantic Monthly, Commentary, Current, Fortune, Harper's Magazine, The New Republic, The New York Times Magazine, The Progressive, The Public Interest, The Reporter,* and *The Saturday Review*. How impoverished the American political scene would be without these journals!

If this book helps readers form more well-considered opinions on national policies, it will have served its major purpose. If it also helps shatter a few disabling myths, so much the better.

In conclusion, I wish to note my appreciation to Miss Barbara Gagel, whose sterling assistance during an unusually hectic period went far toward preserving my sanity.

REO M. CHRISTENSON

Oxford, Ohio
October, 1966

CHAPTER

◂ 1 ▸

RACE AND RIGHTS:
Yesterday, Today, and Tomorrow

Among the enduring and insistent issues confronting this generation, perhaps none has been of greater moment than the struggle to insure a growing measure of political, economic, and social equality to more than 22 million Americans—the Negroes. Our failure to accord them the dignity and equality that are the birthright of every American has cost us dearly. It has deprived us, to an appalling degree, of creative abilities and productive potentialities among more than 11 percent of our people. It has led to a combination of bitterness, alienation, frustration, and apathy among those same citizens. It seriously impaired our capacity to command the respect of nonwhite countries and complicated our efforts to guide them into the political and economic channels we believe will promote the interests of human freedom and welfare. It armed the Soviet Union with its most effective cold-war instrument—the propaganda of devastating truth. And it took its toll of the nation's spiritual resources—for no nation with our pretensions to democratic and religious ideals can do what was done to the Negro without practicing gravely destructive moral evasions and hypocrisies.

The urgency and gravity of the problem broke upon America like a flood in 1963. Mass Negro demonstrations throughout the nation, repeated outbreaks of violence, a new and determined militancy on the part of Negroes everywhere, the demand for full and equal rights now—these took the nation by surprise and catapulted the "Negro problem" to the forefront of national issues. Writing in 1963, Newspaper columnist (and CBS newsman) Eric Sevareid described developments in these moving and prophetic words:

> By its dominant voices, its most unforgettable faces and its chief acts of bravery does a generation recognize itself and history mark it.
>
> For America, this postwar period is surely the era of the Negro passion. The most moving voices are now those of Negroes; the most searing, lasting words are put on paper by Negro writers; their music is the American music most penetrating and persuasive to other parts of the world; no cause is now so fundamental to the health and integrity of this society as the Negro cause; of no other leaders are so much stamina and courage demanded as are now required of Negro leaders.
>
> They are bound to win, somehow, not only because their present aims are so limited and unarguable, but because they have succeeded in involving us all, whoever we are, wherever we live within the nation's frontiers.
>
> They have caught the attention of the whole American people and, more than that, they have caught up the conscience of the whole people, however many of us may try to deny this ourselves.
>
> A newspaper or television picture of a snarling police dog set upon a human being is recorded in the permanent photoelectric file of every human brain.
>
> This generation is not likely to find surcease from the Negro passion; its source springs and the resistance to it are too deeply grounded for easy resolution, and its present outburst too long delayed.
>
> Its more violent manifestations are not going to be confined to the deep South. The head of black steam building up in places like New York,

Washington and Chicago are finding outlets too few and too small, at the present rate, for the permanent avoidance of combustion.

Because this unfolding drama involves the automatic reflexes of the instinctive sense of justice, because it involves namable, hearable, countable individual persons of flesh and blood, it is going to dwarf the general and social pageants of this domestic era, whether they be the struggles to rationalize the inchoate megalopolis, to preserve the open spaces, to eradicate a disease, to "conquer" space, or whatever.

The time is coming, soon, when the Negro passion will truly dominate American politics. . . . An education in the facts of life and history is in store for those pained by the messy contradictions built into the Negro passion. Those bewildered at the Negro uprising ("after all, they had made a lot of progress") may learn that this is one of the eternal lessons from past rebellions against oppression. It is not when the oppression is most complete that these revolutions begin to revolve, but when concessions are given, hopes are born, light is glimpsed at the end of the dark tunnel. It is when an oppressed people feels close to its goal, not far from it, that their action becomes frenetic.

Those who are cynical or upset by the moral duality in the Negro phenomenon, by the spectacle of lofty courage and self-sacrifice among the Negro leaders, side by side with the spectacle of spreading crime and moral squalor in the slum-bound masses of the Negro poor, may learn that the first is a direct reflection of the second, its natural, not its unnatural, partner.

Desperation, like war, ennobles some among its victims and debases others. No true people's revolution was ever neat, clean or devoid of sad anomalies.

If the Negro passion of today is not a true people's revolution, it is as close to one as we have ever known in our land.[1]

Mr. Sevareid seems to have read his history aright when he observes that long-submerged groups become most frenetic when their goals are within sight. Groups mired in the very depths of poverty, injustice, and exploitation are more prone to feel a sense of futility and fatalism than a determination to rise from those depths. But when an upward movement has mitigated or overcome many of their torments, the grievances that remain

[1] Eric Sevareid, *The Blade*, May 12, 1963. Reprinted by special permission of The Hall Syndicate, Inc., New York.

tend to bring forth a mood of frenzied resolution to wipe out every vestige of their rankling presence. Thus the Negro Revolution may acquire a more strident character in the years ahead.

This theory of revolutions, however, does not provide an adequate explanation for the racial riots and bloodshed which have occurred in so many American cities. Other factors may be equally important. While the statutory triumphs over racial discrimination in recent years have been impressive, their principal benefits have accrued to the Negro middle class. The millions of Negro poor, largely cooped up in central city ghettos, find their lives about as cheerless as before. They continue to work at low-paying jobs, to send their children to inferior schools, to live in squalid and cramped housing, to receive inferior public services. The cultural encrustations of three centuries of oppression continue to hamper their efforts to share equally in the affluence so tantalizingly flaunted before them by the mass media. Thus while the Negro Revolution has provided psychic gratifications and nourished their self-respect, it has also aroused aspirations that seem maddeningly far from fulfillment. That this should lead to irrational acts of defiance and violence is hardly surprising.

In general, the urban riots that have broken out in so many cities have been the work of teenagers, acting partly in response to some inflammatory incident (or interpretation of an incident) and partly in response to a tempting opportunity to "raise hell" under the guise of a protest against social injustice and "police brutality." (Neither Negro nor white adolescents are distinguished these days for their Spartan self-discipline and self-restraint). The 40 percent of Negro children who live in fatherless homes often lack the respect for authority that an adult male in the household normally tends to provide. Many of the others whose fathers are present are, nevertheless, the psychological victims of the matriarchal character of Negro culture (described at a later point). Moreover, while the adolescent Negro rioters incur the disapproval of many of their elders, many other Negroes have decidedly ambivalent feelings about the riots. Along with some whites, a majority of Negroes in 1966 believed that outbreaks of Negro violence were an effective way to convince "Whitey" of the seriousness of the Negro's plight and of the imperative necessity to take drastic remedial social action.[2] As a result, something less than the maximum social disapproval may be visited upon the young roustabouts who take part in the burning and shooting and looting that erupt in our cities.

James Reston has written: "The facts of life in Harlem in New York, in Watts in Los Angeles, and Hough in Cleveland were well known to the governments of those cities. All officials there knew that the conditions in their slums encouraged violence, but they did not or could not react to reason as well as they could react to violence. It is the same the world over. Most of the time, just grievances are removed only after the aggrieved resort to the uses of power." [3]

A combination of factors, then, seems to prophesy an increase in racial violence in the years ahead. The slum-swaddled lower-income Negro lives within wretched conditions that naturally produce a deep sense of injustice—conditions with an especially combustible potential during the current Negro mood. (Attorney General Nicholas Katzenbach says the true agitators of social riots are "disease and despair, joblessness and hopelessness, rat-infested housing and long-impacted cynicism.") Economic progress for these people is bound to be much slower than Negro impatience can readily brook. There is a natural tendency for the long suppressed to want to "get even" with members of the race which suppressed them. There is the extreme difficulty of sustaining a mass revolutionary movement on the high moral plane advocated by Martin Luther King—especially when competing leaders are peddling more dramatic, visceral, and cut-rate strategies in an effort to seize the reins of leadership. There is the inherent tendency of revolutions to move from the control of moderates to extremists before their emotional force is spent and self-correcting influences come to fruition. There is the certainty that Negro excesses will provoke white excesses, touching off chain reactions of unpredictable magnitude. A mounting mood of hostility among certain classes of white Northerners, a hostility which can erupt into violence even when defensible

[2] "Crisis of Color, '66," *Newsweek,* August 22, 1966, p. 22.
[3] *The New York Times,* July 24, 1966, p. 10.

Negro goals and protests are involved, also bodes ill for the years ahead.

Finally, the above exist in the context of an age in which traditional moral values are under attack from many quarters, in which traditional authority figures and symbols are viewed with shrinking respect, and in which change proceeds at such breakneck speed that instability, confusion, and a sense of rudderlessness abound.

Perhaps this will yet turn out to be the most moderate of revolutions—largely because the Negro is so greatly outnumbered—but one wonders if major bloodletting must convulse the nation before passions subside and a sobered nation takes stock of itself.

Since 1962, the nation has moved far—farther than once seemed possible in so short a time—toward achieving political and economic equality for the Negro. But although progress has been striking in the political sphere, full equality in the economic and social spheres is still in the distance. As for the gravity of the uncompleted task, Charles Silberman, one of the nation's more acute observers, wrote in 1965 that ". . . the U.S. now faces a racial crisis every bit as serious as, and in some ways more urgent than, the one that tore the nation asunder a century ago. Indeed, it is no exaggeration to say that unless we make the plight of the Negro American the central concern of all Americans, there will be no social peace in this country for generations to come."[4]

In selecting the means for achieving greater equality and in interpreting the meaning of equality as it applies to concrete situations, opinion is widely and often sharply divided. What role remains for Congress, the Executive, and the Judiciary in these realms? For state and local governments? At what point does zeal for the fulfillment of Negro rights imperil the legitimate rights of others? Or arouse such hostile sentiments among whites that progress toward full equality is jeopardized? What about the responsibilities of Negroes themselves?

[4] "Beware the Day They Change Their Mind," *Fortune Magazine,* November, 1965, p. 151.

Because the Negro revolution challenges many of the nation's economic practices, its balance of political forces, its stubbornly held (although often unacknowledged) class concepts, its mores and its folkways, progress in this realm almost inevitably entails bitterness and strife. How, then, can the optimum rate of progress be reached by methods that minimize friction, that are regarded as legitimate by men of understanding and good will, and that invoke our often dimly perceived common interests? This is the problem to which Negroes and whites alike must address themselves.

The Great Retreat

A brief recapitulation of the struggle for racial equality since the Civil War will help provide a background against which analysis of current alternatives can better take place.

The story of the effort to elevate the Negro to a position of relative equality during the Reconstruction period is sufficiently well known to merit no more than passing mention. With the ratification of the Thirteenth Amendment, formal slavery disappeared from the American scene, even if the attitudes accompanying that institution have persisted. Historians generally agree that the drafters of the Fourteenth Amendment intended a sweeping reform when they inserted the words ". . . nor shall any State deprive any person of life, liberty, or property, without due process of law; nor deny to any person within its jurisdiction the equal protection of the laws." It seems, too, that the radical reconstructionists intended to insure the suffrage to Negroes when their Fifteenth Amendment proclaimed that "The right of citizens of the United States to vote shall not be denied or abridged by the United States or by any State on account of race, color, or previous condition of servitude." That they took their task seriously was shown by a succession of federal laws and acts, notably the establishment of the Freedman's Bureau, the struggle with President Johnson over Reconstruction policies, and especially the Civil Rights Act of 1875. The key provision of the latter reads as follows: "That all persons within the jurisdiction of the United States shall be entitled to the full and equal enjoyment of the accommodations, advantages, facilities, and privileges of inns, public conveyances on land or water, theaters, and other places of public amusement. . . ." Although the Negroes made signal advances in some respects, the South was not long in erecting a network of subtle and not-so-subtle resistances designed to "keep the Negro in his place." As the crusading zeal of northern politicians and other groups subsided, culminating in the withdrawal of Northern troops during President Arthur's administration, a Great Retreat began.

The Supreme Court played a major part in the Great Retreat by invalidating the Civil Rights Act of 1875, declaring that it proscribed acts of discrimination by private individuals rather than acts by the states themselves. Although many historians believe the drafters of the Fourteenth Amendment intended to authorize legislation such as that embodied in the 1875 act, the court's decision temporarily ended the effort to effectively implement the Fourteenth Amendment on behalf of Negro rights. Much of the pattern of discrimination which white Southerners wanted to create or maintain could be accomplished by private citizens acting in a nonofficial capacity.

When the court further upheld "separate but equal" facilities in public transportation (if the Negro regarded this as discriminatory, the court declared, this was only because he *chose* to put that interpretation upon it!)[5] the way was opened for the creation of an entire social fabric based on "separate but equal." Not only was "Jim Crow" enthroned in transportation systems and terminals but in the educational system and in other public facilities as well. Combined with the discrimination permissibly practiced in hotels, restaurants, and places of amusement (as well as in other economic and social relationships), the white South needed only to restrain Negro voting to insure the perpetuation of the white supremacy system.

It was not only in areas where the Negro predominated that the white South determined to keep him from the polls. Experience had shown that white politicians, faced with a hard-fought election battle, tended to woo Negro voters with promises that threatened to disturb the developing pattern of white

[5] *Plessy* v. *Ferguson,* 163 U.S. 537 (1896).

supremacy. To eliminate the Negro as a political factor, it was necessary either to keep him away from the polls entirely or reduce his vote to insignificant proportions. Threats, intimidation, economic pressures, night-riding Ku Klux Klanners—these could be, and were, used effectively. Naturally, however, the white South preferred more genteel methods. The election laws lent themselves admirably to this end through suffrage requirements that, although ostensibly impartial, in practice bore down heavily on Negroes.

Literacy tests were made prerequisite to voting—tests that were administered rigorously to Negroes and leniently or not at all to whites. Similarly, Negroes seeking to register were required to prove that they understood the meaning of obscure passages in the state and national constitutions, while white registrants were given perfunctory exams or the requirements were waived altogether. In addition, "grandfather clauses" were enacted by Southern states, exempting from suffrage tests those who had voted before the Civil War or whose parents or grandparents had voted. Poll taxes were legislated, affecting whites and Negroes alike but proving more burdensome to the economically hard-pressed Negro. Persons convicted of even the most petty crimes (loitering, vagrancy, petty theft—crimes understandably more prevalent among Negroes) were denied the suffrage. Finally, because the Democratic party was overwhelmingly dominant in the South, and the primary nomination was tantamount to final election, some states specifically reserved the privilege of Democratic party primary voting to whites—or gave the party the privilege of restricting party membership to white voters. In the aggregate, these laws succeeded in whittling Negro voting percentages to trivial levels.[6]

Victory was nearly total for the white South, because the Negro had found no effective way to fight back, and the North had turned its attention to other matters. Gradually a mood of defeatism and apathy settled over the Negroes, a mood that was to endure for generations.

[6] For a general treatment of Southern efforts to deny suffrage to the Negro and to impose a sweeping pattern of segregation, see C. Vann Woodward, *The Strange Career of Jim Crow*, New York, Oxford University Press, 1955.

In a few spotty instances, the Supreme Court had opposed the white South's obvious intent to circumvent the Fourteenth and Fifteenth Amendments. It frowned on the grandfather clauses as constituting too obvious an evasion of the Fifteenth Amendment (the other barriers to Negro voting were sufficient, in any case). It struck down a West Virginia law excluding Negroes from jury service (then opened the way for exclusion in a subsequent case by observing that the absence of Negroes from juries was not *prima facie* evidence of illegal discrimination). It invalidated a Texas law barring Negroes from taking part in Democratic primaries (but later permitted the Democratic state convention to take such action) and it upheld a federal law aimed at limiting the terroristic activities of the Ku Klux Klan. In general, the court presented no serious obstacle to Southern efforts to deny the Negro first-class citizenship.

The Great Awakening

From the 1870s to the 1930s, the American conscience largely slept, so far as the plight of the Negro was concerned. Then a series of developments took place that gradually changed the climate of opinion and set in motion a movement of protest that gained increasing momentum and culminated in the explosive racial mood and demands of today. We will pause a moment to examine these developments.

Probably the first of these factors was the depression and the Roosevelt Administration. The depression focused attention on the needy and underprivileged in general; the spirit of the New Deal was one of active concern for these groups. This increasingly humanitarian spirit was stimulated in significant measure by the courageous and persistent efforts of Mrs. Franklin D. Roosevelt to dramatize the plight of the submerged groups, including the Negroes. During the New Deal and its aftermath, moreover, the nation came to see government—especially federal government—more as a positive instrument to achieve social justice than as a negative force destructive of human liberty when it strayed beyond traditional limits.

As so often proves true of social and political outrages, the ugly phenomenon of Hitlerism played its part in stirring the national conscience. Hitler's emphasis on racial purity and on superior and inferior races was of course repugnant to the American people. Indignation over Hitler's racism prompted the uneasy realization that America was practicing a racism of its own, based on concepts of the superior white and inferior black races. Anthropologists and psychologists also were devoting an increasing amount of research to racial qualities and differences, and their almost unanimous conclusion that there is no innately superior race and that Negroes have potentialities equal to whites, played its part in altering public opinion. This part was augmented by the rapidly increasing number of persons graduating from high school and particularly from college; the correlation between racially prejudiced views and retarded educational experience has been shown by repeated tests to be very high.

The emigration of large numbers of Negroes from Southern farms to Northern cities during and after World War II was of major importance. Urban candidates for public office in the North found it prudent to heed the aspirations of a swelling Negro constituency. Exposed to the more stimulating environment of the cities and to the better-quality schools in the North, educated and aggressive Negro leaders began to appear in larger number—leaders who would hardly have emerged from a Southern agrarian environment. Emboldened by the influx of Southern Negroes into their cities, these men responded to the temper and pressures of their time by demanding "Freedom Now." Such developments insured that Congress would pay increasing attention to the Negro problem in general and especially to the more glaring forms of racial discrimination in the South.

The waning of the era of international colonialism was also instrumental in hastening the Negro Revolution. As the leading power in the West, with leadership aspirations to match its military and economic might, the United States found its leadership potentialities constricted by the continuance of conspicuous and degrading forms of discrimination against American Negroes —discrimination deeply resented by the nonwhite populations in Africa and Asia. The appearance of newly independent African states also helped produce an enhanced dignity and self-respect on the part of American Negroes. The conclusion was inevitable: freedom and equality for Negroes abroad should be matched by freedom and equality for Negroes at home. ("T.R.B." of *The New Republic* has noted that ". . . European nations had their colonies outside their borders, and had to get rid of them. But in America the colony was right inside the country itself. . . ."[7])

In addition to these fundamental historic factors, a number of more superficial but still significant developments within the United States hastened the culmination of the Negro Revolution in 1963. The Supreme Court decision in *Brown* v. *Board of Education,* in 1954, outlawing school segregation and foreshadowing the imminent constitutional downfall of other forms of public racial discrimination, not only had a stunning effect on the South but was remarkably successful in focusing public attention on the Negro problem. The vast outpouring of discussion and literature following this decision enabled long-range forces working on behalf of the Negro to flower more rapidly.

Negro exhilaration over the championing of their cause by the prestigious court gradually gave way to a combination of discouragement over the painfully slow rate of school desegregation in the Old South and growing impatience to harvest the fruits of equality promised by the court. The year 1963 marked 100 years since the Emancipation Proclamation, 100 years of agonizingly slow progress. How long, O Lord, how long? When Negro demonstrations in Birmingham and elsewhere triggered the use of fire hoses, police dogs, and electric cattle prods, Negro and white indignation reached new heights. The role of television should not be overlooked; it produced an immediate, widespread, and vivid awareness of the brutalities involved and sent shock waves throughout the nation that had major political effects.[8] The aroused conscience of the nation provided a milieu

[7] "T.R.B.," *The New Republic,* June 29, 1963, p. 2.

[8] In this connection, Saul Alinsky, director of the Industrial Areas Foundation, said that "A Bull Connor with his police dogs and fire hoses down in Birmingham did more to advance civil rights than the civil-rights fighters themselves. The same thing goes with the march from Selma to Montgomery. Imagine what would have happened if instead of stopping the marchers that first day with clubs and tear gas, chief state trooper Lingo had courteously offered to provide protection and let them proceed. By night

favorable to President Kennedy's sweeping and historic civil rights message in 1963.

The chronology of major developments moving toward first-class Negro citizenship is an interesting one. The Supreme Court and the executive branch have played leading roles, but the Congress has, until recently, lagged well behind.

The court's interest in reviving the Negro's constitutional rights can be said to have begun in 1935, when it altered the effects of an earlier decision by declaring that the systematic exclusion of Negroes from juries deprived a trial of legal validity. The court followed with a ruling in 1938 that required states either to permit Negro residents to attend their own state law schools or to construct separate law schools for their use. Ten years later, in notable decisions affecting the Universities of Oklahoma and Texas, the court set the stage for its 1954 ruling by declaring that separate law schools could not be truly equal, inasmuch as the quality of the faculties, the prestige of the institutions, the influence of the alumni, and so forth, could not be equal. Then in the celebrated *Brown* v. *Board of Education* decision the court declared that segregated schools were "inherently unequal" (even if equal sums were spent for Negro schools) because "To separate [children] from others of similar age and qualifications solely because of their race generates a feeling of inferiority as to their status in the community that may affect their hearts and minds in a way unlikely ever to be undone."[9]

---

the TV cameras would have gone back to New York and there would have been no national crisis to bring religious leaders, liberals, and civil-rights fighters from the North into Selma. I've always thought that just as King got the Nobel Prize there should be an IgNoble prize for people like Sheriff Rainey of Philadelphia, Mississippi, Governor Wallace, and Governor Barnett." ("A Professional Radical Moves In on Rochester," *Harper's Magazine*, July, 1965, p. 53.)

[9] The reversal of *Plessy* v. *Ferguson* in *Brown* v. *Board of Education*, 347 U.S. 483 (1954) disturbed many who believe the meaning of the Constitution should not reflect changing currents of opinion and the changing composition of the court. A possible answer might be found in Justice Louis Brandeis' celebrated observation, "No constitutional question is ever settled until it is rightly settled." Perhaps it should be noted that although segregationists have often contended that the control of education is one of the reserved rights of the states under the Tenth Amendment, the "equal protection" clause of the Fourteenth Amendment governs *all* state actions.

Although the court never declared that desegregation must take place overnight, it did call for prompt action in its carefully phrased demand for "all deliberate speed." Where local communities failed to act "in good faith," suits could be brought before federal district judges, who might order suitable desegregation plans to be submitted by a certain date, or themselves draw up plans for desegregation to take place. In the case of graduate schools, the court would tolerate no delays whatever for qualified applicants.

In subsequent cases, the court extended its ruling to outlaw segregation in public recreational facilities, such as municipal swimming pools, golf courses, and parks.

The court also invalidated white primaries in 1944 and later struck down attempts to gerrymander voting districts where these attempts were patently aimed at isolating the Negro vote. And it undermined so-called restrictive covenants by declaring that agreements restricting the sale of housing to Caucasians were not enforceable at law.

Turning to the executive branch, Franklin D. Roosevelt during World War II established by executive order a Fair Employment Practices Commission designed to promote equal employment opportunities for Negroes in government employment or defense-contract work. The desegregation of the armed services, begun during World War II and completed by the Truman and Eisenhower administrations, has ended segregation in this segment of American life.

The Eisenhower administration established the Government Contracts Compliance Committee to enforce an executive order requiring that business concerns granted federal contracts must make jobs related to those contracts available to applicants on a nondiscriminatory basis. (The committee, renamed the Committee on Equal Employment Opportunity and given a broadened role, now appears to be on a permanent footing.) Persistent efforts have been made by the federal government in recent years to place an increasing number of Negroes in federal positions. Under pressure from the administration, the Interstate Commerce Commission issued orders implementing the court's decision on interstate transportation by forbidding separate but equal facilities in bus and railroad stations serving interstate commerce. The Kennedy administration also issued an executive order prohibiting discrimination in federally supported housing. Finally, the Department of Justice quietly used its influence to facilitate desegregation proceedings in local communities where trouble was anticipated, and has begun a more active enforcement of the various civil rights acts.

From the ill-fated Civil Rights Act of 1875 until 1957, Congress passed no legislation designed directly to ameliorate the lot of the Negro. The watered-down act of 1957 broke the ice, however, by authorizing the attorney general to take the initiative, where persons are illegally deprived of the right to vote, by seeking federal court injunctions forbidding interference with the franchise. It also permits defendants to be tried and convicted by a federal judge (rather than by the jury method preferred by the white South) in cases of civil contempt as long as the penalty does not exceed 45 days in jail or a $300 fine.

This act also upgraded the Civil Rights Section of the Department of Justice, which prosecutes public officials who violate a citizen's civil rights and private citizens who conspire to injure those rights. A Civil Rights Commission was established by the act to investigate civil rights violations and make legislative recommendations to the Congress.

In 1960, Congress passed another civil rights act that authorizes federal courts to appoint voting referees after finding, in any suit brought under the 1957 act, that Negroes have been subjected to voting discrimination. If a second attempt to register fails, the referees can issue voting certificates that must be honored on penalty of contempt of court.

In 1964, the most impressive civil rights legislation since Reconstruction broke through the previously potent Southern defenses in the Senate. The Civil Rights Act of 1964 empowered the attorney general to take legal steps toward the prompt desegregation of schools and public facilities; forbade job discrimination in larger firms; made bias illegal in hotels, motels, restaurants, gas stations, theaters, sports arenas, and public places of amusements; and authorized the suspension of federal funds where states used them in discriminatory fashion.

It also sought to strengthen voting-right guarantees by forbidding election registrars to maintain their long-cherished double standard for interpreting literacy tests and passing on the adequacy of registration-form data. (Negroes with advanced degrees had often been found illiterate by Southern registrars, while whites who had never finished the eighth grade were not given the test or somehow passed it with ease.)

Despite this act, Negroes continued to experience massive difficulties in reaching the polls. State and local ingenuity in inventing new or applying old evasions and resistances showed no signs of abating. The prospect of further prolonged litigation and of spotty, delayed, step-by-step progress finally spurred Congress into enacting legislation that could properly be termed drastic. The Voting Rights Act of 1965 prescribed that any state or county in which less than 50 percent of the voting age population was registered or voted for President in 1964 must suspend *all* suffrage tests except those of age, residence, and criminal record. If compliance is not forthcoming, the attorney general can dispatch federal examiners to protect the right to register and insure that all ballots are fairly counted. Fines up to $5,000 may be imposed on anyone seeking to intimidate would-be-voters or those encouraging them to vote.

Although much Negro nonvoting is the product of apathy rather than discrimination, a sharp increase in Southern Negro voting is expected. In 1964, of 5.2 million adult Negroes in 11 Southern states, only 2.2 million were registered and only 1.6 million voted. In many counties with a high proportion of Negroes, Negro voting was inconsequential. Threats, terror, and economic pressures will doubtless continue to plague Negro voters, but the apparent determination of the federal government to wipe out suffrage inequality promises to steadily diminish the various forms of intimidation. Elimination of the poll tax as a prerequisite for voting in either federal or state and local elections should also accelerate Negro voting. By early 1966, Negro registration figures in the five Southern states with the lowest prior Negro voting records were up 50 percent and still rising.

Direct action by Negroes themselves has aided the struggle in some of these areas as well as extended it into new fields. The well-publicized "sit-in" movement brought about desegregation of many departments stores, restaurants, theaters, and other privately owned establishments serving the public. "Freedom Riders" dramatically challenged segregation practices in facilities connected with interstate commerce. Picketing, marches, demonstrations, and boycotts have been used to protest discrimination in hiring, housing, and access to public and private services. Stand-ins, kneel-ins, wade-ins, and a variety of ingenious pressure techniques have been used by Negroes in an effort to bring down the racial walls of Jericho.

The Negro has made signal advances in other areas. Both political parties (at least outside the South) are willing or even eager to nominate Negro candidates for elective offices. In parts of the South, where the standard formula for political success has been to "shout nigger first and loudest," Negro registration is leading to a more conventional campaign style. Many Negroes are reaching such high elective positions as judgeships and membership in city councils and in Congress. Although constituting only 11 percent of the population, Negroes hold 13 percent of governmental jobs. Managerial and professional positions are opening up to Negroes; in some instances, well-trained Negroes may even enjoy a preferential advantage over whites with equal training as corporations seek to avoid boycotts and unfavorable publicity by demonstrating their lack of prejudice. Little by little, unions are yielding to pressures to permit Negro entry into skilled jobs that have traditionally been reserved for whites. Negro incomes rose 73 percent from 1950 to 1960; in Chicago, 30 percent of Negro families have incomes exceeding those of one half of the white families.[10] The percentage of Negroes living in "dilapidated" housing has been cut in half during the past 10 years. Inadequate as slum housing may be, it is usually an improvement on the rickety shacks that housed rural Southern Negroes before they streamed North.

School integration, which has proceeded at a sticky pace in the South for years, is speeding up under the threat of the withdrawal of substantial federal educational funds for school districts failing to integrate by 1967. Fraternities and sororities are outlawing offensive racial clauses (and occasionally inducting

[10] Eli Ginzberg, "The Negro's Problem Is the White's," *The New York Times Magazine*, February 9, 1964, p. 66.

Negroes). Segregated churches are dwindling; many laymen and church leaders are among the most dedicated and effective champions of the Negro cause. And—of no small significance—the commitment of the younger generation of college students to Negro equality has auspicious portents for the future.

Yet, although much has been achieved, the equality gap is far from closed. The difference between the median annual incomes of Negro and white families gradually widened from 1954 to 1964, largely because jobs for unskilled and semiskilled Negroes were in short supply during most of that period. (The economic boom of the mid-1960s altered this trend, however.) The median income of Negro men is only about 60 percent as much as that of white men. Though one fifth of the nation's families are officially labeled "poor," fully one half of nonwhite families are in this category. Whereas one white worker in three has a professional, technical, managerial, or sales job, only one Negro in 10 is in this group. For years, unemployment was twice as high for Negroes as for whites; for Negro teenagers it has been almost three times as high. Job discrimination remains a serious problem in many fields. Housing segregation in both North and South has actually increased in recent decades, producing *de facto* school segregation on a massive scale.[11] Fears persist that school integration in the South will remain on a token level despite federal pressures. In 1966, for example, only one Southern Negro child in 13 was attending integrated classes. Equal justice in Southern courts remains an unachieved goal.

The ugly legacy of centuries of oppression has produced Negro social traits that will take generations to overcome.[12] During the

[11] Before World War II, Negroes frequently lived among whites in many Southern cities—although they were often concentrated in clusters here and there throughout the metropolitan area, or on one side of a street. New suburban developments in Southern cities, however, are now usually as lily-white as in Northern cities. See Everett C. Ladd, Jr., "Civil Rights: The Continuing Revolution," *The Yale Review*, Autumn, 1965, p. 14.

[12] See Charles Silberman, *Crisis in Black and White*, New York, Random House, 1964, ch. IV. Also see *The Negro Family: The Case for National Action*, report of the Department of Labor, 1965; Thomas Meehan, "Moynihan of the Moynihan Report," *The New York Times Magazine*, July 31, 1966; and Paul Good, "The Thorntons of Mississippi: Peonage on the Plantation," *The Atlantic Monthly*, September, 1966.

slavery era, the disorganization of the Negro family gave rise to familial characteristics that are the Negro's heaviest burden today. The male slave had no opportunity to be a normal father and exercise normal parental responsibilities. He could not legally marry, own property, sign contracts, or even testify in court against a white man. In the eyes of the law, he was a cipher. At any time he might be wrenched from his family and sold to another master. He had to surrender his "wife" to his master's lust and often live with the fact that his "children" were not truly his own. He could not carry himself like a man, but had to abase himself before his owner—and before all whites. (This condition was not corrected by Appomattox, of course, because the freed Negro seldom dared to be "uppitty" in the presence of whites.)

After the Emancipation Proclamation had "freed the slave but ignored the Negro," fresh difficulties arose. Lacking a job, lacking the self-discipline and sense of responsibility that only freedom can develop, lacking strong family ties, the Negro male often became a drifter—rootless, promiscuous, covering up his insecurities and lack of self-esteem with a happy-go-lucky air.

Necessarily, then, the Negro mother became the family's mainstay, the one stable element in the children's life. She earned the family bread in the husband's absence, cared for the children, and assumed the dual role of mother and father. Aside from the economic and emotional insecurities generated by this pattern, the children could not look up to their father as a loved, trusted, dependable masculine figure. Theodore White quotes Police Commissioner George Edwards of Detroit as saying of Negro delinquents that ". . . in many cases we are dealing with children who never, in all their lives, have met a decent man—a kind man, an honest man, a responsible man."[13] Yet the absence of such a relationship wreaked heavy psychological damage on the children, especially the boys, who needed a responsible adult to emulate.

The economic disasters of the Depression aggravated these

[13] Theodore H. White, *The Making of the President, 1964,* New York, Atheneum, 1965, p. 241.

abnormalities. During the 1930s and during the national economic slowdown of the late 1950s and early 1960s, Negro women often could find jobs when their husbands could not, further contributing to the male's lack of status and self-respect. In recent years, a program intended to be humanitarian has also accentuated the problem—Aid to Dependent Children (ADC). In many states ADC checks are available only to mothers with no husbands because of death, divorce, or desertion. Since desertion, in some states, will thus enlarge the family income, unemployed fathers have often felt obliged to leave home.

These conditions, combined with a decline in manual labor jobs when muscle is all many Negro males have to offer, have produced the tragedy that Negroes widely refer to as the "castration" of the Negro male. Add to these the stinging humiliations endured by a black skin in a white man's world, the poverty, the squalor, the crowding, the slums, the frustration, the despair, the hopelessness—all have played their dismal part in producing the breakdown of the Negro family. The statistics are depressing. As of 1965, 62 percent of all illegitimate children came from Negro homes; Negro women were divorced or separated from their husbands three times as often as white women; almost one half of ADC checks went to Negro homes; and less than one half of all Negro children at age 18 had lived all their lives with both parents. All of this undoubtedly had much to do with the fact that one half of all violent crimes were committed by Negroes.[14]

Meanwhile, the Negro birth rate remains 40 percent higher than for whites. Infant mortality among Negroes, on the other hand, is five times as high as for whites; nevertheless, as Theodore White observes, in 1960, one person of 10 was Negro; in 1965, it was one of nine; in 1972, it will be one of eight. Furthermore, in 1965, one of seven children under the age of 14 was Negro and of infants under a year old, one in six![15]

[14] "How Far the Negro Has To Go and What It Will Take," *U. S. News and World Report,* June 21, 1965, pp. 52–53. Daniel Moynihan believes that when ". . . young men grow up in broken families, dominated by women, never acquiring any stable relationship to male authority, . . . crime, violence, unrest, disorder . . . are not only to be expected, they are very near to inevitable." Meehan, *op. cit.*, p. 5.

[15] White, *op. cit.*, p. 240.

Nowhere do the circumstances of the Negro background lead to more tragic effects than in the preschool environment. This environment will handicap Negro slum children for life, unless major remedial measures are taken.

Charles Silberman's superb *Crisis in Black and White* explains why the Negro child's reading skills are so poorly developed and why his IQ tends to drop about 20 points from the first to the twelfth grade.[16] (White children from the same socioeconomic class experience somewhat similar difficulties.) The noise in the slum household is so high that the preschool child learns how "not to listen." He does not develop the capacity to distinguish between relevant and irrelevant sounds and to block off all but those necessary to cope with a learning situation. Nor do his parents, unlike middle-class parents, correct his baby speech and help him discriminate between subtle phonic differences. His questions go largely unanswered. "Because they are preoccupied with the problems associated with poverty and their crowded living conditions, the parents are only irritated by what they consider the senseless questions of a prattling infant."[17] Thus the spirit of curiosity is dampened, the desire to learn is smothered.

Because his parents speak in short sentences and in monosyllables, the child's attention span is abnormally short, and he is unable to follow the conversation of the middle-class teacher when several long sentences are spoken consecutively. His parents' nonverbal characteristics prevent the child from acquiring the simplest bits of information: The child does not learn the names of common objects, which his parents have identified only by pointing or by saying "get that" or "put it there." The visual and tactile poverty of his environment further contributes to his preschool education deficiencies. There are few objects in the home—"few toys, few pictures, few books, few magazines, few of anything but people and noise." He does not learn about colors, shapes, sizes; he does not handle a wide variety of objects and learn to use them. He often travels no more than a few blocks from home, and fails to absorb the knowledge and stimu-

[16] *Op. cit.*, p. 241.
[17] *Ibid.*, p. 275.

lation that novel sights and sounds bring. As Silberman puts it, "... mental alertness and, in particular, the ability to handle abstractions depend physiologically on a broad diversity of experience in the environment of early childhood."[18] Lacking this diversity and confronted with the stifling conditions of his home, the Negro child is at a staggering disadvantage when he enters the first grade. The difficulties he then experiences, and the irritation of his teachers with his slow learning, tend to produce a sense of failure that deepens as the school years pass. Self-confidence fades, to be replaced either by forms of apathy or by aggressive or hostile behavior reflecting his inability to meet the requirement of the school environment. Or perhaps the school expects so little of him that he accepts its low estimate of his ability. Negro sociologist Kenneth Clark believes the Negro child's main problem lies in his teachers' contempt for him and their disbelief in his capacity to learn.[19]

Recognizing the critical nature of the handicaps that so many Negro (and white) children carry with them to the first grade, the administration launched its widely publicized "Operation Headstart" in 1965. This federally financed program drew over half a million children into experimental summer programs designed to compensate for the deficiencies to be found in so many homes. The program is not expected to have spectacular results. There is no disposition to minimize the fact that not enough is known about *how* to stimulate and encourage children from backward homes. There is a shortage of well-trained teachers and of the assistants they need. Making the administrative arrangements for the millions of children who should be involved is a formidable task. Notwithstanding, the experiment has immense potential significance for the future and may soon be regarded as indispensable for bringing about genuine education equality. Even the first fumbling summer experiment led to an average IQ increase of 8–10 points for participating children.

That the Negro's learning capacity is equal to that of the white was dramatically proven in an educational experiment in St.

[18] Silberman, *Crisis in Black and White,* p. 273.
[19] "Light on the Ghetto," *Newsweek,* May 31, 1965, p. 81.

Louis.[20] Dr. Samuel Shepard, Jr., is assistant superintendent for 23 elementary schools, with about 500 Negro teachers, that accommodate about 16,000 children, nearly all Negroes. At the beginning of the school year 1957–1958, the Iowa Basic Skills tests showed that 47 percent of these children were below average in achievement, 46 percent were average, and only 7 percent were superior. Within six years, only 11 percent of Dr. Shepard's charges were scoring below average, 67 percent were average, and 22 percent rated superior.

How did he do it? He insisted that the teachers forget about IQ's and teach as if every child had an IQ of 120. He urged the children to stop feeling sorry for themselves and to rise above their environment. If you take full advantage of your educational opportunities, he insisted, you can successfully compete with whites. To dramatize the point, he brought successful Negroes into the schools to talk to the students and encourage them to think in terms of hope and success.

Dr. Shepard initiated field trips to zoos, museums, parks, city markets, radio and TV studios, a planetarium. Special programs were created for the more gifted students. School libraries stayed open evenings. When St. Louis schools prepared to replace 6,000 used dictionaries, he obtained them and sold them for 25 cents each to families in the school district. (In many instances, it was the first book the family had ever owned!)

Of perhaps equal importance, Dr. Shepard organized Operation Motivation. He held a series of meetings with parents, poorly attended at first but with rapidly rising attendance as the word spread of Dr. Shepard's plans. He assured them that a new day had dawned, that Negro children could achieve success if they gave their best. He emphasized the dollars-and-cents advantages of an education, citing figures on the average incomes of those, respectively, with an eighth grade, a high school, and a college education. He asked them to turn off the radio and TV when children should be studying, to take an interest in their work, to see that their youngsters got to school on time. The cooperation many parents gave to the program proved gratifying.

[20] Sam Shepard's Faith," *The PTA Magazine,* March, 1964, p. 32.

Unfortunately, there are not many Dr. Shepards on hand, but those who wish the Negro well are delighted by this concrete evidence that, given the proper conditions, Negro children can make the kind of educational progress that the goal of equality requires and the premises of democracy assume.[21]

The Whys of Prejudice

The struggle toward equality is waged in the context of deep-lodged attitudes and fears of national as well as regional dimensions that yield only slowly to education and experience. To fully understand the difficulties the Negro and the nation face, these attitudes must be briefly discussed.

The reasons most Southerners (and some Northerners) give for opposing school integration are by now commonly known. They insist there are valid grounds for supporting "separation" (as opposed to "segregation") and for racial "preference" (rather than "prejudice"). Negro children often have inferior educational backgrounds, and integration into all-white schools at comparable grade levels can complicate the teacher's job, as well as lead to lower-level educational standards. Many of these children come from homes with lax moral and sexual standards. They are exposed to and afflicted with more social diseases, are more prone to violence, and have a lower general cultural tone that would tend to rub off on white children.[22] Furthermore, the "mixing" of the races in the schoolroom will inevitably, it is believed, lead to an increase of intermarriage, a development most Northerners would surely deplore.[23] Would self-righteous

[21] Also see Kenneth Clark, *Dark Ghetto,* New York, Harper & Row, 1965, pp. 139–145.

[22] Thomas R. Waring, "The Southern Case Against Desegregation," *Harper's Magazine,* January, 1956, pp. 39–45. Also see James J. Kilpatrick, *The Southern Case for School Segregation,* New York, Crowell-Collier Press, 1962.

[23] Herbert Ravenel Sass, "Mixed Schools and Mixed Blood," *The Atlantic Monthly,* November, 1956. For rebuttal, see letters to editor, *The Atlantic Monthly,* January, 1957, and Oscar Handlin, "Where Equality Leads," *The Atlantic Monthly,* November, 1956. Also see Paul Douglas and Herman Talmadge, "Plain Talk on Civil Rights," *The Reader's Digest,* July, 1960, and Milton Mayer, "The Issue Is Miscegenation," *The Progressive,* September, 1959, pp. 8–18.

Northern critics, if confronted with the concrete Southern problem, want their children to mix with masses of culturally backward Negro children, in the interests of some abstract principle? Is not the alacrity with which Northern parents change their residences or withdraw their children from schools penetrated by Negro children eloquent testimony to the true Northern attitude?

It is easy to demonstrate that many of these attitudes represent rationalization rather than reason. Objective circumstances as well as federal court flexibility usually preclude the necessity for any "mass integration," with the admitted difficulties this would bring. Yet many Southern communities opposed even a modest amount of integration by raising many of the same arguments. That their concern for educational and cultural standards was less crucial than they may sincerely believe becomes apparent when one reflects on typical Southern (or Northern) community reactions when culturally and educationally backward white families move in. There is no community crisis, no protest meetings are held, no riots occur, no teenagers hurl stones at the "poor white trash" when they enter the schools. Yet they pose precisely the same educational and cultural "threat." And because the yahoo elements raise the most vociferous objections to school integration, their behavior conceivably represents something more than a profound commitment to high educational and cultural standards.

Will "mixing" in the schools lead to an increase in intermarriage? Over the short run, the probabilities are that the increase will be slight, if any, judging by the experiences of long-established Negro communities in northern Michigan, western Massachusetts, and Ontario.[24] After-school fraternization among Negroes and whites of different sexes is rare, and the tendency of persons to marry those in their own social and cultural group would preclude intermarriage in the overwhelming majority of cases. Most young people are aware of the psychological, familial, social, and economic problems that marriage brings to Negro and white partners. Increasingly, too, Negroes tend strongly to dis-

[24] Handlin, *op. cit.*, p. 53.

approve the marrying of whites, regarding it as an indication that the offender thinks Negroes are "not good enough" for him or her. While Negroes resent statutory restrictions on whom they may marry, there is wide professional agreement that the Negro has little interest in marrying outside his race.[25] Dr. Martin Luther King observes, "We ask only to be the white man's brother, not his brother-in-law." Although a certain amount of intermarriage has taken place throughout American history, and will doubtless continue, most authorities doubt that it will be appreciably increased over the short run by school integration, and may in fact be reduced. William Faulkner asked, "Why do we have so low an opinion of our blood and traditions as to fear that, as soon as the Negro enters our house by the front door, he will propose marriage to our daughter and she will immediately accept him?"[26] The long run, of course, may be another story. If race prejudice eventually disappears or is reduced to negligible proportions, sociologists agree that absence of social disapproval would lead to an increase in intermarriage.

Few, if any, close students of the subject believe that either Northern or Southern opposition to school integration is based, rock-bottom, on fears of racial "mongrelization." No great social stigma attached to pre-Civil War slave-masters who often enjoyed black concubines. A certain tolerance has attached to Southern white males who have sexual adventures with Negro women—so long as they do not actually marry.[27] (An estimated 70 to 80 percent of Negroes have some white blood.) It is noteworthy that the most strident opponents of intermarriage seem not to be fearful that integration will cause *their* sisters to marry Negroes, but they are highly resolved that racial impurity shall not take place among others. Perhaps, but there is always ground for skepticism when one finds such passionate devotion to the welfare of others and to the long-run interests of the race among

[25] W. S. M. Banks II, "The Rank Order of Sensitivity to Discrimination of Negroes in Columbus, Ohio," *American Sociological Review,* August, 1950, p. 532. Also see "Intermarriage—And the Race Problem," *U. S. News and World Report,* November 18, 1963.

[26] William Faulkner, "On Fear: The South in Labor," *Harper's Magazine,* June, 1960, p. 32.

[27] Mayer, *op. cit.,* pp. 9, 15.

those who are most unconcerned about the general welfare in other respects. Is this reason given because it meets with social approval and masks the deeper—and uglier—reasons?

If the professed reasons for opposing school integration are not very convincing, what are the *real* reasons? A number of hypotheses have been advanced that deserve brief exploration if we are to understand better why the road to full equality for Negroes is such a long and tortuous one.

The spirit of racial intolerance exists with greatest intensity in the South because of special historical circumstances associated with events leading up to and following the Civil War. Prolonged association with Negroes in their capacity as slaves inevitably left its impact on Southern attitudes. Southern-style slavery was particularly demeaning, because slaves had no legal rights to own property, make contracts, testify in court (except against other slaves) or even to marry. By law, Negroes could not be taught to read or write; they could not practice a religion without their master's consent; they could not assemble with other Negroes for any purpose unless white persons were present.[28] Even the attitude of Northerners has been affected, consciously or unconsciously, by the Negro's slave background, just as most of us are affected, conversely, by the knowledge that a given family has ties with a royal bloodline. The aroma of low caste and degradation inescapably associated with slavery clings stubbornly to the valuations people unconsciously place on groups unfortunate enough to have endured that background.

The white South's attitude toward the Negro is also influenced by the fact that the South's greatest period of travail, suffering, and humiliation was associated with the struggle to free the Negro and, later, with the Northern effort to establish a heavy-handed dominion over the South in the alleged interests of Negro rights. Negro excesses during the Reconstruction era also left an enduring imprint on white Southerners. The latter, then, can hardly avoid harboring an unpleasant association between the campaign for Negro rights and Southern suffering, defeat, and humiliation. This carry-over from the Civil War is bound

[28] "The End of the Beginning," *Current,* November, 1965, p. 9.

to affect the efforts to reach a more satisfactory relationship between the Negro and the Southern white.

Racial intolerance also draws on factors that influence Northern whites as much, or almost as much, as Southern whites. In the interests of brevity, these will be mentioned, rather than fully explained.

Whites are of course dominant in our society, largely monopolizing the political power, the economic power, and the more choice social fruits of that society. History records no instance of a self-conscious social group surrendering its powers and privileged position without a struggle. Certainly there have been economic advantages for whites in reserving much of the nation's menial and "dirty" work for Negroes. The existence of a cheap and docile labor force is a white asset that will dwindle as Negro education and social status improve. In the nature of things, then, it is to be expected that whites in North and South alike who feel their status and privileges threatened will seek to magnify real or imagined grievances associated with the challenging group.

Negroes are the victims of prejudice, in part, simply because of their poverty. Those mired in a low economic status are always "looked down on," regarded as culturally inferior, and discriminated against. The Irish, Italians, Greeks, Bohemians, and other immigrant groups suffered social penalties partly because of their poverty and partly because their Old World customs and practices made them "different." The Negro is also poor, usually, and he, too, is different—because of his skin. Unfortunately for the Negro, his skin color persists, whereas other minority groups could gradually merge indistinguishably into the general population as income rose and "Americanization" did its work. (For a thoughtful comparison of the similarities between Negroes now and the Irish and other immigrant groups in the nineteenth century, see Irving Kristol, "The Negro Is Like the Immigrant Yesterday," *The New York Times Magazine,* September 11, 1966.)

Still other factors contribute to racial prejudice. Persons near the bottom of the social totem pole have a special need to feel superior to some social group, and the Negro fulfills this need in their emotional economy. Those who feel frustrated or defeated, or who are deeply disturbed about their personal deficiencies, may take comfort from feelings and expressions of racial or cultural superiority over Negroes, Jews, Mexicans, Catholics, *et al.*

Much racial prejudice, however, does not rest on a need to identify a group over which one can feel superior. Many well-adjusted and "successful" persons are infected with racial prejudice simply because they absorbed it, along with the totality of their attitudes, from family and community conditioning. In the South, this type of prejudice has been strengthened by the social necessity to hold "correct" attitudes—especially in public—on the place of the Negro. But many Northern "liberals" will confess, in their more candid moments, that the valuation of the Negro that has pervaded almost our entire society has left its mark on them.

The usages of the English language also militate against the Negro's aspiration to be thought of as a normal individual rather than as a member of a somewhat inferior racial group. The word *black* is connected with dirt and filth, with sin and crime, with misfortune and sorrow and disgrace. "That was a black day in history." "He was in a black mood." "They blackened his reputation." White, on the other hand, is associated with purity and cleanliness, with sinlessness and virtue. The angels are white but Satan is dark.

The seeming desirability—and normalcy—of whiteness is also underscored by American mass media advertising, which usually pictures only attractive white men, women, and children. The family-type TV program revolves about a white family. Until very recently Dick and Jane—white children—virtually monopolized reading primers. Our great historic national heroes are all white men.

Thus the characteristic uses of the words white and black, plus the premiums placed on whiteness by our cultural heritage and folkways, add yet another burden to a race confronted with a disheartening array of obstacles.

The so-called "self-fulfilling prophecy" has also had a role. Assuming the Negroes to be inferior, whites consigned them to menial, unskilled labor and then declared, "See, that is all they are good for." Whites gave them an inferior education and shook their heads over Negro backwardness. Whites denied Negroes the vote while deploring Negro apathy. Whites refused Negroes economic opportunities while lamenting their lack of ambition. Thrust for generations into this milieu, many Negroes began to wonder if they really *were* equal to whites and really could compete with them. The myriad subtle destructive effects of these blows to Negro self-confidence further assured many whites that their low estimate of the Negro was indeed well founded.

Finally, there may be another cross for the Negro to bear in a predominantly white society. Gerald Johnson has observed that

> . . . Above and beyond all this, there is a psychological, or perhaps a biological, block, ignored by the thoughtless, but formidable nevertheless. It is the primeval impulse, not monopolized by man but shared by bird and beast and creeping thing, to equate "alien" and "enemy." Jeremiah, who antedates the Confederacy by a very considerable time, took note of the speckled bird that "the birds round about are against her." Whatever is not of our kind is *ipso facto* objectionable, and a definite exercise of the intelligence is required to neutralize the repugnance. The Negro merely by his coloration is, of all other races, the one most completely alien to the white man, hence the one surest to arouse—and to reciprocate—this ancient hostility. The primitive, or in ordinary parlance, the natural relation of black and white is one of dislike.
>
> This is no defense, but it is a partial explanation of such policies as segregation. Morality may be defined as the conscious suppression of destructive biological urges, and the advance of civilization is measured by the success of that suppression, so the appearance of any instinctive reaction is a slip backward toward Neanderthal man. But that such reactions do appear constantly is attested by trials everywhere and every day for homicide, theft, rape, and abduction. It will be a very long time before they are eliminated. Race prejudice will not be eliminated soon; the hope is not to eliminate it but to prevent its expression in race injustice, at least as far as the forms of law are concerned.

The theory cherished by idealists that race prejudice is exclusively the product of miseducation and bad environment is only about 90 percent true. There is a residue that can be traced back certainly into prehistory, and the attitude of the animals toward a variant strongly suggests that it can be traced back into prehumanity. However well suppressed, the thing exists, in Detroit as certainly as in New Orleans, in Massachusetts as in South Carolina. Latent everywhere, it needs only a certain combination of evil chances to become manifest. And its existence is one more complication added to the other troubles of the South. . . .[29]

Many psychologists and sociologists disagree with Mr. Johnson's appraisal, believing race prejudice to be purely a matter of social conditioning. Although the tendency of social groups to look askance at whatever is "different" is undoubted, why should prejudice attach more to a dark skin than to red hair or freckles? Perhaps, then, the felt "differentness" of a dark skin is a handicap to normal and uninhibited social relations only because of special societal circumstances rather than because of a natural biological tendency. Or is there something to what Mr. Johnson says?[30]

We have discussed the roots of prejudice at some length in the conviction that the problems and injustices associated with it can be intelligently approached only if its sources are clearly understood. If the difficulties attending the elevation of Negro status and rights are grounded in stubborn social, psychological, and economic factors that yield only slowly to education, experience, and legislative reforms, adequate recognition needs to be taken of that fact if we are to realistically plot the wisest course forward.

[29] Gerald W. Johnson, *The Man Who Feels Left Behind,* New York, Morrow, 1961, pp. 75–76. Copyright © 1960, 1961, by Gerald W. Johnson. By permission.

[30] "Intermarriage—And the Race Problem," *op. cit.,* p. 87. Dr. Ernest van den Haag believes that although skin color differences do not necessarily produce antipathy, "people will consider skin color as part of their aesthetic and psychological evaluation of another person . . . skin is the most visible part of the body and I cannot believe that people will ever disregard it."

What Tools for Washington?

Following the Birmingham demonstrations in 1963, President Kennedy called on Congress to provide federal guarantees of equal access to public facilities, including hotels, motels, restaurants, lunch counters, and public places of amusement. Stating that these facilities served interstate and international travelers and that "their goods come from all over the nation," the President found constitutional warrant in Congress' power over interstate commerce as well as in the Fourteenth Amendment's guarantee of equal protection of the laws. Although the Civil Rights Act of 1964 is here to stay, the controversy over its wisdom and constitutionality lingers in certain quarters. Because of its recency and importance, as well as the intensity of the feelings it generated, it will be instructive to review the positions staked out by the rival camps in the debate.

Equal accommodations legislation, it was argued, far from being radical in character, was in accord with long-established traditions and with English common law. Blackstone's *Commentaries* declared that ". . . when a man professes the keeping of an inn or public house, he thereby gives a general license to any person to enter his doors."[31] As early as 1450, an innkeeper was convicted for refusing to serve a customer. There were other convictions for similar offenses in later centuries. Thus the administration was seeking to effectively reinforce ancient rights rather than establish new ones. Those who accuse Washington of "grasping for power" overlook this background.

The administration contended that the needs of interstate commerce are not adequately met unless there is uniform and nondiscriminatory access to goods and services involved in interstate commerce. Although the Supreme Court had struck down the Civil Rights Act of 1875, it was believed that both public opinion and the court would now sustain an interpretation of the commerce clause and the Fourteenth Amendment that seemed harmonious with the modern imperatives of a progressive democratic society. (The Supreme Court did promptly uphold

[31] *The Congressional Record,* March 30, 1964, p. 6318.

the constitutionality of the act in *Heart of Atlanta Motel, Inc.*, v. *U.S., et al.*, 379 U.S. 241, December 14, 1964.)

In support of the President's proposal, Walter Lippmann wrote:

> [Public accommodations] discrimination is a public humiliation based solely on color. It is a public declaration that the descendants of the slaves are not full American citizens. The victims of this discrimination are for the most part the very Negroes who are the natural leaders of the Negro people. They are the ones who can afford to travel, and it is they who have begun to be part of the American public way of life. They suffer acutely from the stigma put upon them when they want a room in a motel or a sandwich at a lunch counter or a glass of water. This stigma injects poison continuously into the relations of whites and blacks . . . of all the grievances, this one is the most blatant. It is also the most easily redressed.[32]

Attorney General Robert F. Kennedy dramatized the grievance by observing that while a dog—if traveling with a white man—could find overnight accommodations "in at least five establishments in Montgomery, Alabama, and four in Danville, Virginia," a traveling Negro would be served by only one establishment in Montgomery and none at all in Danville.[33] Downtown Birmingham, moreover, offered not one general restaurant that would accommodate Negroes, nor one public restroom for their use, nor one theater for them to enter—yet the city (population 635,000) was one-third Negro.[34]

Others pointed out that many concerns serving the public raised no objections to serving nonwhites so long as they were foreigners, but drew the line where American Negroes were concerned. (Harry Golden observed that a Negro would be served almost anywhere if he wore a turban!) It was particularly galling for American Negroes to realize that they were often denied access to public facilities only because they are Americans.

[32] Walter Lippmann, "The Negroes' Grievances," *Newsweek*, September 16, 1963, p. 21. For a poignant account of a Negro's attitude toward segregated public accommodations in the North, see Fletcher Martin, "We Don't Want Your Kind," *The Atlantic Monthly*, October, 1958, p. 51.

[33] "Civil Rights: It's a Two-Way Street," *Newsweek*, July 29, 1963, p. 36.

[34] White, *op. cit.*, p. 175.

The opposition principally rested its case on two propositions. Some cited the civil rights cases of 1883 that held that (1) Congress has no direct powers over civil rights, but can only enact legislation required to counteract state laws violating constitutional rights associated with United States privileges and immunities, due process of law, and equal protection; and (2) the Fourteenth Amendment protects the citizen against encroachments on his rights by state law and state officials, but not against encroachments by individuals acting in their private capacities. Stretching the commerce clause to the point where it permits the national government to limit the businessman's discretion in deciding whom he will and will not serve carries that clause far beyond the intentions of those who drafted the Constitution. Unless some limits are placed on the interpretation of the commerce clause, federalism is virtually dead, and the states might as well close up shop.

Many of these critics asserted that because businesses in general are privately owned, private property rights are impaired if the federal government or any other government regulates the furnishing of their service. They deny that this is a case of human rights versus property rights, insisting that the rights of property are among the most important of human rights. If the federal government can use the commerce clause to abridge the rights of business, large or small, to conduct its relations with customers as it sees it, there is no logical limit to the scope of federal intrusions into business freedom.

The position of numerous dissenters was roughly as follows:

> It is going too far . . . to fasten a public obligation to forsake all prejudices and serve all comers in every country store, perhaps on the local bowling alley, and in Mrs. Murphy's boarding house. There must be some limit set by a right to privacy, a right to be ornery and unmannered and even immoral—some limit on the intrusion of public policy, and especially of distant, federal policy. The owner of an establishment and his accustomed patrons must in some circumstances be able to rely on a right to just be as they are. How homogenized do we wish to become?[35]

[35] Alexander M. Bickel, "Civil Rights and the Congress," *The New Republic,* August 3, 1963, pp. 14–15.

Of what value is a law which compels service to Negroes without close surveillance to make sure the service is on the same terms given to whites? It is not difficult to imagine many ways in which barbers, landlords, lunch counter operators, and the like can nominally comply with the law but effectively discourage Negro patrons. Must federal law enforcement agencies become in effect public utility commissions charged with the supervision of the nation's business establishments or will the law become an unenforceable symbol of hypocritical righteousness?[36]

Others found an acceptable case for outlawing discrimination in the larger establishments that serve the public, but wanted to exclude smaller entrepreneurs from federal restraints. This would be in line with other applications of federal law under the commerce clause that apply only to businesses with a certain number of employees or that do a certain volume of business. It would also be in line with common-law practices that distinguish, for example, the householder who rents rooms to supplement his income from the commercial operator who runs a hotel or inn as a primary business venture. (Householders renting five or fewer transient rooms were exempted from the 1964 act).

Finally, others balked at any compulsory law of this nature, but said they would support federal efforts to *persuade* businesses engaged in interstate commerce to desist from discrimination.

The administration claimed it had neither an interest in, nor constitutional justification for, carrying the commerce clause to unreasonable lengths. It only wanted to insure that commerce would be, in effect, desegregated. Because it sought to prevent individual choice where that choice denied basic human rights, this was no logical precedent for a denial of business freedom that did not impair those rights. Furthermore, the small businessman has just as great an obligation to respect human rights as the larger entrepreneur. If limitations on the applications of the law were needed, it would be because of administrative feasibility rather than of logic.

[36] Robert Bork, "Civil Rights—A Challenge," *The New Republic,* August 31, 1963, p. 23. See also James J. Kilpatrick, "Civil Rights and Legal Wrongs," *The National Review,* September 24, 1963.

Admittedly, some businessmen might serve Negroes in such an insulting and obnoxious manner that Negroes would decline to patronize them. But this would hardly be a common practice, if for no other reason than that human beings are normally uncomfortable when they treat other human beings rudely—particularly when the mistreated persons have been guilty of no offense.[37]

And speaking of the right of free choice, an employer who chooses to discriminate does not extend the right of free choice —to serve or not to serve customers—to his own employees. The latter must follow the practice dictated by their boss, whatever their personal preferences. Thus it is clear that it is not so much individual "rights" at stake as property "rights."[38]

If the right of "free choice"—and the rights of property—was violated by federal laws requiring merchants to serve all customers, what about the rights of Southern merchants who preferred to serve both white and black, but were denied this choice by state segregation laws? Why the curious silence about the denial of their rights during all these years?

Public eating places and places of lodging have been regarded as quasi-public enterprises since the days of Chaucer, because they perform services of such an essential character that they are vested with the public interest. Even in the laissez-faire heyday of the late nineteenth century, there was no questioning the authority of state governments to license them and impose special regulatory controls on them. Such businesses, then, are of a sufficiently public character to bring them under the discipline of the Fourteenth Amendment's equal protection clause.[39]

Property rights, it was added, are not absolute rights. Property rights exist only because society has decided they promote the individual and collective welfare of mankind. Having created the right, society can also limit that right in the interests of

[37] Howard Zinn, "A Fate Worse Than Integration," *Harper's Magazine*, August, 1959, pp. 53–56.

[38] "Civil Rights–A Reply," *The New Republic*, August 31, 1963, p. 24.

[39] Some judicial students believe the Supreme Court would soon have applied the equal protection clause to hotels and restaurants, even if Congress had failed to act.

human welfare. Zoning regulations, child labor laws, minimum wages and maximum hours, licensing requirements, tax laws, the Sherman Act, liquor regulations—these and many more demonstrate conclusively that business freedom and property rights have never been and are not now absolute in character.

It is generally conceded that no one has a right to use his property so as to injure the health of others (through impure food and drugs or the discharge of noxious fumes or equipment unduly dangerous to employees). If no one may use his property to injure another's health, can someone engaged in serving the public claim a right to impair a man's equal status as a human being? Does not the latter injury cut as cruelly and deeply as the former?

The disagreement between differing interpretations of property rights and human rights is a fundamental one. When pressed, the spokesmen for property rights conceded limitations to the rights of property, but insisted that the particular restraint proposed went beyond the realms of reason. Their opponents, in turn, conceded that restraints on property usage could be so unreasonable as to be unconstitutional. In the end, the difference boiled down to an interpretation of what is or is not reasonable —a difficulty long familiar to the courts.

Civil rights forces argued, furthermore, that it made no sense to outlaw discrimination against customers while permitting discrimination in the selection of employees who wait on the customers. The Civil Rights Act of 1964 did, in fact, also prohibit racial discrimination in the hiring, firing, compensation, or promotion of persons working for firms employing 25 or more persons, as well as in labor union and employment agencies. Those favoring this provision believed the federal government had both the authority and the obligation to bring its maximum moral and legislative influence to bear against racial inequality. The knowledge that discrimination based on race, color, creed, or national origin was illegal in these firms would not eliminate the practice overnight, but the presence of the law would encourage compliance. Because the government could bring adverse publicity to bear, supplemented by court sanctions, on those who flouted the law, a significant measure of enforcement could be expected. The fact that more than a dozen states had enacted fair employment practice laws that had enjoyed a moderate degree of success and had led to no unusual abuses suggested that the federal government could achieve constructive results if it took vigorous action against business engaging in conspicuously discriminatory hiring practices.

Constitutional? Because Congress had already made it illegal (with the Supreme Court's blessing) for an employer to discriminate against an employee because of his membership in a union, what constitutional objection could logically be raised against extending the ban to include racial discrimination as well?

Aside from repeating the objections against straining the interpretation of the commerce clause and deforming the face of federalism, opponents charged that such a law would inexcusably interfere with the right of a businessman to hire and fire as he pleases. Surely this, at least, ought to be beyond the long reach of the federal arm, if economic freedom is to mean anything at all. In any case, the law would be extraordinarily difficult to enforce because of the near impossibility of establishing the facts in specific cases. Is a Negro denied employment or fired because of his race, or because he lacks certain qualifications of ability and/or training? Is it discrimination, or a recognition that his personality, temperament, or character unfit him for a particular job? The complexities and imponderables of human motivations in cases of this kind are reason enough for keeping the federal government out. Moreover, the government would either give the law skimpy and haphazard enforcement (with more than 200,000 firms involved) or build up a huge federal bureaucracy to police the already overregulated businessman. Even though defending Negro rights is a worthy objective, we must not lose sight of other social values. (The pro forces contended that the Equal Employment Opportunity Commission would concentrate on the more flagrant violations of the law, just as the National Labor Relations Board [NLRB] had done in enforcing the Wagner Act ban on discrimination against union members. And they denied the complexities and subtleties involved in making a determination of racial discrimination were any greater than where union discrimination is alleged.)

To the surprise of both opponents and proponents of the new law, the public accommodations enforcement problem proved less troublesome than predicted. The normally law-abiding tendencies of the American people led to rapid compliance in the larger cities in the Deep South, though smaller towns and villages were slower to yield. As for the fair-employment provisions, it has been difficult to evaluate their impact during a period of unexampled prosperity. The real test will come during an economic downswing.

School Integration: Slow-down, Speed-up, and Pause

After the Supreme Court declared segregated schools to be "inherently unequal" in 1954, high hopes (and grave fears) were entertained that integrated education would rapidly become the norm throughout the public schools. But while the remnants of *de jure* segregated education were soon wiped out in the North and considerable progress was made in the border states, segregation's grip remained largely unshaken in the South for more than ten years. A number of Southern states did integrate their schools on a "token" basis, using the so-called pupil-placement plan as a court-approved device for complying with the letter of the law while essentially maintaining their schools unchanged. (This plan permitted Negro transfers to previously all-white schools if certain "nonracial" qualifications such as "psychological suitability," place of residence, and "educational preparedness" were met. Few Negro children managed to meet these tests.) By 1964, only about one half of 1 percent of Negro children in the South attended integrated schools. Not until the Civil Rights Act of 1964 threatened the receipt of federal educational funds did integration make much headway in many Southern states. And the degree to which this threat would lead to fully integrated schools in the deep South remained highly uncertain. The strategies for complying with the law on the surface while actually retaining the traditional character of Southern schools have not yet been exhausted.

Although all Negroes want the opportunity to decide for themselves whether to send their children to the nearest school, many prefer to keep their children in an all-Negro school—because it has always been the family school or because other members of the family are now attending the school or because the children feel more comfortable in a school in which their race predominates. Others strongly prefer to have their children integrated into white schools, feeling that these schools have superior instruction and that their children will be better able to compete and make their way in a white-dominated nation if they understand white behavior, attitudes, and values from firsthand experience. They further believe that school associations on an integrated basis tend to reduce the tensions that often result when Negroes previously accustomed to a virtually all-Negro environment are thrown into racially integrated employment situations. If they have learned from school that they can compete successfully with whites and win a measure of acceptance and approval from them, they are psychologically better adapted to postschool economic competition.

The feeling of some Negroes and some educators that the struggle for racial equality cannot be won unless Negroes achieve actual school integration instead of merely the right to attend has led to experiments at "forced" integration. Negro students have been transported considerable distances from their racial ghettos into schools located in all-white or predominantly white neighborhoods.

The experiment has ardent defenders and ardent foes. The former are convinced it is the only realistic way to end school segregation growing out of housing segregation patterns that, although not supported by law, are extremely difficult to alter. Schools should be leaders in social progress, it is said, and unless the schools take the lead in integration, they have failed to meet their full responsibilities.

Some opponents regard this effort to move large numbers of Negro students out of their neighborhood into distant white schools as a flagrant example of sacrificing common sense on the altar of ideological purity. They believe it bespeaks a determination to achieve the appearance of progress, whatever the effects may be on the substance of education. If Negro children from culturally inferior backgrounds are educated among more fortunate white children, their educational backwardness will become conspicuously evident. They will either have to be set back several grades or be resegregated into the backward sections of a given class. The blow to their self-esteem may have grave consequences, possibly confirming and deepening a previous feeling of inferiority. White children, observing the Negro's educational shortcomings as well as the personality distortions that grow out of frustration and shame, may conclude that Negroes really *are* somewhat inferior, after all. What the educationally disadvantaged Negro child really needs, these opponents believe, is better teachers in his neighborhood school, better equipment, smaller classes, and perhaps longer hours.

Agnes Meyer, a well-known champion of the Negro, has observed:

> . . . The situation in New York City, where Negro children have been transported by bus to distant white schools, has proved that this is a trivial, costly, ineffective solution to desegregation, and in the case of the elementary-school children, may even be detrimental. There are in the New York City school system about 170,000 Negro children in the kindergarten and grades one to eight. Of these, slightly more than 6,000, or a little more than 3 percent, are transported to white schools. How was this token group chosen? I do not know, but if such an experience is essential for all Negro children, it seems a great injustice to the vast majority, since tossing 170,000 children around the city is impossible. Why make an exception for a handful? Why not use the money, instead, for improving the schools?
>
> Moreover, is it not too great a strain for Negro children to have to journey every day to a remote white school for a few hours, and then return to their Negro neighborhoods? I discussed this procedure with some Negro high school students in another city, who, after attending a distant white high school, had returned to their Negro high school, and I am convinced that artificial desegregation is harmful. "When I left my friends and went to the white high school," said one tall young athlete, "it made me so nervous to compete with white children who are strangers to me that my hands would sweat." What, then, does being tossed between a strange white school and a familiar Negro neighborhood do to a little boy or girl?
>
> Another point is of major importance. How can the teacher in some

remote white school know the imported Negro child's home and background? Yet, without such knowledge, she is handicapped in teaching the child. No, the little elementary school children are much better off in their community schools, with their friends, in a familiar background, even though it may be a slum.[40]

Dr. James Bryant Conant agrees, in the following words:

> In some cities, political leaders have attempted to put pressure on the school authorities to have Negro children attend essentially white schools. In my judgment the cities in which the authorities have yielded to this pressure are on the wrong track. Those which have not done so, like Chicago, are more likely to make progress in improving Negro education. It is my belief that satisfactory education can be provided in an all-Negro school through the expenditure of more money for needed staff and facilities. Moreover, I believe that any sense of inferiority among the pupils caused by the absence of white children can be largely if not wholly eliminated in two ways: first, in all cities there will be at least some schools that are in fact mixed because of the nature of the neighborhood they serve; second, throughout the city there ought to be an integrated staff of white and Negro teachers and administrators.[41]

To these admonitions, several answers are given: Negro schools, in terms of instructional quality and often in other ways, are usually inferior to all-white or predominantly white schools. If housing segregation continues to produce *de facto* school segregation, big city school systems will remain essentially separate and *unequal*. One way this can be overcome is by opening all city schools on a first-come, first-served basis. Furthermore, only if some white parents' children are transplanted into inferior Negro schools will aroused white parents take seriously the formidable task of rapidly upgrading the quality of Negro schools—through adequate financing and quality teacher recruitment. Otherwise the predominantly white-controlled school system will

[40] Agnes Meyer, "Slums and Schools," *The Atlantic Monthly*, February, 1962, pp. 78–79. Also see Inge Lederer Gibel, "How *Not* to Integrate Schools," *Harper's Magazine*, November, 1963, pp. 59, 66.

[41] *Slums and Schools*, New York, McGraw-Hill, 1961, p. 28.

pay lip-service to the ideal of equal educational opportunity but will make only token gestures to achieve that end.

Many educators will concede that a considerable measure of truth adheres to these charges. For the most part, however, they regard it as hopelessly unrealistic to expect significant numbers of white parents to permit the transportation of their children, often at considerable distances, to second-rate schools in Negro neighborhoods. Stepped-up Negro demonstrations to achieve such reshuffling will only lead to militant and adamant white opposition—or to a rapid exodus of white families to areas in which such practices are not followed. While rejecting the feasibility of bussing large numbers of white students to schools in Negro residential areas, these educators are willing to support less drastic measures. They would agree that Negro children should be given the privilege of filling up any empty seats in predominantly white schools. (The better-prepared Negro students can adjust and profit from the switch.) Some believe that extraordinary efforts should be made to upgrade the quality of the so-called transitional schools (where integrated schools are being eroded by white withdrawal from the communities concerned) to improve their appeal to whites and arrest the process of resegregation. Many would also agree that white unwillingness to give all children equal access to the best public schools—where bussing white children to primarily Negro schools would be demanded—imposes a heavy moral obligation on whites to make the major and costly effort that is required if Negro schools are to achieve educational parity at the earliest possible date.

Negro Neighbors?

What, if anything, should government do about the Negro's persistent complaint that he lacks equal access to good housing? It has been said, now that the 1964 Civil Rights Act has largely guaranteed equal access to public places offering food and shelter, that housing is the one commodity the Negro cannot purchase on equal terms with other Americans. Resentment over this situation is growing among Negroes (and many whites), and the pressures to reduce or eliminate this grievance are sure to produce abrasive social conflicts in the years ahead. For reasons to be developed later, the Negro regards this struggle as critically important, just as many whites regard the right to sell or refuse to sell their homes to whomever they please as a matter of equal importance. Few issues are likely to be more enduring or produce more heated controversy.

The background of the housing problem reveals that government once played an active role in helping develop segregated housing in the United States. The use of restrictive covenants (contracts obligating the purchaser of a house not to resell to non-Caucasians) began around 1915 and was enforced in the courts until 1948. In *Shelley* v. *Kraemer*,[42] the Supreme Court ruled that courts could not enforce restrictive covenants without becoming parties to discriminatory practices forbidden by the Fourteenth Amendment. The latter, it will be recalled, forbids a state to deny the equal protection of the laws to its citizens.

Meanwhile the federal government established the Federal Housing Authority (FHA) in 1935 to spur the construction industry by offering to guarantee housing loans.[43] From 1935 to 1950, however, FHA manuals specifically warned against housing plans involving "incompatible racial elements" or "inharmonious racial and national groups." A sample racial covenant was prepared for builders containing a blank space in which "undesirable" groups could be specified. Thus the FHA, although an arm of the government, helped shape housing patterns that discriminated against Negroes and other minority groups over a prolonged period.

During the Eisenhower administration, efforts were made to persuade the President to issue a housing order barring discrimination in government-supported housing. Steadfastly maintaining that the elimination of segregation was principally a concern of education rather than of legislation, the President declined to act. However, he did appoint a commission to investigate the question. The commission recommended an executive order

[42] 334 U.S. 1 (1948).

[43] The author draws heavily upon Charles Abrams, "The Housing Order and Its Limits," *Commentary*, January, 1963, in treating this subject.

against discrimination, but Mr. Eisenhower chose to abide by his initial inclination.

During the 1960 Presidential campaign, John F. Kennedy reproached the Republicans for not wiping out federally related housing discrimination "with a stroke of the pen." But, fearing to antagonize southern Congressmen whose votes seemed crucial to his New Frontier programs, he delayed signing the long-awaited executive order until November, 1962. Since only an estimated 25 percent of new housing was affected by the order, it proved something of a disappointment to civil rights groups. Although it banned discrimination in housing thereafter insured by the FHA or the Veterans Administration (with single family dwellings or duplexes exempted), housing owned by the federal government or receiving federal loans, and future urban renewal projects partially financed by Washington, it did not cover housing loans emanating from building and loan associations. The latter are major mortgage lenders; as members of the federally created Home Loan Bank system, with deposits insured by the Federal Deposit Insurance Corporation (FDIC), they were subject to federal restraint had the President chosen to include them.

Until 1963, only about 2 percent of housing insured by the FHA had been available to Negroes. Middle-income Negroes were increasingly confined to ghettos in which housing was not only inferior, but often bore excessive rents. Knowing that Negroes had fewer options than whites in the same income brackets, landlords often charged whatever the traffic would bear.

Although discriminatory barriers have been lowered in many respects, housing segregation in the North, at least, seems to be increasing. In Chicago, in 1910, 35 percent of the Negroes lived in areas that were less than 10 percent nonwhite; by 1965, 92 percent of the Negroes lived in ghettos. Other cities seem to be moving in a similar direction—both Northern and Southern.[44]

A variety of activities and strategies were promoting this trend. Many realtors will not inform Negroes of openings in white

[44] C. Vann Woodward, "After Watts—Where Is the Negro Revolution Headed?" *The New York Times Magazine*, August 29, 1965, p. 81.

neighborhoods, and vice versa. Banks usually decline to lend to Negroes who seek to buy or build in all-white communities. If Negroes are able to make the necessary financial arrangements, white residents have an ingenious arsenal of violent and non-violent devices for letting them know that they are not welcome. If they do move in, "For sale" signs spring up on the lawns of nearby white residents. As Dick Gregory once put it, "In the South, white folks don't care how close I get, if I'm not too big. In the North, they don't care how big I get if I'm not too close." "Would you want one living next door?" is often the Northern equivalent to the South's "Would you want your sister to marry one?"[45]

Cynics have defined housing integration as "the period of time that elapses between the arrival of the first Negro and the departure of the last white." Some white neighborhoods do not object to having a few Negro families live among them, but when 30 to 40 percent of the families are Negro, a "tipping point" is reached at which a mass exodus of white families occurs. And because good residential property salable to Negroes is hard to come by, it is natural that the first Negro families in a pleasant residential area will be followed by others who seek the best housing available.

There are said to be over 100 relatively stable integrated neighborhoods in the United States, but they achieve their stability from unusual circumstances and measures. In virtually every case, a so-called benign quota is informally established by community leaders, limiting Negroes to not over 20 percent of the homes in the neighborhood. This quota, although offensive to many Negroes (and whites) is accepted by others as the realistic price to be paid if integrated housing is to persist. University communities, or communities in which white civil rights groups are active, or housing projects run by convinced believers in integration, provide the best milieu for the development of integration stability.

In an effort to promote more interracial housing, the National

[45] See Harry M. and David H. Rosen, *But Not Next Door,* New York, Ivan Obolensky, 1962.

Conference on Religion and Race has urged interested members of local communities to solicit open occupancy housing pledges from as many members of their communities as possible, to establish service centers for bringing together potential Negro purchasers and sellers willing to do business with them. It has, further, urged churches to invest some of their funds in housing loans for Negroes, when banks find excuses for withholding funds.[46] More than 1000 communities have established interracial housing organizations designed to bring about increased integration in their localities. Many of these groups have run advertisements listing the names of persons agreeing not to discriminate; provided Negroes with the location of housing for sale to all comers; sought to introduce or strengthen state or municipal fair housing laws; and tried to help communities accept integration in a spirit of good will.

Many states and cities have passed legislation making illegal certain forms of housing discrimination. In general, the legislation applies only to commercial housing projects or to projects financed in whole or in part by public funds. Landlords having four or fewer rooms to rent are generally excluded from the provisions of this legislation and owners of individual homes or duplexes are also exempt.

In 1966, President Johnson took the nation by surprise when he called for "the first effective Federal law against discrimination in the sale and rental of housing." He appealed for legislation covering "all dwelling units," making illegal false statements by realtors concerning the availability of housing, prohibiting discrimination by banks and other lending institutions which make home loans or fix down payments or interest rates, and permitting the objects of discrimination to sue in federal courts. Congress, however, balked at passing a housing law of such scope.

Opponents of housing legislation, particularly when it involves the sale of noncommercial housing, rely on a number of the following arguments to sustain their positions:

Unless a person's property rights include the power to sell or

[46] "Inter-Racial Housing," *Editorial Research Reports,* February 6, 1963, pp. 88, 103.

to refuse to sell his home to the customer of his choice, those rights are shrivelled. Selling a home is unlike selling food, or automobiles, or amusement tickets. A home is (or can be) a uniquely personal possession—the object of our creative efforts in building or decorating, the scene of our most cherished personal relationships, invested with some of our most sacred memories. It is so deeply a part of many of our most vital life experiences that its sale can be a traumatic experience. To deny the privilege of selling a possession of this nature to the person of your choice is to grant the state a power over the individual that no government with a sense of the fitness of things should even want to exercise.

Aside from these sentiments, a member of the community has not only the right but the obligation to respect the wishes of his neighbors when he sells his home. These people are often his friends, or persons with whom he has engaged in the sundry human relationships that make a group of homes a neighborhood. If they want to keep a community white, for whatever reasons, their wishes should not be ignored. If we are to do unto others as we would wish others to do unto us, we cannot introduce undesired elements into a community in the pursuit of some abstract notion of justice. Should the state, then, statutorily force the disruption of peaceful communities by requiring the sale of property to anyone who wishes to buy? Negroes have rights, but do not whites have rights as well? Are not their preferences as deserving of legislative respect as the preferences of Negroes? Besides, why should a person want to enter a community where he is unwelcome? Why force yourself on others, acting behind the shield of an offensive statute? Is this the way to win the respect and friendship of others?

Surely a person should have the right to refuse to sell or rent to someone who is dirty, uncouth, belligerent, uncivil, or possessed of other characteristics that would make him an unwelcome neighbor. Yet, suppose that a Negro with one or more of those qualities sought to purchase your house. If you refused and he charged racial discrimination, how could you prove that your action was unrelated to race? Can a fair-housing commission be expected to plumb the subtleties of human motivations?

Governments are well advised to stay within the limits of those problems they can hope to handle effectively.

A neighborhood that cannot protect itself from Negro entry cannot protect its property values. Once a Negro has entered a previously all-white community, or a considerable number of Negroes have entered, the community will no longer be as attractive to white purchasers. The resultant loss of property value would be, in effect, the taking of property without just compensation. Although such an action would not be a technical violation of the Constitution, it would be in violation of the spirit of that instrument.

Attempts to evade the provisions of law would be so widespread as to make it unenforceable except in cases so scattered as to be virtually capricious enforcement. It is of the essence of a lawful and orderly state that law should apply evenly to all, and be enforced evenly. It would take a monstrous bureaucracy to enforce a housing-discrimination law uniformly. Perhaps even this would be impossible, for when a sufficiently large number of persons disapproves of a law, it can never be successfully enforced. (Remember the Prohibition Amendment.) Minority pressure-group activity might be able to intimidate a state legislature or city council, but yielding to such pressure would invite unwelcome repercussions. Any attempt to ram through "forced housing" legislation could boomerang on civil rights groups, because the presence or imminence of such legislation will often touch off a referendum showdown. Anti-forced-housing groups that have taken the issue to the people have carried the day in every community or statewide test to date. In California, the voters defeated a so-called fair-housing law in 1964 by a margin of two to one; California voters presumably have about the same views on such legislation as other Americans. Civil rights advocates have fought for many a just cause, perhaps, but they should know when to call a halt.

As for federal legislation such as that suggested by President Johnson, this is patently unconstitutional. The sale of a citizen's private residence is strictly his own affair, unlike discrimination involving state or local laws or officials. To argue that the commerce clause empowers Washington to determine to whom a homeowner may or may not sell or rent his property is pushing the commerce clause to ridiculous lengths. Of course materials used in housing move in interstate commerce; of course persons moving from state to state want to rent and buy housing. But if such factors furnish an adequate constitutional ground work for such legislation, pray what is left of the reserved rights of the states?

Garbage cans are made from materials which move in interstate commerce; so are marriage certificates. People who travel from state to state want their garbage collected; some of them want to marry. Is Washington constitutionally authorized to regulate garbage collection and prescribe marriage practices? Is it possible to conceive of *any* statute which doesn't have some remote connection with interstate commerce? To have a flexible Constitution is one thing; to permit one phrase to swallow up all the others is quite another matter.

Proponents of fair-housing legislation respond that property "rights" involve a two-edged instrument: Why confine property rights to the right to sell? How about the right to buy? Is that not a legitimate property right also? Where two alleged rights come into conflict, it is up to the government to decide which right has the greatest priority—as nearly as that can be determined by our hearts and minds. Is not the right of an individual to fair and equal treatment more important than the right to discriminate on the basis of race, religion, or nationality? The "right" to discriminate is actually a privilege, not a right, a privilege that ultimately rests on an unwillingness to respect human dignity and human equality. It is a raw affront to human dignity when a property owner tells a Negro, in effect, "I don't want to sell to you because my friends and neighbors just don't like the color of your skin. You should pay your taxes and be prepared to die for your country, but don't ask me to treat someone with your color as a fully equal human being."

What kind of logic underlies the notion that no Negro, even the best educated and the most refined, can be fit to dwell in a household treasured by a white person? Shouldn't fitness be determined by the character, temperament, personality, and training of an individual, rather than by his skin pigment? It is interesting to note that there are many "plush" residential areas where a gambler, a narcotics pusher, or the owner of a string of brothels can buy a home without any difficulty, but where a Negro with a graduate degree and a spotless record of personal conduct is denied entrance. This is justice?

Property rights are not endangered by fair housing laws. States and cities that have enacted such laws have not found that a decline in property values or a reduction in construction has followed. The most searching investigation into the impact of integration on property values led to the conclusion that the chances are 4 to 1 that Negro entry will either leave property values stable or raise them somewhat.[47] Panic selling can indeed lead to financial losses, but if persons confronted with Negro neighbors sell with their usual deliberation, they can often obtain more than the prevailing price simply because Negroes are often willing to pay premium prices for good housing. If some folks' *real* concern is about a fall in property values, why are they disappointed when they learn that it just does not happen? It makes one wonder!

State fair-housing laws may help stabilize housing values. If all communities within a state are subject to Negro "infiltration," the presence or absence of Negroes in a particular community at a particular time will become a much less important selling factor.

Proving that discrimination is responsible for the rejection of a Negro seeking to buy a house might well prove difficult in many instances. Civil rights commissions, however, would give primary attention to the more clear-cut cases of housing discrimination (as they now do in equal employment opportunity cases), using them as object lessons to publicize the law and discourage other potential discriminators. It is better to have a law that

[47] Luigi Laurenti, *Property Values and Race: Studies in Seven Cities*, Los Angeles, University of California Press, 1960, p. 52. Using census figures covering 1,323,762 homes, Sherwood Ross notes that property values in all-Negro neighborhoods rose 61 percent from 1950 to 1960; in areas changing from all-white to all-Negro, they rose 42 percent; in areas remaining all-white, they rose only 35 percent. Ross concludes that "no white home-owner in America need lose a dollar on his house." *The Progressive*, March, 1966, p. 8.

constrains the conscience of the people and makes modest progress than no law at all. Admittedly, the elimination of all housing discrimination is a long way off, but law can be one of the pressures that will reduce it. As Martin Luther King has said, "Laws may not change the heart but they can restrain the heartless." Furthermore, psychologists tell us our attitudes are conditioned by our behavior; acting in nondiscriminatory ways helps to reduce prejudiced feelings.

Currently, some persons with homes for sale are willing to sell to Negroes but fear to do so lest they incur the displeasure of their friends and neighbors. If fair housing laws were passed, they could act on their essentially decent impulses and receive forgiveness from friends who would recognize that they were obeying the law. Thus, such laws would facilitate the reduction of racially prejudiced behavior. Negroes are quite properly willing to enter communities where they are not wanted by some (although rarely all) of the people. Many of them hope, by their exemplary conduct and by the human contacts that will invariably occur, to soften prejudice and gradually make friends. This, of course, often does happen. Perhaps they are even doing members of the community a favor by giving them an opportunity to rid themselves of racial prejudice.

State open-occupancy laws may be the only way to put a halt to the white practice of fleeing from one part of a metropolitan area to another when Negroes enter. If Negroes were free to buy anywhere in the city or state, there would be little point to selling out when the next all-white neighborhood might be desegregated the following day. The reduction of Negro ghettos is a social objective devoutly to be desired, yet it seems unattainable unless something is done to make housing available to all comers able to pay the price. As for housing referenda forbidding fair housing legislation, these may be invalidated by the courts. (This has already happened in California.) If they are not, proponents will take comfort from polls showing that the percentage of Americans who would object to having a Negro live next door is declining.

It is widely recognized that Negro schools are unable to attract as good teachers as the white suburban schools. Because *de facto* housing segregation leads to *de facto* school segregation, the

Negro will never be able to achieve equality of educational opportunity for his children unless he can buy into neighborhoods with good schools. Thus truly integrated education can only be won if the struggle for housing equality is won.

The constitutionality of state and local fair housing legislation is beyond question. As for federal action, President Johnson's proposal rested its case on Washington's power to "regulate commerce among the several states." More specifically, "The interstate movement of funds for housing; the interstate travel of individuals, which can be impeded by segregation in housing in various areas; and disturbances resulting from housing segregation that can have an adverse effect on the interstate movement of people and goods." This does not mean that Washington can legislate on local matters whenever it pleases. Washington may prevent all forms of discriminatory action where interstate commerce is directly or indirectly involved, but it cannot regulate local activities that do not involve equal protection of the laws or some other constitutional right.

Finally, buying a home is more than buying some real estate. It means buying ready access to good neighbors, good schools, museums, parks, and various cultural facilities. It involves raising your family in a neighborhood atmosphere conducive to the healthiest and fullest development of your children. The entire quality of one's life is affected by the quality of a neighborhood. To arbitrarily deny persons equal access to all of the advantages of a fine neighborhood is to strike deeply at the heart of fair play, justice, and equal opportunity. And how are whites to understand—really understand—that Negroes are "just people" unless they live together?

President Johnson put it this way: "The ghettos of our major cities . . . represent fully as severe a denial of freedom and the fruits of American citizenship as more obvious injustices. . . . If we are to include the Negro in our society, we must do more than give him the education he needs to obtain a job and a fair chance for useful work. We must give the Negro the right to live in freedom among his fellow Americans."[48]

The importance of these considerations helps explain why

[48] *The New York Times,* May 1, 1966, p. 2E.

Negroes place such high priority on housing equality and why they will never be content with anything less than full parity in this field.

Beyond Civil Rights

The Negro has a legal (although not necessarily a *de facto*) guarantee of equal employment opportunity with larger firms, but is employment equality enough? Many Negroes and some whites believe that the policy of "compensatory hiring," which temporarily favors Negro applicants, is fully justified. For example, Guichard Parris, an assistant to the executive director of the National Urban League, declares, "It's time to discriminate in the Negro's favor for five or ten years. . . . The veterans of World War II got a break—the GI bill and extra points in Civil Service examinations—because they were out of the mainstream of the economy for three or four years." The Negro, he contends, has never been in that mainstream, and compensation is entirely in order.

Mr. Parris' superior, Whitney M. Young, adds:

> An intensive special effort may appear to be in conflict with the principle of equal treatment for all. But such effort is required to overcome the damaging effects of generations of deprivation and denial and to make it possible for the majority of American Negroes to reach the point at which they can compete on a basis of equality in the nation's increasingly complex and fast-moving industrial society. . . . The intense needs and problems which are a direct result of past and present discrimination and exclusion based on race. Thus, as a matter of historic equity, compensatory effort is justified and may well be the only means of overcoming the heavy aftermath of past neglect.

James Farmer, former national director of the Congress of Racial Equality, says, "It is no longer acceptable . . . for an employer to say there are no qualified Negro applicants for a job. The employer . . . is now obligated to find a qualified Negro. If he cannot . . . he should train a Negro for the job."[49]

[49] Quotes are from "Is Equality in Employment Enough?" *Current*, August, 1963, pp. 13–14.

A dissenting view was expressed by Kyle Haselden, managing editor of the *Christian Century:*

> . . . Compensation for Negroes is a subtle but pernicious form of racism. It requires that men be dealt with by society on the basis of race and color rather than on the basis of their humanity. . . . Racism, whoever may be its temporary beneficiary, should be eliminated from the social order, not confirmed by it.
> Second, preferential economic status for Negroes would penalize the living in a futile attempt to collect a debt owed by the dead. The 20th-century white man is no more to blame for the fact that his ancestors bought and held slaves than are 20th-century Negroes for the fact that some of their ancestors captured and sold slaves. . . . Preferred status for the Negro, however much society may owe him a debt, will inevitably destroy in him the initiative and enterprise required of a minority people in a highly competitive society. Slavery corrupts ambition and self-reliance; so, too, does patronizing social status. . . . Compensation for Negroes would be unfair to other minorities handicapped by their history or by rapid social and industrial change: Puerto Ricans, Mexican-Americans, migrants of all races, Indians, coal miners and others. . . . Our goal should be parity, not preferment.[50]

Currently, many business firms are scrambling to obtain Negro employees in an effort to ward off possible picketing, demonstrations, or other "unpleasantness" by Negro organizations. It appears that Negroes with employable skills are enjoying better job opportunities than they have ever known before—with "discrimination in reverse" apparently occurring in some cases. How far this trend will go remains to be seen. Although many whites will be understanding of or sympathetic to employers who give a degree of preference to Negro applicants, any persistent and widespread policy in this direction is sure to arouse persistent and widespread white antagonism.

Now that the Negro has won about as much equality (housing

[50] "Should There Be Compensation for Negroes?" *The New York Times Magazine,* October 6, 1963, p. 128. Copyright © 1963 by The New York Times Company. Reprinted by permission. Also see Robert Carter, Dorothy Kenyon, Peter Marcuse, and Loren Miller, *Equality,* New York, Pantheon Books, 1965.

aside) as the law can offer, the over-all potentialities of dramatic protest seem to be declining. Obtaining full equality now becomes a matter of effectively using normal political channels to insure adequate funds for, and proper administration of, programs to help the poor and illiterate improve their education and job skills. Demonstrations may not accomplish much here, except to antagonize those whose help the Negro needs. As for destructive and bloody riots by wanton teen-age vandals, these call for stern Negro condemnation and more effective Negro restraint than has yet been forthcoming.

Will Negro leadership be able to measure up to this challenging assignment, an assignment that calls for a less conspicuously "heroic" and visible role with more emphasis on the hard work, self-discipline, and responsibility required of their followers? In this connection, John Fischer, editor of *Harper's Magazine,* once called for the establishment of a new Negro organization, "A First-Class Citizens' Council," carrying the motto, "Let's Make Every Negro a First-Class Citizen."

Mr. Fischer believes Negroes should face up squarely to the fact that there are some rational grounds for white uneasiness about the influx of large numbers of Negroes into American cities. He observes that in cities such as Washington, Chicago, Philadelphia, and Detroit, Negroes account for far more than their proportion of serious crimes. If whites are assaulted and robbed by Negro gangs, Negro bystanders may watch passively and later refuse to cooperate in apprehending the offenders. Policemen, too, lead unusually hazardous lives in Negro sections, the rate of attacks on them reaching shocking levels at times. He adds, "A neighborhood where I once lived in Washington is now occupied almost entirely by Negroes; it has indeed gone downhill, swiftly and unmistakably. In part this is due to overcrowding, and to incomes so low that the owners can't afford to keep their places up properly. But it is also partly due to plain old don't care. Garbage, broken bottles, and old bed springs accumulate in many a backyard . . . a loose porch board goes unfixed for weeks, though all it needs is one nail and two licks with a hammer . . . broken windowpanes get stuffed with rags." The editor says, "Similar examples can be cited in almost any

American city. Still—nothing about this matter is simple—I know of communities in Atlanta and the S. F. Bay area which have improved, rather than deteriorated, after an influx of Negro families." Another legitimate white complaint is that Negroes seem unwilling ". . . to invest time and effort in the web of civic, political and voluntary organizations which holds every American community together." Mr. Fischer cites nonvoting statistics and adds, "How many [Negroes] attend the meetings of their Parent-Teachers' Association? How many help collect for the Community Chest or offer to lead a Girl Scout troop?"

He readily concedes that whites bear a heavy share of responsibility for this irresponsible and undisciplined behavior. But he says that Negroes must not seek easy absolution by pointing to white shortcomings. They should make it their major objective to acquire the personal habits that will induce respect and disarm their critics. He cites Martin Luther King approvingly. "Even the most poverty stricken among us can purchase a ten-cent bar of soap; even the most uneducated among us can have high morals. . . . By improving our standards here and now we will go a long way toward breaking down the arguments of the segregationist."

Fischer adds that ". . . Negroes need a great deal more help than they have yet had, to overcome the cultural lag that has been imposed upon them. They need—and deserve—the same concentration of money, talent, and organization that we are devoting to underdeveloped people in Asia, Africa, and Latin America." But, he insists, they also need to make a greater effort to help themselves.[51]

Henry Lee Moon, director of public relations for the National Association for the Advancement of Colored People, dispatched a hot answer to Mr. Fischer. Among other things, he charged that Negroes are often apprehended and convicted in the South on charges that would never be pressed against whites—including arrests for demonstrations against discrimination. He ridiculed the notion that whites move out when Negroes move in largely because of Negro standards of behavior. They move out, he said,

[51] "What the Negro Needs Most: A First-Class Citizens' Council," *Harper's Magazine,* July, 1962, p. 14.

in response to the "oft-exposed myth" that Negro entry will bring depreciated property values. He also said that instances can be cited where whites have stood passively by when Negroes were beaten up by white ruffians. Regarding much if not all of the statistical evidence used against Negroes as inaccurate or suspect, he concluded ". . . we are damn tired of having to be nicer than white folk."[52]

A friend of the Negro revolution wisely emphasizes the important distinction between true integration and desegregation. Writing in *The Saturday Review,* William Sloane Coffin, Jr., chaplain of Yale University and a Freedom Rider himself, declared:

> The former gets to the heart of the matter, the heart of every man, and thus refers to something personal and subjective. Desegregation, on the other hand, refers to something impersonal and objective, a state of affairs in which rights and opportunities are guaranteed to all citizens despite the objections of some.
>
> From any religious or moral point of view integration is the only acceptable goal, for the brotherhood of man is a farce if it is not finally a matter of the heart. Moreover, in an explosive world, integration may well be an absolute necessity. But the fact that a thing is right and necessary still does not make it possible; ironically, the very insecurity of the world, increasing as it does individual insecurity, tends to enhance rather than to diminish the possibility for racial discrimination. For racial discrimination, or prejudice of any kind for that matter, is deeply rooted in a sense of individual insecurity—which is why it is at once so universal and so ineradicable . . . what the segregationist fears is finally less the Negro than himself—his own insecurity inevitably felt most acutely when change and strife render horribly insecure the world about him. . . . Those who believe that prejudice can be eradicated simply by education do not properly assess these emotional and moral dimensions of the problem, do not realize how inadequate a solution education is for people whose lives are motivated not by love but by hate and fear of the truth. Thus, while all individuals surely have a clear religious or moral obligation to overcome their prejudices, it seems only realistic to anticipate that far from all will succeed. "Human nature," as a shrewd observer of the human

[52] "Letter to Editor," *Harper's Magazine,* October, 1962, pp. 26, 28, 29.

scene remarked, "is very prevalent." As far as whole societies go, integration appears an unattainable goal.

Dr. Coffin believes desegregation is an attainable goal, however, noting that "while it is true that morality cannot be legislated, it is also true that one can legislate conditions more conducive to morality."[53]

The struggle for full equality will be long and painful, with heavy responsibilities weighing on both Negro and white to help build an America measuring up more faithfully to its professed ideals. Certainly the decades ahead will demand the most skillful and balanced blend of our courage and our restraint, our good will and our pragmatic estimate of what will work. Bringing a once enslaved people into a position of fruitful equality with those who enslaved them is as noble and challenging an undertaking as any nation has ever faced.

[53] "Desegregation: Will It Work? Yes," *The Saturday Review,* November 11, 1961, pp. 20–21. For a rebuttal, see William F. Buckley, "Desegregation: Will It Work? No," *The Saturday Review,* November 11, 1961, pp. 21–22.

CHAPTER

◂ 2 ▸

LABOR LEGISLATION:

Which Road Is the Road Ahead?

The power and place of labor unions in American life has divided Americans since 1935, much as the power and place of the "trusts" divided them decades earlier. Although labor union acceptance has intermittently gained ground during much of this period, the feeling persists with varying degrees of intensity that (1) labor unions should enroll their membership by persuasion only, not by the coercion implicit in the "union shop"; (2) labor unions should either stay out of politics altogether or confine themselves to political activities financed exclusively by purely voluntary contributions; (3) labor union power has reached dimensions that threaten the public interest, and this power should be scaled down through the elimination or reduction of certain legal privileges that invite the abuse of power.

Before evaluating the controversies surrounding these issues, it will be well to take a brief backward glance at the evolution of unions and legislation affecting them. This glance must perforce be hasty, too hasty to give the student an adequate historical perspective, yet providing enough familiarity with major trends and landmarks to prevent the grosser errors of judgment to which the unhistorically minded are prone.

Labor unions have faced a relatively hostile environment throughout most of American history. Ours was a predominantly rural nation until recent years, and even when an urban majority appeared and enlarged, many of its members carried their rural attitudes into the city. Farmers are rarely friendly to unions, for quite understandable reasons. The farmer cannot go on strike, cannot work an eight-hour day, gets no time-and-a-half for overtime, lacks a minimum wage, receives no paid vacations, and usually has no workmen's compensation or pension plan (although he was recently covered by Social Security). These benefits, which are often available to nonunion workers, too, combined with farmers' traditional mistrust of urban morality and city-slickerism, has meant that unions could expect little sympathy and support from either a farming population or its legislators.

Until the New Deal, the courts quite consistently interpreted common law, statutory law, and the Constitution in such a way as to cramp union activities.[1] Thus, early efforts to form unions, to strike, and to conduct boycotts met a series of hostile court interpretations based on common-law provisions forbidding conspiracies to injure others. After strikes became legal, employers faced with strikes often sought and won injunctions that forbade even legitimate union activities on grounds that violence was impending. These injunctions, frequently issued on an *ex parte* basis (after hearing the employer's side only) were of a sweeping character and placed unions under a heavy handicap.

Meanwhile it was commonplace for employers to refuse to hire persons known to be pro-union (blacklists were often maintained and circulated among employers), to fire employees who sought to organize, to employ spies who infiltrated employee groups, to

[1] Lloyd G. Reynolds, *Labor Economics and Labor Relations,* 3rd ed., Englewood Cliffs, N.J., Prentice-Hall, 1959, pp. 118–121.

hire provocateurs to goad unions into illegal and hence punishable activities, and to enlist bullyboys, on occasion, to use whatever violence might be needed when outbreaks occurred.[2] The unions fought back with rough tactics of their own: mass picketing, threats, and physical violence to prevent nonstrikers from going to work; destruction of company property; sabotage of plant equipment; and intimidation of workers who were indisposed to join the union.

Unions formed first among the more skilled workers and grew most rapidly during prosperous times. During depressions, when the employer had large pools of unemployed labor to call on, unions usually lost ground. But, as an ever larger proportion of the working population found nonfarm employment, unions tended to gain in numbers, popular acceptance, and political influence.

Labor's first great national legislative victory was the passage of the Clayton Anti-Trust Act in 1916. This act contained a provision that seemingly exempted labor unions from the provisions of the Sherman Anti-Trust Act of 1890. Although the latter had forbidden conspiracies in restraint of trade and monopolistic activities, it was aimed at industrial combinations rather than at labor. Nevertheless, the courts began applying the act to secondary boycotts (union attempts to persuade members and friends to coerce third parties, not concerned with the labor dispute, to discontinue business relations with an offending employer). To clarify the original intent of the Sherman Act, the Clayton Act declared that labor was "not a commodity or article of commerce," and affirmed that the Sherman Act did not forbid the existence of labor unions or deny their lawful pursuit of legitimate objectives. To the dismay of labor and its friends, however, the courts continued to outlaw secondary boycotts on grounds that they were unlawful interferences with interstate commerce and thus unaffected by the Clayton Act.

Unlike previous depressions, the Great Depression of the 1930s

[2] Robert R. R. Brooks, *When Labor Organizes,* New Haven, Yale University Press, 1938, ch. III.

ushered in a golden era for the United States labor union movement. In 1932, Congress passed the Norris-LaGuardia Act, making the "yellow dog contract" unenforceable in the courts. (Under these contracts, employees agreed not to join a union while working for a given employer.) This act also placed stringent limits on the power of courts to issue injunctions in labor disputes, while specifically recognizing the right to organize.

The Wagner Act, sponsored by an administration friendly to union objectives, gave organizers long-sought protection. It forbade employer interference with organizing activities and discrimination against union members; it required employers to bargain "in good faith" with representatives of unions once an election supervised by the newly formed National Labor Relations Board had certified that a majority of employees wanted to join the union. When a union was legally formed, its spokesmen were free to bargain collectively for the union shop, requiring all employees to join the union within 30 to 60 days as a condition of retaining their jobs, or the closed shop, requiring membership as a precondition to obtaining a job.

Shielded by the Wagner Act, encouraged by the Roosevelt administration, and operating in a climate of opinion that was more critical of the chastened business community, union membership zoomed from 3.5 million in 1930 to 8.7 million in 1940. With this growth came greater public awareness of the theoretical values of unionism, including:

1. Representatives of a union can bargain far more effectively for improved wages, hours, and working conditions than can a single employee.
2. Unions protect workers from arbitrary managerial decisions, protection that is of special importance to the worker where possible dismissal is involved. With the union to back him up, an aggrieved worker can appeal what he regards as an unfair or high-handed decision with far greater assurance that his grievance will be given due consideration.
3. Unions confer an element of dignity on the worker, by offering him an opportunity to participate in plant decisions that vitally

affect his welfare. Decision-making shared by the worker provides a more democratic and self-respecting atmosphere than exists in a plant where decisions are handed down from on high.

4. Unions can block wage cuts that would otherwise be made during recessions and depressions. Employers naturally seek to cut costs during "hard times," and were previously able to reduce wage costs by recruiting unemployed persons sufficiently hard pressed to accept employment at almost any wage. Economists generally agree, however, that reducing wages and hence purchasing power only intensifies economic declines.
5. Unions provide a disciplining counterbalance to the economic and political power of giant corporations. Major economic decisions must be made with an eye to considerations uniquely important to the working man as well as to those traditionally important to business. Public policy-making bodies are subjected to labor as well as to business pressures, thus assuring a less one-sided evaluation of measures affecting business, labor, and the public.[3]

In the words of Clark Kerr, "A rough balance among private and public power centers is the essence of a pluralistic society, and a pluralistic society is the only firm foundation for democracy in an economy based on industrial production."[4]

In theory, then, labor unions won acceptance during the depression and postdepression years as legitimate social institutions that could potentially serve the general welfare. Critics, however, deplored the gap between the potential and the performance, and a hard-core minority has never been willing to accord even lip-service to the value of unions.

During World War II, although labor's normal strength was cramped by no-strike pledges, strike legislation, and by wage and price controls, unions continued to increase their membership. When the accumulated grievances of the wartime years, fed by rapidly rising prices, led to a succession of major national strikes in the immediate postwar period, demands increased for legislation to correct the "one-sided" character of the Wagner Act and to protect the nation against strikes that might have

[3] John Kenneth Galbraith, *American Capitalism: The Concept of Countervailing Power,* Boston, Houghton, Mifflin, 1952, ch. IX (for paragraph 5).

[4] Clark Kerr, *Unions and Union Leaders of Their Own Choosing,* New York, Fund for the Republic, 1957, p. 8.

paralyzing national economic consequences. The Wagner Act spelled out a series of unfair employer acts, but what about unfair union acts? Should they not come under legislative condemnation also?

Led by the redoubtable Senator Robert A. Taft, a Republican Congress pushed through the Taft-Hartley Act against the combined and bitter opposition of the labor unions and President Truman. This Act outlawed a long list of union activities, including:

1. The closed shop (union shops were permissible if a majority of workers voted for them in states that had not forbidden their existence);
2. Secondary boycotts;
3. Featherbedding (which requires employers to pay unneeded workmen or which limits the amount of work done in a day as a means of stretching out work);
4. Excessive union dues (the term "excessive" was to be interpreted by the NLRB);
5. Refusal to bargain with employers;
6. Jurisdictional strikes (strikes that grow out of disputes between unions, each of which claims the right to do a particular job);
7. Political expenditures in connection with federal elections, if financed from union dues.

The law also restored to the employer the privilege of discussing unionization with his employees so long as neither threats nor promises of special benefits were made. He was also permitted to sue the union for breach of contract. National strikes that threatened the public health or safety could be delayed for 80 days while the NLRB attempted to bring about a settlement of the disputes.

The Taft-Hartley Act, labeled a "slave labor act" by its foes, was the object of both vituperative attack and immoderate praise for many years. Although it did not achieve many of its ends (for example, featherbedding continued to persist, the closed shop continued in practice in many industries, jurisdictional strikes still broke out, loopholes appeared in the secondary boycott provision, and the political spending provision was evaded), relatively objective students believed it achieved many constructive results. The predictions of disaster for the union movement have not materialized, and unions made some of their greatest material gains between 1948 and 1956.[5]

Although dissatisfaction with union behavior found continuous expression in the press, no new labor legislation was seriously considered by the Congress until charges of corruption in the biggest single labor union, the Teamsters, as well as in some other unions, shocked the nation. The employment of racketeers on the union payroll; the raiding of welfare funds; the use of millions of dollars of union funds for speculative purposes, for payment of union officials' salaries while in jail, and for the purchase of box seats at horse races; lavish expense accounts; income tax evasion —these and many other charges made before the McClellan Rackets Committee aroused the nation.[6] Even George Meany, the president of the AFL-CIO, said, "We thought we knew a few things [about the Teamsters] but we didn't know the hundredth part." Fed by over 100,000 letters from citizens all over the nation, the McClellan hearings turned up numerous examples of misuse of union power and money in other unions.

The McClellan hearings stimulated a deluge of general attacks on labor unions. Critics charged that many unions, in addition to being corrupt, were run in high-handed fashion by despotic and arbitrary leaders; that rank-and-file members were often intimidated and denied free participation in union meetings; that unions had invaded managerial prerogatives to the detriment of plant efficiency and in violation of management "rights"; that unions forced certain firms out of business if they did not knuckle under to union demands; that unscrupulous union picketing often halted the delivery of goods or discouraged prospective customers or harassed employers until employees

[5] Benjamin Rathbun, "Taft-Hartley and the Test of Time," *Harper's Magazine,* March, 1953; Daniel Bell, "Taft-Hartley: Five Years After," *Fortune,* July, 1952. Also see Sumner Slichter, "The Taft-Hartley Act,' *The Quarterly Journal of Economics,* February, 1949.

[6] Clark Mollenhoff, "The Teamsters Defy the Government," *The Atlantic Monthly,* November, 1958; John Dos Passos, "What Union Members Have Been Writing to Senator McClellan," *Reader's Digest,* September, 1958.

were virtually coerced into joining a union; that union power had become so great that even powerful companies could not compete on equal terms, leading to inflationary contracts and other unfortunate developments.

No responsible authority believed that more than a small minority of unions were corrupt, racketeer-ridden, or run by despots indifferent to member wishes or rights. But a public aroused by the Teamster stench demanded action, and Congress responded with the Labor-Management Reporting and Disclosures Act of 1959 (also known as the Landrum-Griffin Act).[7] Originally designed to eliminate union corruption and to curtail the kind of abuses to which Teamster boss James Hoffa was believed to be addicted, the bill eventually broadened into a general reform measure aimed at reducing labor's economic power and guaranteeing democratic processes within unions.

Among other things, the 1959 act placed tight restrictions on the use of union funds; set up stringent reporting requirements concerning the use of those funds, and forbade certain categories of convicted criminals or former Communists to hold union office for five years after conviction or after leaving the Communist Party. A "Bill of Rights" was included to insure free speech in union meetings; free, reasonably frequent, and secret elections with fair play for opposition candidates; the right of appeal in disciplinary cases; no dues increases or special assessments unless approved by a majority vote; and the rights of members to sue the union. All of these rights could be vindicated in federal courts, where desired.

The act also narrowly limited the right to picket, forbidding virtually all picketing for a twelve-month period following union elections in which workers elected to join no union or in which a particular union was certified. (Purely "informational"

[7] For explanations of, and comments on, the act, see "House Adopts Strict Labor Union Reforms," *The Congressional Quarterly,* No. 33, 1959, pp. 1113–1115; Joseph E. Finley, "Understanding the 1959 Labor Law," Public Affairs Institute, 1960; Benjamin Aaron, "The New Labor Bill," *The Nation,* November, 1959. For the debate preceding passage of the bill, see "Congress Acts to Curb Labor Abuses," *The Congressional Digest,* August and September, 1959.

picketing, which doesn't lead to work stoppages or strikes or nondelivery of goods, is still legal and is believed to be protected by the First Amendment.) Secondary boycott provisions were tightened, "hot cargo" contracts ruled out (contracts in which employers agree not to ask their employees to handle "struck goods," that is, goods produced while a strike is proceeding). State courts, which are normally less lenient with unions than are federal courts and the NLRB, were given wider latitude for handling labor cases.

Whether the 1959 act has reduced the power of the Teamsters is not altogether clear. It has, however, made Teamster officials more prudent about their financial transactions and general behavior, and there are high hopes that James Hoffa will eventually be put behind bars. As for other provisions of the law, not enough evidence is in to permit a reasonably objective evaluation of its merits.

A Dialogue on Right-to-Work Laws

Section 14(b) of the Taft-Hartley law declares: "Nothing in this Act shall be construed as authorizing . . . agreements requiring membership in a labor organization as a condition of employment . . . [where] prohibited by state or territorial law." Acting under this provision, 19 states have passed "right-to-work" laws forbidding union-shop contracts that require workers to join a union within 30 to 60 days of obtaining a job. Unions in these states, then, are "open shop"—that is, they may exist so long as they are supported by a majority of the workers, but no worker is compelled to join as a condition for holding his job.

The 1964 Democratic platform called for the repeal of Section 14(b). With what may be termed "underwhelming" enthusiasm, President Johnson, in 1965, asked Congress to honor the pledge. The House supported his recommendation by a vote of 221 to 203, but a late-session Senate filibuster, well timed to capitalize on the senators' desire to go home, blocked passage of the bill. A factor of some importance in the struggle was a Gallup poll (June 13, 1965) showing that the American people, by 49 to 43 per cent (8 per cent were undecided) supported the belief that no one should be compelled to join a union in a unionized plant.

Under AFL-CIO pressure, President Johnson renewed his request for abolition of 14(b) in 1966, but once again a filibuster blocked action on the bill. Apparently a majority of senators favored repeal, but the two-thirds majority needed to terminate debate could not be found.

Let us construct a conversation about "right-to-work" laws that might take place between "Pro," who fervently favors them, and "Con," who fervently opposes them.[8]

Pro: This is primarily a moral issue. The right to join or not to join an organization is one of the inalienable rights of a free man. Each individual should have the right to decide for himself whether or not he believes an organization claiming to promote his welfare will accomplish that end, and whether he chooses to identify with it. But when the element of compulsion enters in, and contracts protected by law demand that you join a private organization or else—well, this is in about as direct a conflict with the American way of life and with the general concepts of freedom as any action I can imagine.

Con: I am inclined to agree that this is a moral issue, but in my view the morality concerns the question of responsibility versus irresponsibility. If a union bargains for a group of employees and wins benefits for them that they would not otherwise enjoy, every worker has an obligation to help support those who have improved their lot. The worker has rights, to be sure, but he exercises these when he votes in an election to determine whether a union shall represent him or not. Once a majority decides to form a union, the latter has rights, too, one of which is to ask a

[8] For discussion of the right-to-work issue, see "The Growing Controversy Over 'Right-to-Work' Laws," *The Congressional Digest,* February, 1956; "The Case for Voluntary Unionism," United States Chamber of Commerce (undated); W. L. White, "Right To Work: Our Hottest Labor Labor Issue," *The Reader's Digest,* August, 1958; Clinton S. Golden and Harold J. Ruttenberg, "The Union Shop is Democratic and Necessary," *Union, Management, and the Public,* 2nd ed. (E. Wright Bakke, Clark Kerr, and Charles W. Anrod, eds.), Harcourt, Brace, and World, 1960, pp. 78–84; "The Case for the Union Shop," AFL-CIO Publication No. 11; P. Sultan, *Right-to-Work Laws: A Study in Conflict,* Los Angeles, Institute of Industrial Relations, University of California Press, 1958.

reasonable financial support from those it represents. And let's never forget that rights must always be balanced against responsibilities.

Pro: You seem to be assuming that once a majority votes for a union, minority rights disappear. This is not sound democratic theory. Ours is a country based on both majority rule and minority rights. The majority's rights are exercised when the union bargains for all the workers in a plant. The minority's rights are respected only if individuals are free to join or refuse to join the union. This right cannot be wiped out in the name of "majority rule." Majority rule can be tyrannical rule, as we know from current experience as well as from advice given us by the Founding Fathers.

By the way, I'm sure you are appalled by the old "yellow dog contract" that required a worker to pledge not to join a union as a precondition of employment. If it is morally wrong and contrary to national policy to exact contracts *forbidding* union membership, why is it morally acceptable to have contracts *requiring* union membership before a man can get a job? Isn't that a double standard? Besides, the union shop actually is in violation of a provision of the Taft-Hartley Law that forbids an employer to ". . . encourage or discourage membership in any labor organization." When an employer signs a union-shop contract, he becomes a party to encouraging membership in unions.

Con: You've slid over an important difference between the yellow dog contract and the union shop. The former denies a man a right tacitly guaranteed under the Constitution, the right to freely associate with his fellows to promote legal ends. But under the union shop, the right not to associate is protected by the election that must precede the establishment of any union at all. You must look at Congress' intentions as well as the specific wording of Taft-Hartley. Congress was concerned with employers who threaten their employees not to form a union or offer inducements so they will refrain from joining. Every member of Congress who voted on Taft-Hartley understood that the union shop would remain legal except where it was specifically outlawed by the states.

I think you have this freedom issue confused. When a worker accepts employment, he accepts the responsibility to live up to the rules of the plant. These rules are jointly worked out by unions and management. I have never understood why it is perfectly all right for the worker to be compelled to live up to a thousand and one rules affecting the conditions of employment—hours, wages, lunch hours, wash-up time, disciplinary rules, safety rules, and what have you—and none of them impair that priceless freedom you are so concerned about. But if the contract adds one more rule, that workers shall help support those who make the rules, the American Way cf Life is threatened and majority tyranny has set in! Why is it all right to require adherence to these other rules and all wrong to require financial support for those making the rules?

I might add that the choice is not between freedom and the tyranny of the union or the union boss. There will always be rules, and they will either be made by the employer or by the employer in conjunction with employee representatives. Union membership simply gives the worker an opportunity to participate in the making of the rules within which he works. Is it bad to offer him that privilege, or does it actually extend his freedom?

Pro: If the worker prefers not to take advantage of this "privilege" for any one of a number of reasons, he is exercising his freedom in making that choice. Besides, there are reasonable rules and unreasonable ones. Coerced union membership falls into the latter category. It goes beyond mere plant regulations into a fundamental right of man—the right of association or non-association.

Getting back to your earlier point about the benefits unions allegedly win for their members and the consequent obligation to support the union, this lends no support to compulsion. Churches do many good works in this country and help maintain morals and ideals, but we don't compel people to join. The Red Cross does noble humanitarian work, but we don't demand that people join. The farm organizations lobby for farmers in Washington, but we don't oblige all farmers to join. Even if organizations are doing useful work, the element of voluntarism in supporting or not supporting them is an attribute of liberty. You keep slipping away from that point.

Con: But there is a basic difference between churches, the Red Cross, the National Grange, and labor unions. No law authorizes any of these to make rules binding on all persons directly affected by their activities. But federal law does require that properly established unons bargain for *all* the employees, whether members or not. If the law has seen fit to permit this authority, workers should also be obliged to pay for services rendered. Their work helps pay, willy-nilly, for the services of their employer, who helps make the rules. Why shouldn't they help pay for the services of union representatives who also help make the rules? These "right-to-work" laws are misnamed. They should be called "right-to-shirk" laws.

Pro: We're back where we started from on this point. Let's move to other terrain. Unions are actually better off without the union shop. If the leaders act in arbitrary fashion, misuse union funds, or are unresponsive to rank-and-file wishes, members can effectively express their dissatisfaction by discontinuing their membership. This threat compels the leadership to respect workers' rights and desires, insures more democratic union policies, and is the best possible protection against abuse of union powers. Even former Justice Louis Brandeis, who was one of the strongest champions labor had ever known, favored the open shop for this very reason. Good unions run by honest, conscientious, capable men who faithfully reflect membership wishes have nothing to fear from the open shop. They can win the voluntary support of the workers, and support voluntarily won makes for a stronger organization than support that is compelled. If the leadership does a good job, moreover, the rank and file will bring heavy social pressure to bear on the worker who resists membership, pressure that is almost irresistible, because we all want the approval of those with whom we work. If a man still holds out, it must then be because of some conviction so deeply held that it deserves to be respected. So few will fall into that category in a well-run union that it will be no threat to the union at all. It will, instead, be a tribute to the magnanimity of the union and a testimonial to both its self-confidence and its deep respect for the uniqueness of the individual.

Con: I concede more to your eloquence than to the soundness of your arguments. It is true that the better unions need not fear their destruction will follow the establishment of right-to-work laws—at least during normal times. The members' attachment is too strong for that. But you have overlooked some important aspects: Employers often favor the union shop because it serves their interests well. Plant morale is better where the union shop exists, because there is always discord and ill will when some workers refuse to carry their share of the load. Workers snipe at one another, some refuse to cooperate with nonmembers, various accidents seem to befall nonmembers, and a perpetually festering grievance has been introduced into a plant that will reduce over-all efficiency and complicate the employer's managerial job.

Nor is that all. Where some members belong to the union and some do not, anything that can be interpreted as managerial favoritism to a nonmember is bitterly resented. There is, in fact, an atmosphere of suspicion present that tempts the union to read favoritism into perfectly legitimate employer decisions. It is always fearful that the employer will try to woo members away from the union by giving a better break to nonmembers. Naturally employers want to avoid this kind of problem, and hence many of them—especially the larger corporations—prefer the union shop.

I should add a final point. You say that the union leadership must be responsive to member wishes under the open shop or risk the loss of membership and, hence, of dues. What actually happens is that the union leaders become responsible to the minority of gripers and malcontents rather than to the majority of good members. I can cite you a number of authorities who say that under these circumstances the leadership must cater to the cry-babies and the disgruntled by processing grievances they know are trivial or unfounded and that only exasperate the employer and should not be processed at all. But the union dares not exercise restraint, lest the worker drop out of the union and start spreading rumors that will lead to the disaffection of others. As one fellow put it, under the open shop "every grievance becomes a crisis."[9]

Furthermore, union leaders are goaded into making more excessive contract demands than they would otherwise seek, in order to convince this minority of trouble makers that it is really going all out "for the boys." And it is tempted to manufacture issues and maintain a kind of battle atmosphere in order to keep the ranks united. Don't tell me the open shop makes a union responsible—or at least responsible to the right people. No wonder so many experienced employers want the union shop and feel that they are being denied freedom of choice if they cannot bargain for it.

Pro: I suspect you are considerably exaggerating the effect of the open shop on plant morale, even if the results you stress sometimes may occur. In general, employees are able to take the measure of their fellows and to recognize the trouble maker for what he is. His gripes won't hurt the union much if its general performance is good. Remember that the railroad unions got along very well from 1934 to 1951 even though the law forbade compulsory membership. And some of the nation's strongest unions—steel, automobile, airplane, and others—won their positions of union eminence despite the absence of union-shop provisions.[10] Their experience demonstrates clearly enough to me that the open shop doesn't weaken unions—where they deserve to remain strong.

Another point. Under union shop contracts, truckers would be and often are compelled to join Hoffa's organization and to pay tribute to him. Is it all right with you if legislation compels truckers to pay Hoffa's price and submit to this indignity in order to work?

Con: I'll confess that this doesn't set too well with me, either. But I doubt that the open shop would help matters much. Even if this were imposed, do you think workers would dare to drop

[9] Frederic Meyers, *Right to Work in Practice*, New York, Fund for the Republic, 1959, pp. 37–39.

[10] "The Case for Voluntary Unionism," United States Chamber of Commerce, 1955, pp. 10–11.

out of the Teamsters? The Teamster lieutenants are a rough bunch as you well know, and they could make life pretty unhealthy for a Teamster brash enough to stop paying dues. The same would go for a longshoreman who had become fed up with Harry Bridges. In general, I'd say that the more unscrupulous the union bosses, the less chance the average member has of dropping out and making that decision stick.

Remember that the right to secede from a union is not the only effective pressure members can bring against a union that disregards workers rights and wishes. They can always vote out the current leaders in the secret elections required by the 1959 act. And, if enough members are persuaded that they don't want a union at all, they can demand an election and have the existing union decertified by the NLRB. This is more than a theoretical possibility, too. It happens many times every year. These contingencies are enough to insure that the leader doesn't ride roughshod over the members. Where it doesn't serve to prevent union autocracy, as with the Teamsters, it's because the workers accept autocracy—so long as it delivers the goods. Every newspaperman who has ever had much experience with the Teamsters agrees that the overwhelming majority of members support Hoffa—and enthusiastically, too.[11] Situations like that cannot be changed by law.

Pro: Acting on one's rights is often hazardous, I'll admit. But that is no reason these rights shouldn't be asserted by law or that the individual shouldn't be given the opportunity to decide for himself whether he wants to take the risk.

No private organization, to proceed a bit further, should have the power to demand that private individuals pay taxes, in effect, to that organization in return for the privilege of earning a livelihood. This is a governmental type of power, and one that should never be conferred on a private body. I can never accept the proposition that a private association has the right to determine whether or not a man shall work. If the right to work at the

[11] A. H. Raskin, "Why They Cheer for Hoffa," *The New York Times Magazine,* November 9, 1958; "Hoffa'll Take Care of Hoffa," *The New York Times Magazine,* March 26, 1961; "The Power of James R. Hoffa," *The Atlantic Monthly,* January, 1964, p. 42.

occupation of your choice isn't a basic right of man, I'd like to know what is?

Con: Just a minute, there. You keep referring to the unions as purely private organizations, when I doubt that you really believe they are that at all. When Congress passed the 1959 labor act it did so because it regarded unions as quasi-public organizations, exercising powers affected with the public interest. How else could it justify the mass of controls imposed on the internal life of the union? In a democratic state, unlike a totalitarian state, the government does not presume the power to control the internal rules of private associations. Certainly the Congress would not try to interfere with the meetings and by-laws and constitutions of farm organizations or the Red Cross or the churches. But it did enact a host of union regulations in this area. Isn't it a little late to be insisting on the private character of labor unions? Considering your attitude toward unions, you should be the last to take this position.

Sometimes it seems to me that the case for the open shop, which once had a degree of merit, is essentially the case for the Bill of Rights that was incorporated into the 1959 act. Because unions do exercise impressive authority over the lives of men, and because authority is sometimes abused wherever it exists, there was once a strong argument for erecting legal safeguards against that abuse. But once this was done, and the worker could vindicate his rights in federal court, the case for the open shop vanished.

Pro: One right has not yet been guaranteed, so far as I'm concerned, and that is the right to freely associate or decline to associate. But we've been over that ground before. The right of states to require an open shop has certainly been a boon to the South. Open-shop provisions and an abundance of nonunion labor have attracted a great deal of industry to the South—which it needed badly. It has been in the national interest for northern capital to move south and give that once underdeveloped region a chance to make some of the economic advances that will eventually enable it to catch up with the rest of the nation. Right-to-work laws have played a part in promoting that great economic transformation.

Con: I doubt that the open shop has been as important a factor in attracting business investment as the absence of unions altogether, plus the low wage level that exists in the South. Are you really arguing that low wages and a docile nonunionized labor force are in the public interest? If so, this debate will break down for the lack of common premises.

Pro: Low wages in the South aren't attributable to the open shop. I am aware that some union studies show that wages are much lower in open-shop states, but this is primarily because these states were slow to industrialize in the first place, and wage levels were lower before right-to-work laws were ever passed.

Con: There's some truth to that, although right-to-work laws tend to prevent the gap between wage levels from being narrowed. In fact, the gap in hourly earnings between the right-to-work states and the other states increased from 21 cents in 1950 to 23 cents in 1961. And whereas 15 of 19 right-to-work states had per capita incomes below the national average in 1947, 18 were in this category in 1961.[12] Quite a tribute to the sterling economic impact of these laws!

Pro: In that connection, I have some figures that tell a different story. Hourly earnings of manufacturing employees rose almost 47 percent in right-to-work states from 1953 to 1963, while climbing only 42.4 percent in other states. Jobs rose almost 5 percent more rapidly, unemployment was lower, and per capita personal income rose 8 percent more than in union-shop states.[13]

Con: Statistics are tricky. Maybe both of our statistical supports are accurate. Your remarks about the South intrigue me. I have always suspected that those who argue for these mislabeled right-to-work laws are using the most respectable way to express their antagonism to unions *per se*. They aren't satisfied with the open shop. They want the open shop as a half-way station to eliminating unions entirely. If the open shop were nationally accepted, they'd move on from there to attack the whole concept of unionism.

[12] Milton J. Nadworny, "The Impact of Right to Work Laws," *Challenge*, April, 1963, pp. 25–26.

[13] Press Section, *The Reader's Digest*, July, 1965, p. 11.

Pro: I emphatically dissent. This may be true of some people, but I trust you will concede my sincerity as I do yours. It does not logically follow that because one dislikes coerced union membership, he therefore opposes voluntary membership. You wouldn't put Brandeis in that company, would you?

Con: O.K., I should have qualified my charge, even if I do think it applies to most of the noisiest advocates of right-to-work laws.

Wouldn't you, at the very least, be willing to accept the so-called "agency shop"? Under this arrangement, those who have moral or religious objections to joining a union can pay a sum roughly equivalent to union dues and assessments to compensate for union services rendered, but they need not formally join the union. There are "conscientious objectors" to joining unions, I will admit, and I expect any bill repealing Section 14(b) to contain a clause protecting them.

Pro: You are drawing a very fine line. Although I don't find the "agency shop" an entirely satisfactory solution, it does represent an improvement over the typical union-shop system.

Con: Because you are adopting such a reasonable pose, maybe I should admit that right-to-work laws may not have as much effect on union activities as union spokesmen believe. A Texas professor did a study for the Ford Foundation a few years ago, analyzing the effect of ten years of right-to-work experience in Texas.[14] Texas was chosen, in part, because it is one of the more industrialized states that has a right-to-work law. The study showed that things were about the same as before the law passed. Organizing efforts hadn't been noticeably impaired, closed shops still existed where they had existed before, union membership held firm, and the law was widely evaded, often with the tacit consent of employers. Another case of "the more things change, the more they remain the same."

Pro: Yes, I'm familiar with that study. The results were about as you describe them, and I believe your comment about "every grievance a crisis" came from that pamphlet. The writer did insist that union leaders had to cater more to the malcontents. Still,

[14] Meyers, *op. cit.*, p. 40.

the study does suggest that the issue may be much less important than either of us is disposed to concede. *The New York Times* contends, for example, that right-to-work laws have no important impact on either the economy or on labor relations.[15]

Con: Maybe, but Henry Wallich, a prominent member of President Eisenhower's Council of Economic Advisors, declares that "small and medium sized firms have proved harder to organize under right-to-work." He adds that "corporations have their limited liability, without which they could not operate. Labor seems entitled to its union shop."[16] Besides, labor is getting sick and tired of raising millions of dollars to fight right-to-work referenda in so many states. This money could be spent far more constructively than that.

Pro: Corporations couldn't function without limited liability, but history shows unions can thrive with the open shop. And don't forget it costs the proponents of right-to-work laws plenty of money to fight the union treasuries when right-to-work referenda are at stake. Still, I suppose if both of us were more objective, we might concede that the struggle revolves more about symbols than substance. From history we learn that groups which have long been competitive often continue to battle fiercely over certain symbols even after the conditions which originally gave the symbols meaning have largely passed away. I've never yet determined whether homo sapiens is basically a rational or an irrational creature.

Should Labor Stay Out of Politics?

Pro: I have one more point to make before concluding this discussion, though, and it is a pretty important one. It involves the question of political participation by labor unions. Taft-Hartley forbade unions to give or spend money in connection with any federal election, yet this provision is flagrantly evaded by the unions. Union dues are collected by compulsion and then spent to advance partisan political interests that a minority strongly opposes.

[15] *The New York Times*, August 1, 1965, p. E3.
[16] "Right to Work," *Newsweek*, June 28, 1965, p. 74.

You can make a case for the AFL-CIO's Committee on Political Education, which frankly spends for partisan purposes but relies on voluntary political contributions to finance its work. But when union dues are collected from every worker in the plant, and then spent for partisan purposes, that is something else again. The money, as you well know, goes almost exclusively to Democrats, whereas from one fourth to one third of union members are Republicans. Under the union shop, workers are thus coerced into financing the campaigns of candidates they oppose. To me, this is intolerable, because if anything is sacred in a democracy, it should be the right of each man to support, or decline to support, the candidate of his choice. Chip away at that, and you chip away at the very cornerstone of man's political freedom.[17] On this point, I emphatically endorse the statement of Thomas Jefferson: "To compel a man to furnish contributions of money for the propagation of opinions which he disbelieves and abhors, is sinful and tyrannical."

Con: Would you please explain yourself? The law forbids the expenditure of union dues in national elections, and state laws forbid such expenditure in state elections. What do you mean, "flagrantly evaded"?

Pro: Of course the unions don't take union dues and hand them over to favored candidates. But they indirectly finance their campaigns by carrying out so-called "education" programs that attempt to educate the union and nonunion voter to support Democratic candidates. It amounts to the same thing. Specifically, union publications carry glowing or glowering reports about certain candidates and their opponents. Editorials beat the drums for policies, parties, and candidates of which the union bosses approve. Unions distribute analyses of the voting records of incumbents, analyses that list a dozen or so major issues, identify certain votes as "pro-labor" or "anti-labor," and put candidates in a good or bad light. Radio commentators financed by union dues interpret the news with a pro-Democratic bias that, incidentally, reaches union and nonunion members alike.

[17] Barry Goldwater, "Who Speaks for Labor?" *Reader's Digest,* November, 1960, p. 85. Also see W. L. White, "Why Should Labor Leaders Play Politics with the Worker's Money?" *Reader's Digest,* October, 1958, pp. 157–174.

Democratic officials and candidates are invited to address union meetings and conventions, thereby according them an excellent opportunity to propagandize their political wares. Sometimes unions will invite their favorites to take part in "educational" radio or TV programs, during which they are asked the "right" questions, and are pcrmtited to expound their special views and political "line." It's very nice to be on radio and TV and have the unions pick up the tab, but I wonder how a lot of union members like to have their money spent like that. Nor is this all. Union officials spend some of their time, for which they are paid from general dues, to carry on other political activities helpful to party organizations and candidates. Finally, the unions carry on a massive registration and voting effort among their members, knowing that the bulk of them will vote Democratic as a matter of habit. All of this saves the Democratic party a lot of money, but doesn't it also pollute the wellsprings of a free political system. I know your views about Barry Goldwater. How would you like to have money extracted from you against your will and then spent to promote his political ambitions? Okay by you?

Con: You've covered a lot of ground. Let's go back and retrace it step by step. You've conceded that unions don't use union dues to directly contribute to parties or candidates. That is all the law actually forbids, according to my interpretation.

If you want to outlaw most of the other union activities you regard as objectionable, you'll have to make some drastic changes in the Constitution. Freedom of the press applies to organizations as well as to individuals. If you want to deny editors the right to write editorials and to comment on public issues and candidates, you'll have to abolish the First Amendment. And then you'll have to apply the same rule to other organizations. In a number of "right-to-work" states, no lawyer can practice unless he joins the state or local bar association. It is practically imperative for doctors to belong to the American Medical Association (AMA) if they are to have hospital privileges. Some teachers are coerced into joining the National Education Association. So you will need to forbid the AMA and the NEA and some of the bar associations to write editorials on political issues, too.

The same thing applies to the distribution of voting analyses and to news commentators. How can you forbid the AFL-CIO to have a news analyst without abridging the First Amendment? You aren't really suggesting, are you, that unions don't have the right to invite whom they please to address their meetings and conventions? As for getting its members registered and to the polls, this should be regarded as a commendable rather than an illegitimate activity. We have had a lot of public exhortations and big advertising campaigns encouraging people to vote. As a nation, we regularly deplore the fact that national elections bring out a much smaller part of the electorate than in West European and Commonwealth countries, and now you are deploring the most effective step toward increasing voting participation that this country has been able to take.

Pro: I didn't deplore the registration effort; I just mentioned it as an example of political activity by unions that is a major asset to the Democratic party. I do deplore unions granting favored candidates free radio and television time, and I deplore union officials giving part-time, union-financed political aid to a party or candidates. How do you justify those?

Con: I suspect those activities are rare, but I can understand why you would regard them as indefensible.

Pro: It has been responsibly estimated that unions spend about $20 million during a presidential campaign year for political activities on all levels.[18] In Michigan, in 1956, for example, labor claimed to have spent only $79,939, but a Senate investigating committee discovered that the state's 700,000 union members had been required to contribute $1.20 apiece toward a "citizenship fund," which was then dipped into for political activities. That alone provided almost a million-dollar kitty.[19] Probably over 90 percent of union political money goes to Democrats. Is it desirable for one of our major political parties to be indebted so deeply to a special-interest group? Can the Democratic party approach legislation affecting unions with a balanced outlook when it must rely so heavily on campaign contributions from the unions? From the standpoints of both worker rights and a

[18] *Congressional Quarterly,* January 21, 1966, pp. 56–57.
[19] Goldwater, *op. cit.*

healthy political system, union political spending should be restricted as nearly as possible to funds collected on a strictly voluntary basis.

Con: You know the answer to your comment before I give it. If it is iniquitous for the Democratic party to be so heavily indebted to the unions, then it must be equally wicked for the Republicans to be so deeply indebted to the contributions of corporation officials. You've seen the figures, I'm sure, showing that corporation officials' outlays for the Republican party are lopsided, too.

Pro: But at least business contributions are voluntary.

Con: If you think the social pressure to contribute to the GOP isn't heavy, you are more naive than I believe you to be. Generous giving establishes the fact that a man is both politically sound and politically concerned, and a man is regarded as a bit suspect who doesn't give.

Pro: You can't legislate against social pressures, but you can against overtly illegitimate activities.

Con: Let me make a further defense of union political spending, as long as the law is not violated. Inasmuch as the estimated total political spending in a Presidential election year now runs to about $200 million, that $20 million you cited for labor constitutes a pretty modest portion of the total. The reported figure is considerably less than that, but I am willing to concede that unreported help might approximate that figure. Considering the margin by which the GOP outspends the Democratic party in almost every national election, it isn't very sporting of the Republicans to try to slash union contributions while keeping corporation officials' contributions intact.

The GOP, I might add, gets huge amounts of free propaganda from the nation's press in every election year, and in between as well. The daily newspapers are at least 3 to 1 Republican (unless Barry Goldwater is the GOP candidate!), and the weekly small town papers are probably more lopsided than that. Furthermore, the biggest and probably most influential mass-circulation magazine in the world, *Reader's Digest,* averages about two articles per month expounding right-wing political and economic doctrine. Have you ever read an article in the *Digest* that had an even moderately liberal economic orientation? Then there are *Life* and *Time*, consistently pro-Republican in overt or subtle ways, to say nothing of David Lawrence's conservative *U. S. News and World Report*. Ben H. Bagdikian, one of the foremost students of the press, recently observed that a cross section of small dailies and weeklies revealed that "84 percent opposed any government-sponsored medical or hospital aid to the aged, were strongly opposed to federal aid to education, and were generally found in the right-wing Republican camp."[20] The literature distributed by the AFL-CIO is almost the only material friendly to the Democratic Party that reaches the mass of voters—or rather, a considerable portion of that mass. And yet Barry Goldwater and his conservative buddies ceaselessly clamor for labor to get out of politics. Some people are never satisfied.

Pro: Things aren't as one-sided as you like to paint them. I wouldn't necessarily term them "liberal," but mass-circulation magazines like *Newsweek*, *Look*, and *The Saturday Evening Post* can't be properly labeled "conservative" in recent years. Some pretty liberal material appears in their pages from time to time.

Con: As for the alleged brainwashing of union members by their leaders and the supposedly decisive part unions play in so many elections, I suspect this is vastly overrated. In the first place, union propaganda has to compete with propaganda from innumerable other sources, most of which is pro-Republican. Moreover, the average American is a pretty independent fellow when it comes to making up his mind about voting. If you think union members meekly accept the voting advice of union leaders, look at the evidence. In 1940, the miners idolized John L. Lewis, but when he asked them to support Willkie instead of Roosevelt, they rejected that advice by almost 9 to 1. The unions went all out to defeat Senator Robert A. Taft in 1950 in Ohio, and Taft won a sweeping victory—widely attributed in part to union member disgust with the opposition candidate foisted on them. Despite the vigorous support accorded Adlai Stevenson by the AFL-

[20] "Behold, the Grass-Roots Press, Alas!", *Harper's Magazine*, December, 1964, p. 103.

CIO, Dr. Gallup says that working-class people shifted to Eisenhower in about the same proportions as the rest of the population. To me, this is immensely significant; and it goes far to refute all this "brainwashing" talk. It is doubtful if over 10 percent of union members can be influenced by any propaganda whatever. Most union members are solidly Democratic because of family inheritance, economic interests, and class identification. Others are Republican because of inherited family leanings or other causes. And because less than half of union members are registered, this would only leave a small number of union members open to persuasion in national contests. Some estimate it as low as 500,000.[21] This hardly leaves the unions in a position to massively manipulate the voting public and dominate American politics, as some labor critics are wont to imply.[22]

Pro: So far as presidential politics are concerned, there may be much to what you say. But in state and local contests, where the union member isn't exposed to the countercurrents of propaganda that blow nationally, the situation may be quite different. Having much less interest in these contests and knowing less about the opposing candidates, union members can be persuaded. Take Michigan, for example. The United Auto Workers (UAW) virtually dominated the Democratic party for years through its vigorous political activities. No one can tell me this is good for state government.

Con: The UAW and the Democratic party were natural allies in Michigan. It's easy to charge the UAW with having run the state, but I suspect your evidence is pretty meagre. The Michigan press, by the way, is overwhelmingly Republican, so the crosscurrents still move in that state.

Pro: I'm wondering if unions should be engaged in politics at all. Unions are formed for collective bargaining purposes, to help workers improve wages and hours and working conditions. When they get into the realm of politics, they venture into areas alien to a union's central purpose and take positions that represent the

[21] Robert Bendiner, "Labor Vote: Monopoly or Myth?" *The Reporter,* November, 1955, pp. 20–21.

[22] Also see Neil W. Chamberlain, "Union Support: Asset or Liability," *Challenge,* October, 1960, p. 29.

union oligarchy's views far more than they do the members' views. If I may quote Barry Goldwater, "Unions should be forbidden to engage in any kind of political activity. I believe that the Federal Corrupt Practices Act does forbid such activity. . . . I see no reason for labor unions—or corporations—to participate in politics. Both were created for economic purposes, and their activities should be restricted accordingly."[23]

Con: Are you proposing that labor shouldn't even testify in Washington or in the state capitols on legislation affecting working men? Surely you can't mean that, and yet when you say labor shouldn't be engaged in politics, that seems to be implied. It is an unthinkable position, as you surely must recognize. And you recognize it even though a minority of union members are bound to disagree with the labor lobbyists on the positions they advocate. If we are going to be purists about labor expenditures in politics, no union official could ever testify before a congressional committee until 100 percent of the members agreed with his stand; otherwise the minority would be involuntarily financing causes with which it disagreed, and you say that would contaminate the political process and infringe on individual rights. We have to be a bit realistic about these things and acknowledge that all organizations operate on a majority-will basis. And there is certainly no more reason to suppose that unions misrepresent their members than any other organization that testifies on legislation or distributes literature with an ideological or partisan bias.

Pro: I'm not talking about lobbying, as you should know. I'm talking about labor participation in election campaigns.

Con: Well, I'm glad to know that, as the term "politics," to me, embraces policy-making as well as elections. To continue, then, I challenge the whole proposition that labor should stay out of politics, however that is defined. I submit that a healthy democracy is one in which the maximum number of individuals and groups concern themselves with both policy-making and elections. This promotes the spirit of individual and group responsibility, involves a maximum number of persons in democratic

[23] Goldwater, *op cit.*, p. 86.

problems, promotes the growth and development of citizens, and insures legislation that most accurately reflects the will of the people. You can't seek to politically emasculate labor without applying the same medicine to other associations.

Do you really want labor to be concerned with its narrow self-interest, with getting as much as it can for the union member without regard to the interests of other Americans? Since you quoted Barry Goldwater, permit me to quote Gus Tyler:

> . . . the trade union needs a greater goal than the contract, a broader religion than the dollar sign. It must be concerned with industry as a whole, with the economy, with the nation, with democracy. The social view has a double value: it makes the union an integrated and contributory force in the community; and it raises the spiritual level of both the leadership and the rank and file.[24]

Let me further quote from one of the most respected labor experts in the country, A. H. Raskin of *The New York Times:*

> . . . the demise of the strike; increased mechanization of bargaining; increased bureaucratization of the work process itself; automation and unemployment—will require for even their proximate solution a degree of political commitment American labor has never shown. They demand that politics become a principal business of unions, not a haphazard adjunct of their narrowly economic purposes. . . . Labor has no more urgent job in the Sixties than the focusing of its political energies on the conquest of want, illiteracy, intolerance; the building up of both health and decent housing; the realization of the limitless promise of this scientific Golden Age. And apart from their general social necessity, these undertakings would be vastly more inspiriting, to union membership and leadership alike, than the present ever more routine function in the policing of day-to-day plant grievance and the writing of mechanized contracts. . . . What is needed from labor is a degree of independent leadership that will give vitality to the concept of direct political action for jobs and an expanding economy.[25]

[24] *A New Philosophy for Labor,* Fund for the Republic, New York, February, 1959, p. 10.

[25] A. H. Raskin, "The Obsolete Unions," *Commentary,* July, 1963, pp. 24–25. Copyright by American Jewish Committee. Reprinted by permission.

Pro: Unhappily, union political pressures seem to be almost invariably directed toward measures that push us deeper into the welfare state and overcentralized government. But I would like to return to my original point. Wouldn't you agree, despite your bias for unions and their political activities, that there should be restrictions on some of their more egregious evasions of the law forbidding spending "in connection with any federal election"? If I were to grant that unions have a legitimate part to play in American politics—including the right to be wrong—couldn't you agree that there are appropriate limits to the indirect as well as the direct use of union dues for partisan purposes?

Con: First, let me say that I am willing to compare the historical record of unions, where progressive legislation has been concerned, with that of the National Association of Manufacturers. But as to your question, we might find some common ground here. If legislation could be enacted that didn't infringe on labor's constitutional rights and focused on specific abuses rather than seeking to choke off political activity in a general sense, it might be a constructive step. In face, it might strengthen labor's hand by depriving its foes of a weapon that could be used effectively against it.

Pro: That isn't exactly what I had in mind, but I'll accept your cooperation toward reform legislation on whatever terms I can get it. Fortunately, the Supreme Court, in 1963, reaffirmed an earlier ruling that union members cannot be forced to pay that portion of union dues used for political purposes of which they disapprove.[26] It's up to the courts to finally decide what is or isn't a political expenditure, and they can require refunds where money is misspent. As Justice Brennan said, this may encourage the unions to set up a voluntary plan for segregating political from nonpolitical expenditures. But if the abuses I object to aren't corrected, the federal and state legislatures may have to spell them out and proscribe them.

Con: Maybe we can agree to await developments before tackling the problem further. On this amicable note, let's go have a cup of coffee.

[26] *The New York Times,* May 14, 1963, p. 29.

Antitrust and Labor "Monopolies"

Should the antitrust laws apply to unions? Many critics of the labor movement believe unions, as currently organized and operated, have become monopolies inimical to the public interest. The National Association of Manufacturers contends that "monopoly powers [are] the power by an individual or a group to control the supply and fix the price of needed goods and services."[27] Because unions monopolize the supply of labor and fix its price in many industries, the Sherman Act forbidding monopolies and combinations in restraint of trade should apply to unions as well as business.

Professor Edward H. Chamberlin suggests that ". . . as a good general rule . . . no employer should have brought against him pressures exerted by anyone other than his own employees."[28]

Others would say we should limit collective bargaining either to a single union and a single employer or to employers in one industry within a metropolitan area, so long as the workers in that area did not constitute too large a percentage of the total employers in the entire industry. Many businessmen and others agree that so-called "industry-wide bargaining," whereby a national union signs a contract with all or most of the employers in a given industry, should be outlawed. They believe that nationally organized unions can make excessive demands on an industry, or at least on certain companies within an industry. They are convinced that such bargaining compels all employers, without regard to their special economic circumstances, to pay

[27] "Should Labor Unions Be Subject to Antitrust Laws?" *The Congressional Digest,* October, 1961, p. 240.

[28] "Can Union Power Be Curbed?" *The Atlantic Monthly,* June, 1959, p. 49. Also see Barry Goldwater, *op. cit.,* p. 87; Stephen F. Dunn and John L. Kilcullen, "Labor Organizations and the Antitrust Laws," U.S. Chamber of Commerce (undated); W. L. White, "Should Unions Have Monopoly Powers?" *Reader's Digest,* August, 1955; Arthur Krock, "Legal for Unions: Illegal for Management," *U. S. News and World Report,* December 7, 1959, p. 124. For a general discussion of pros and cons, see "Should Labor Unions Be Subject to Antitrust Laws," *Congressional Digest,* October, 1961, p. 231; Charles M. Rehmus, "Multi-Employer Bargaining," *Current History,* August, 1965, presents an excellent analysis of this topic.

wages or submit to other demands that may have ruinous effects on some companies.

There is a tendency, in fact, for the highest wages paid by a given firm to become the minimum wage demanded by the union for all related companies. And of course strikes, instead of being localized, spread widely and have a more serious impact on society. Instances are cited where employers have been forced out of business by ruthless union demands.[29]

Union power of this character can also force employers to accept featherbedding practices, whereby workers are paid for useless work or even for not working at all. The record is replete with union pressures that delay the introduction of labor-saving devices, such as ready-mixed cement, prefabricated materials, prethreaded pipe, spray painting, and others. This is particularly serious in the construction industry, where union resistances typically increase the onsite costs of labor from 8 to 24 percent.[30] Industry-wide bargaining also enables unions to force inflationary wage increases jeopardizing the economic health and well-being of the nation. It also generates nation-wide strikes that can have a crippling effect on the economy. Finally, it is doubted that current union power is necessary to protect the wage returns of the laboring man, because the relative proportion of the consumer's dollar going to wages and to profits has remained remarkably stable over the past 50 to 60 years.[31] Real wages (that is, wages in terms of purchasing power) have tended to increase in close correlation with productivity increases, despite fluctuations in union strength and membership.

Labor-union defenders contend that no one can predict with even reasonable certainty what the application of antitrust laws to unions would mean. It has taken the Supreme Court decades to decide what business practices are illegalized by the Sherman Act, and the picture is still far from clear. The confusion and dis-

[29] "Should Labor Unions Be Subject to Antritrust Laws?" *op. cit.*, p. 242.

[30] Reynolds, *op. cit.*, p. 241.

[31] *Ibid.*, pp. 470–472. Also see Daniel Bell, "The Subversion of Collecitve Bargaining," *Commentary,* March, 1960, p. 189. For a dissenting view, see Arthur Goldberg, "Collective Bargaining," *Commentary,* July, 1960, pp. 62–63.

order that would follow if unions were collared by the act could hardly promote the public interest.[32]

Many employers prefer multiemployer bargaining. It enables a competent and professional staff to handle contract negotiations for a large number of companies, thus avoiding the expense of recruiting and maintaining a professional staff for each company. Small concerns (as in trucking, dairying, baking, canning, construction, and clothing) feel they can compete more successfully with a big union if they bargain jointly. Even large corporations may prefer this to avoid the "whipsaw" tactic whereby a powerful union isolates one company and wins a contract that is then forced on all major companies in that industry. There tend to be fewer strikes, also, because the stakes are so high.

If uniform wages within an industry are to be deplored, then uniform prices must be equally deplorable. Yet the phenomenon of price leadership is so well established in major industries that almost everyone takes it for granted. One big company sets a standard price, and practically all the others follow suit as a matter of course. Besides, the Supreme Court long ago accepted the distinction between "reasonable" and "unreasonable" monopolies, permitting the former despite the Sherman Act.[33]

Where unions are weak or where splintered unions bargain with employers separately, each employer will naturally seek to cut his costs by reducing the price of labor. The most successful competitor, therefore, will often be the one who has been able to pay the lowest wages. Isn't competition on the plane of managerial and technological efficiency far preferable to competition based on wage-cutting?[34] Wage demands that drive an employer out of business are extremely rare. Unions are cutting their own throats if they extort wage levels that cost union members their jobs. Self-interest alone normally precludes such action. Since the Taft-Hartley prohibition against featherbedding has not elimi-

[32] Sar Levitan, "An Appraisal of the Antitrust Approach," *Annals*, January, 1961, pp. 113–114.

[33] Alfred H. Kelly and Winfred A. Harbison, *The American Constitution*, New York, Norton, 1948, p. 559.

[34] "The Labor Monopoly Myth," *Labor's Economic Review*, February, 1946, pp. 14–15.

nated the practice, why would another law accomplish that end? So long as workers fear joblessness, they will support certain "make-work" practices. Professor Lloyd Reynolds has noted, moreover, that the practice of limiting the output per worker "is a widespread practice in both union and nonunion shops, particularly where the workers are paid on a piece-work or incentive basis."[35]

Unions deny that they are responsible for the postwar inflation, insisting that they sought only to share in the increasing profits of corporate and private employers.[36] In any case, inflation was minimal from 1958 to 1965. While per man-hour productivity increased 3.4 percent in factories from 1957 to 1962, wages and salaries rose only 2.2 percent during that period.[37] Seen from another perspective, wage gains from 1960 to 1965 increased about 3.5 percent per year, only slightly more than productivity gains of about 3.2 percent. The over-all picture does not sustain the proposition that wage rises have been exorbitant. America's price level was more stable from 1958 to 1965 than that of any other major industrial nation. The inflation that followed was triggered partly by spending for the war in Vietnam, partly by excessive levels of private capital investment, and partly by towering corporate profits. The latter increased 67 percent after taxes from 1961 to 1966, while wages rose only 21 percent. No wonder labor finally decided to get its fair share, adding fuel to an inflationary fire first stoked by government and management.

Have unions protected or increased the share of national income going to the worker? Admittedly this cannot be proved, but neither can it be proved that labor would not have gradually suffered a decline of its income share had unions not existed. If unions do not in fact improve the worker's share of corporate gross receipts, why are they resisted so strenuously by so many employers?

Legislation to break up labor unions would meet with savage

[35] *Op. cit.*, p. 240.

[36] "Should Labor Unions Be Subject to Antitrust Laws?" *op. cit.*, pp. 251, 253, 255.

[37] "T.R.B.," *The New Republic*, November 9, 1963, p. 2.

union opposition touching off a period of labor unrest such as this nation has never known. The upshot would be a poisoned political atmosphere for years to come and a virtual breakdown in the good relations that have existed between many major unions and industrial firms. Even Senator Barry Goldwater reversed his earlier position; he conceded that the antitrust law is a clumsy tool for dealing with unions—one that is difficult to apply equitably and productive of endless litigation.[38]

Some observers, it might be added, believe both unions and management share responsibility for the recent inflation. Even if it is granted that most unions made relatively modest wage demands from 1958 to 1965, considerably less restraint has been manifested since then. A more severe test of labor and management "statemanship" in the realm of wages and prices may appear in the years just ahead.

Are Unions Fading?

Many students of labor believe the question of antitrust action against unions must be evaluated in the light of certain economic and social trends that are clouding labor's future. Not only has labor organizing largely come to a halt, but the economic horoscope seems to indicate a long-run decline of labor's comparative power position.[39] Having organized most of the nation's major manufacturing industries, unions find further organizing efforts make agonizingly slow progress. Today only 17 million jobs out of a labor force of about 75 million men are organized. Since 1945, the proportion of the labor force that is unionized has

[38] "The Public Record of Barry Goldwater," *The Congressional Quarterly* Special Report, September 20, 1963, p. 1603.

[39] See the following articles by A. H. Raskin: "The Squeeze on the Unions," *The Atlantic Monthly*, April, 1961; "The Obsolete Unions," *Commentary*, July, 1963; "Wanted: Statesmanship in Industry," *The New York Times Magazine*, September 4, 1960. Also see Richard Bruner, "Has Success Spoiled the Unions?" *Harvard Business Review*, May–June, 1960; (Anonymous), "Why White Collar Workers Can't Be Organized," *Harper's Magazine*, August, 1957; Edward T. Townsend, "Is There a Crisis in the American Trade Union Movement? Yes," *Annals of the American Academy of Political and Social Science*, November, 1963; Joseph Shister, "The Outlook for Union Growth," *Annals*, November, 1963.

dropped 5 percent. Union membership gains hereafter must be largely found in the service industries, which are steadily absorbing a larger percentage of the work force. But these are precisely the areas most resistant to organizing. The firms are much smaller, in most instances, and the workers have less of a "workingman psychology." White-collar workers have long tended to identify with management rather than with the working class. Most white-collar workers seem to prefer the "psychic income" that comes with this social identification rather than the increased compensation that might come from unionizing. An ever-increasing percentage of workers is female, and women share the conventional white-collar attitude that associates unions with greasy overalls, dirty, horny hands, smudgy faces, and somewhat crude, uncouth manners. However absurd this characterization, it remains a potent barrier to the labor organizer. Younger workers also are disinclined to join unions, never having known sweat-shop conditions, prolonged joblessness, the hardships and insecurity of the depression period, or the bitter struggles with employers that crystallized worker solidarity in days of yore. The memories that help keep alive union loyalty among older workers have little meaning for the incoming generation.

Organizers face other handicaps, also. Although the South constitutes largely virginal organizing soil, that soil is tough and flinty. Most of the employees in the burgeoning industries of the South are fresh from farms and small towns, and feel the typical hostility toward unions that their background creates. The tendency of the Protestant South to look with suspicion on the high proportion of Catholic trade-union leaders does not facilitate the work of the union organizer. Finally, the urgent need the South feels for more industry, combined with its awareness that a relatively low-wage, nonunionized labor environment is attractive to many industrialists, has produced a regional state of mind and restrictive labor legislation that are often the despair of the union organizer.

Meanwhile, the onrush of automation adversely affects unions in three ways: it reduces the proportion of production employees; the remaining jobs tend to be manned by more highly skilled technicians who resist union membership; and the plants themselves tend to become more strike-proof as fewer and fewer highly trained men are able to keep plants in operation. The communications industry is already largely strike-proof, and the utilities and oil refineries are rapidly becoming so. As this trend continues, one of the union's major weapons will be blunted.

It is also becoming ever more difficult for unions to obtain (in peacetime) the rather generous wage concessions that help keep workers loyal. Stiffer competition in the world markets from efficient Western European producers means that wage increases must hereafter be tailored to levels enabling United States industry to remain competitive abroad. This is reinforced by the necessity to prevent a deficiency in our balance of payments abroad—declining exports lead to a growing demand for American gold. Employer strike-insurance plans, stockpiling arrangements, and automated production make it progressively harder for unions to strike without injuring their members more than the employers. Members seem more restive when strikes are prolonged. It is becoming easier for both industry and the federal government to mobilize public sentiment against inflationary wage settlements; public opinion is readily critical of "inflationary" wage demands but notably uncritical of "excessive" profit levels which often trigger those wage demands. These factors suggest that peacetime wage increases will be tied more closely to per-man-hour productivity increases, thereby placing this aspect of collective bargaining on something of a slide-rule basis. If wage increases are determined by a relatively fixed formula (in the major industries, at least, where industry-wide bargaining takes place), the "fighting" role of the labor leader will fade before the encroachments of a mechanistic standard that tends to drain away the prestige and functional importance of the negotiator. (During periods of serious inflation, however, relatively mechanistic bargaining formulas tend to break down.)

Whether labor unions in the future will be able to continue the relatively free collective bargaining they have known in the past is in considerable doubt. Public antagonism to prolonged strikes and threatened strikes in railroads, shipping, airlines, newspapers, and subways and busses seems to have made the public more receptive to compulsory arbitration than it has been.

The opposition to compulsory arbitration among unions and management has always been intense. Such arbitration takes the power of decision out of the hands of the negotiators and into the hands of representatives of the public. Furthermore, since one or the other party to a labor dispute usually feels that arbitration would yield a settlement closer to its interests than can be won by its own bargaining power, that party would be likely to become an intractable bargainer, hoping to force the decision *into* arbitration. Thus the collective bargaining process would tend to be subtly undermined, with more and more contract decisions dropped into the lap of a reluctant government. The result would be to further impair the functioning of a free economy—a development especially unwelcome to businessmen. Yet an exasperated public, faced with the repeated curtailment of vital services by strikes, may well force the enactment of a compulsory arbitration statute applicable to key industries, a statute that neither labor, management, nor government really wants, but which might seem the lesser of two evils.

In some respects, unions are partially the victims of modern prosperity. When unions were fighting for a foothold in the American economy, battling sweat-shop conditions involving pitifully low wages, long hours, unsafe working conditions, and an employer attitude that all too often regarded the worker as a unit of energy rather than a human being, union leaders were inspired by a great sense of mission. Full of enthusiasm for a cause in which they deeply believed, their ardor and idealism not only affected the quality of their labors but infected the working class as well. Now that the battle has been largely won, and the worst abuses of the past corrected in cooperation with employers who are considerably more enlightened than those of 50 years ago, much of the old fire has died down.

Many union leaders have become engrossed in the bureaucratic routines of an established organization, have acquired a vested interest in their jobs and perquisites, and are unmoved by visions of new and worthy worlds to conquer. The leaders still seek the maximum wage and fringe-benefit increases, but the spirit of crusade, of striving for social justice and battling the hosts of evil, has largely disappeared. Because labor leadership requires ever more sophisticated skills to deal with a complex world, the leadership also tends to become estranged from the workers. The workers know little about trust funds, balances of payments, corporation balance sheets, comparative wage costs, and the hundred and one high-level considerations with which the modern labor leader must reckon. Among the latter, then, the feeling grows that the worker "just doesn't understand."

Union members were naturally enthusiastic about the first paid vacation, but the enthusiasm diminishes as paid vacations merely lengthen. They were elated with the first pension plan, but improvements in that plan bring a declining sense of elation. They were grateful for the first life insurance or health insurance benefits, but are less thankful for a liberalization of those benefits.

To cap it off, few bright young labor leaders are being developed these days.[40] Twenty-five years ago a gratifying number of able and idealistic young college graduates were attracted to labor union work. Today there are few potential Sidney Hillmans on the horizon. The waning enthusiasm of intellectuals for increasingly "fat, sluggish, and bureaucratic" unions also bodes ill for the future power and prestige of the movement. As one writer put it, the intellectual can "identify only with certain humanist values or with the plight of the underprivileged. But the labor movement as just another special interest group offers nothing on either score."[41]

In sum, the evidence suggests that unions may become a waning influence in both the economic and political sphere in future decades, although the auto workers could be a major exception. Unless labor can create a new role of social usefulness or overcome the hardened obstructions that block its way among the unorganized, it can hardly hope to maintain the position it has held. These developments do not provide ready answers to the specific labor reform proposals that have been made, but

[40] A. H. Raskin, "Help Wanted (Young) for Unions," *The New York Times Magazine*, September 10, 1961.

[41] H. Harris, "Why Labor Lost the Intellectuals," *Harper's Magazine*, June, 1964. Also see Maurice F. Neufeld, "The Historic Relationship of Liberals and Intellectuals to Organized Labor in the U.S.," *Annals*, November, 1963.

some of these need to be considered in the context of the travails labor is now experiencing.

Can unions continue to justify their existence in a prosperous nation whose government provides many of the protections and securities unions have long sought? No one can know, but a number of potentially useful functions can be served if unions are alert enough and wise enough to seize them.

In addition to the continued necessity for union services previously described (see pages 63–64), unions may be able to insure that automation is introduced into Americans industry with due regard for the human element at stake. Unions may not always use their powers discreetly in this area, but there is clearly a need for pressure on management to guarantee that workers about to be displaced by automation are either properly retrained where possible, given adequate severance pay, or are given every assistance in finding new employment (especially in the case of older workers).

Second, as technological advances quicken, a need for the periodic retraining of workers whose skills are rapidly becoming obsolete will become imperative. Unions can play a beneficent role if they help prepare workers for the practical and psychological adjustments involved in the more or less constant upgrading or transformation of their skills. The resistance of workers to this requirement is bound to be great; the unions' judgment and finesse will be tested to the full as this development occurs.

Finally, if unions can help workers feel that they are not anonymous, insignificant cogs in an immense, impersonal, and faceless enterprise, they will have gone far toward establishing their continued indispensability. The decentralization of union decision-making which this entails may create almost as many problems as it solves, but striking the right balance between overly centralized union decision-making and unduly fragmented decentralization would be a major union achievement.

CHAPTER

◂ 3 ▸

BILLIONS FOR THE FARMER?

"Among the many mysteries which surround the government of the United States, there is none more impenetrable than why anyone should want to be secretary of agriculture." So wrote Professor John Kenneth Galbraith in 1953.[1] And, in 1960, Orville Freeman was quoted as pleading with Senator Hubert Humphrey, "Don't let them make me secretary of agriculture."

But they did make Mr. Freeman the secretary of agriculture. For the first few years he suffered from the same lambasting that had been the lot of his predecessors, Ezra Taft Benson and Charles F. Brannan. Farm program costs continued to rise, Freeman's major legislative recommendations were beaten back by Congress, and the potent American Farm Bureau Federation was bitterly critical of virtually his every move.

Yet, by 1966, a variety of domestic and world conditions had so

[1] "Why Be Secretary of Agriculture?" *Harper's Magazine,* July, 1953, p. 82.

altered the political landscape of agriculture that Mr. Freeman was enjoying an unparalled respite from the abuse normally heaped on our secretaries of agriculture. Writers who had assumed that the farm surplus problem would be with us for decades were blinking at the spectacle of a steady decline in federal farm surplus holdings; some were even predicting that the production control machinery that had become a commonplace feature of American agriculture might be largely dismantled within the next few years. Instead of seeking to restrain the fabled productivity of the American farmer, the Department of Agriculture talked of stimulating production into patterns corresponding to rapidly rising world food requirements.

It would be premature to conclude that the farm surplus and farm income problems were sure to vanish. Unforeseen developments in technology (which was continuing its breakneck forward pace in agriculture) might yet restore the national preoccupation with surpluses. Nevertheless, the prospects for shucking off agricultural controls were brighter than they had been since World War II. In 1966, about half of the 55 million acres previously idled by federal surplus control programs were being returned to production. The prospects for substantially reducing the huge federal farm budget were less bright, however. The vast sums previously spent to brake production and support the Food for Peace program might still be utilized to expand the dimensions of the latter. So long as the government continues to spend about $7 billion a year for the USDA budget, farm policy will remain a national issue.

The Road We've Traveled

The modern "farm problem" arose as an aftermath of World War I. During the war, American farmers plowed under 40 million acres of additional land to feed the Allies. The collapse of the postwar export market led to depressed agricultural conditions throughout the 1920s. When the great Depression struck, the farmer's plight rapidly became desperate. Industrial prices frequently dropped little, if any, but farm prices hit rock bottom; the average farm family made only $237 in 1932. Unable to pay the interest on the mortgage, tens of thousands of farmers were driven off their farms by a wave of foreclosures. Angry farmers sometimes blockaded the highways, overturned milk trucks, and dumped the contents of produce-laden trucks into ditches. In some cases, they armed themselves with pitchforks and shotguns and refused to permit foreclosures to take place. Those who wonder why American agriculture has endured its network of controls for nearly 30 years need only recall the Depression to understand.

President Roosevelt first sought to help the farmer by paying him for taking land out of production. When the Supreme Court declared the Agricultural Adjustment Act unconstitutional, the administration next offered farmers cash for diverting acreage from the production of surplus crops to nonsurplus soil-building crops. When this proved inadequate, the second AAA was enacted. Acreage allotments based on estimated national needs of certain surplus crops were divided among the states, subdivided among counties, and subdivided once more among individual farmers. Farmers who agreed to adhere to their acreage allotments were promised price supports, with the Government prepared to pay a guaranteed price for the output from their remaining acreage. When it appeared that an insufficient number of farmers was "cooperating" with the program to make it effective, the government was authorized to compel adherence to allotments by imposing penalties on the sale of commodities produced on acreage in excess of the quota. Such penalties, however, could be imposed only if two thirds of the farmers growing a given crop agreed to their use. The program was to be administered by farmer-elected committees in each county.

The agricultural programs did help bolster farm income, but they were relatively unsuccessful in reducing surpluses. Land diverted from production of surplus crops went into the production of other crops, thus creating new surpluses. Furthermore, farmers managed to outwit the government by farming their reduce acreage more intensively—applying more fertilizer and planting rows more closely together. However, World War II (and later the Korean War) rescued the program by converting burdensome surpluses into valuable assets.

Farmers enjoyed unparalleled prosperity during World War II. But as postwar fears arose concerning the recurrence of a farm depression, Congress enacted a new "flexible" price support law: It enabled the secretary of agriculture to reduce the level of supports on surplus commodities in direct relation to the magnitude of the surplus—thereby theoretically discouraging output—while raising the level as surpluses declined. However, before this legislation went into effect, a raging Congressional battle centered around the "Brannan Plan," put forward by President Truman's secretary of agriculture, Charles F. Brannan. This plan would have partially replaced price supports with direct payments, with no farmer eligible for payments or supports on output exceeding $25,000 per farm. "Perishable" commodities would sell in the open market for whatever they would bring, and the government would pay the farmer the difference between the market price and a "fair" price. The plan was killed by Congress, partly because the formula for determining a "fair" price was exceedingly generous, partly because it became a partisan issue, and partly because the Farm Bureau resented the plan's suspicious resemblance to National Farmers Union proposals.[2] In its place, Congress continued the price support system, fixing supports at comparatively high levels.

During World War II and the postwar years, agricultural technology was boosting farm output at a phenomenal rate. Output per man-hour in agriculture was increasing from two to three times as fast as in industry. Despite a steady decrease of farm labor, agricultural output increased 140 percent from 1945 to 1963. Hybrid and other kinds of improved seeds; more and better fertilizers; portable irrigation systems; chemical weed-killers; potent insecticides; artificial insemination; livestock and poultry feeds containing vitamins, minerals, and antibiotics; machinery to speed up planting, cultivating, and harvesting; better management methods—these were combining to make American agriculture the economic success story of the twentieth century. For example, wheat production per acre has doubled

[2] For a general discussion of the economic and political aspects of the Brannan Plan, see Reo M. Christenson, *The Brannan Plan: A Study in Farm Politics and Policy*, Ann Arbor, University of Michigan Press, 1959.

in the past 20 years, and corn yields have nearly tripled since 1932. In 1800, it took 344 man-hours to produce 100 bushels of corn; today some producers can match this with 4 man-hours. One outstanding bull has sired 60,000 daughters through artificial insemination; whereas one cow produced enough milk for 5 children in the early part of the century, it now will serve 25 children. Beef cattle, because of superior feeding practices, are brought to market in 1½ years versus 2½ years in 1930. Although cropland in use declined by 6 percent between 1950 and 1959, productivity per acre increased 27 percent.

Thus, while the government has made strenuous efforts to control surpluses, agricultural scientists have quietly confounded its work. Someone has suggested that we could solve both our and the Soviet Union's farm problem by shipping our farm scientists to Moscow!

When the Korean War ended, surpluses promptly reappeared, and the new secretary of agriculture, Ezra Taft Benson, resolved to reverse the direction in which Secretary Brannan had chosen to move. Benson was opposed, as a matter of almost religious principle, to high-level price supports and federal controls over farm production. Although at first it was not politically expedient to fully express his views and shape a program reflecting his massive dissatisfaction with existing farm policy, Benson moved as vigorously as he dared toward a "free" agriculture. In the process he retained the full support of President Eisenhower, but became *persona non grata* to farm-state Republicans who periodically pressed "Ike" to destroy this "albatross" before Mr. Benson destroyed them.

Old MacDonald Has a Choice: Freedom or Security

The critics of the farm production control and subsidy system were never convinced that the farm program really "worked." They believed that the existence of price supports for certain commodities at well above free market price levels encouraged surpluses—they persuaded farmers to continue producing foods and fibres that were not needed—and kept land in production that should have gone back to grass and trees. Acreage controls were frustrated by farmers' removing only their worst land from production while pouring on additional fertilizer and using more intensive production practices on their best acres. Decades of acreage-control experience led not to the elimination of surpluses but to their increase. Accusing the administration program in 1966 of having "failed miserably" to achieve its goals, the Farm Bureau attributed the decline of surpluses almost entirely to expanded exports rather than to effective controls. The housewife was obliged to pay more for her groceries as a result of price supports. The exporter of farm commodities (such as cotton) found his market shrinking as foreign producers were able to undersell him. Meanwhile the taxpayer was shelling out the sobering sum of nearly $7 billion a year to maintain the USDA budget, an amount nearly half of the total net farm income. And a swollen bureaucracy of about 100,000 USDA employees ministered to the "welfare" of only 3.4 million farmers.

Why single out farmers for such a lush bonanza? Are they more deserving of fat subsidies and economic guarantees than other segments of the population—such as small businessmen, for example?

The free segment of American agriculture has gotten along very well during these years without the farm program. The livestock, fruit, and vegetable producers, for example, have never been the beneficiaries of farm subsidies or the victims of farm controls, but market forces maintained a rough balance between supply and demand that enabled them to survive and flourish without the government crutch. Yet that portion of American agriculture that was always being babied by the government remained in chronic surplus difficulty. If the government were to leave the farmer to the self-regulating controls of the free market, there might be some economic difficulties during a transitional period (cushioned, however, by the gradual rather than the precipitous termination of the farm program), but the efficient farmer would be able to demonstrate his self-reliance. The inefficient does not deserve to be propped up by the taxpayer; indeed, he would be better off working in the city at employment of value to the nation rather than producing unwanted commodities on the farm. Nor should it be forgotten that farm subsidies primarily go to the million largest farmers who produced 80 percent of the farm output (and net over $10,000 a year), while only 20 percent goes to the small, low-income farmer who presumably needs them most.

Various polls have shown that farmers favor greater farm freedom and a reduced farm program. Inheritors of a long tradition of freedom and rugged individualism, they resent the controls that have been fastened on them. Yet the continuance of farm subsidies carried dangers that farmer hardihood might yet be undermined. In the words of Charles Shuman, president of the American Farm Bureau Federation,

> . . . government payments have something in common with the narcotics habit. Once on the habit, the victim becomes convinced he cannot live without the drug. In the jargon of the underworld, he's hooked. He'll do most anything to get his next fix, his next check. The pushers, in this case the Government bureaucrats and committees, constantly work to get more farmers hooked. The more that are hooked, the more the payments are and the more assurance of their jobs and the perpetuation of the machine in power. Well, that's the way of socialism.[3]

The defenders of the farm program contested the critics point by point. Farmers, they said, tend to maximize production regardless of price support levels or free market prices, because this is their instinct and it is normally to their advantage. True, the farm program *does* make for a more prosperous agriculture, thereby enabling the farmer to buy more modern machinery and use the most up-to-date production practices. But is an efficient agriculture to be deplored? This very efficiency produces the abundance that has kept food prices so stable until recent years; the American housewife has had almost unparalleled food bargains since the war—compared to the inflation of other prices.

Acreage controls have not worked perfectly, but think of the overproduction we might have had if the 55 million acres of land retired by the farm program had been kept in production. Nor

[3] "How to Shoot Santa Claus," *Time,* September 3, 1965, p. 25.

do price supports keep marginal farmers on the land; agricultural economists agree that the critical factor in accelerating or retarding the movement of labor off the farm is the presence or absence of urban employment opportunities. If termination of the farm program had somehow forced the small farmer off his soil in the 1950s and early 1960s, he would have landed on urban relief rolls—hardly an improvement for him or the nation. Nor would his departure have reduced surpluses; his land would have been purchased by more prosperous farmers who generally use improved practices and wrest still more production from the soil.

It is untrue that the efficient farmer would be able to prosper without the farm program. Studies by Cornell, Iowa State, Oklahoma State, Penn State, and the Legislative Reference Service have unanimously concluded that net farm income would be cut 40 to 50 percent by the elimination of the farm program. Other studies have demonstrated that the larger commercial farmers would suffer the biggest income loss.

The regulated element of American agriculture has not solved its surplus problem, but wheat, cotton, corn, and tobacco had the most severe surpluses under the free market system. If producers of these commodities had switched to other commodities, we would have simply shifted surpluses from one area to another. The root problem is the fantastic advance of agricultural technology, which enables farmers to produce 7 percent more per man-hour per year—far beyond the annual increase of the industrial worker. Technology is the culprit, then, and not the farm program that seeks to alleviate its results. Remember, too, that it was the free market that led to the harsh farm depression of the 1930s.

As for the livestock industry, if the government had not used vigorous steps to curb feed-grain production, grain supplies would have shot upward, prices would have dropped, and livestock producers would have responded to cheap feed by expanding their output. This, in turn, would have depressed livestock prices and shattered the illusion that these producers can get along nicely without any government aid.

The farmer is by no means the only producer who benefits

from government subsidies and protections. The wage earner has his minimum wage and his unemployment compensation and his legal protections for collective bargaining. The airlines receive subsidies, as do the merchant marine, the publishing industry (through second-class mail rates on which the federal government loses money), the housing industry (through FHA and VA assumption of most of the repayment risks involved), small business (through the Small Business Adminstration and certain tax favors), the trucking industry, the banking industry, and businessmen in general through tariff protections and the implementation of the Full Employment Act of 1946. Should those who produce the basic necessities alone be compelled to face the wintry winds of the "free economy" that is lauded in theory but so often abandoned in practice?

Of course farmers who do not receive government aid (or are not aware of the indirect aid they receive) are not enthusiastic about the farm program. Both would sing a different tune if they were actually exposed to the rigors of a free market for a few years.

The farm program is not likely to corrupt farmers' morals any more than other aids and regulations corrupt nonfarmers. The magnificent production record of the farmer in recent years hardly suggests that he has lost his willingness to work or his interest in improving the quality of his farm operations.

Finally, only about $2.5 billion of the $7 billion USDA budget directly supports farm income. The balance goes for such services as Food For Peace; the school lunch program; the food stamp plan; the Forest Service; repayable loans to the Rural Electrification Administration and the Farmers Home Administration; meat inspection; and others that benefit consumers, businessmen, and the general public as well as the farmer.

Freeman: First and Second Thoughts

Rejecting a return to a free market as an alternative that would impose excessive hardships on the farmer, the Kennedy Administration originally concluded that the farmers' tendency to overproduce is a permanent phenomenon to be satisfactorily met only by tightening and enlarging the existing system of controls.[4] Secretary Freeman proposed maintaining or increasing existing price support guarantees for some commodities, while confronting farmers with stark referendum choices. The farmer could choose to accept rigorous production controls, reinforced where necessary by limitations on the number of bushels or pounds on which price supports would be paid, or face the unmitigated hazards of the free market. The latter would respond not only to supposedly increased production, but to the gradual unloading of government supplies held by the Commodity Credit Corporation (which manages USDA's surplus holdings).

The congressional defeat of his mandatory feed grains and dairy programs in 1962, plus the farmers' rejection of his stringent wheat program in 1963, apparently persuaded Secretary Freeman of the political advisability of seeking less coercive methods of dealing with overproduction. In the last few years, the secretary believes, the successful formula that eluded all of his predecessors—a formula that is acceptable to farmer, consumer, and world tradesman as well as to the Congress—has been found. Acting on a principle long endorsed by the National Grange, USDA has helped Congress develop programs tailored on a commodity-by-commodity basis rather than on an across-the-board basis. To make the program palatable to farmers, it has given them the privilege of growing as much as they please—with no direct government aid—or of restricting their output to qualify for attractive incentive payments. Acting on a principle endorsed by the Farmers Union in 1949, it has been reducing price support guarantees close to world market levels and then compensating farmers for the difference between the lowered "floor" and a "fair" price with direct cash payments. Acting on a principle long identified with the Farm Bureau, it hoped to retire about 40 million acres of cropland over a five-year period through five- to 10-year contracts with cooperating farmers (interest in this aspect of the program is waning however). Finally, the administration

[4] *The New York Times,* February 1, 1962, p. 1, and February 1, 1963, p. 10. Also see Orville Freeman, "Freeman Weighs the Farm Surplus," *The New York Times Magazine,* September 24, 1961.

was planning to use various incentives to encourage farmers to produce foods nutritionally desirable for the hungry millions abroad rather than attempting to dispose of the surpluses we happened to overproduce.

The results to date? What was once an 85-million-ton feed grain surplus melted to about 47 million tons in 1966. Wheat surpluses have fallen from 1.3 billion bushels to 535 million bushels. Butter reserves have dropped below 100 million pounds. And since USDA estimates that the nation needs emergency reserves of 50 million tons of feed grains, 700 million bushels of wheat and 100 million pounds of butter, Secretary Freeman was widely proclaiming in 1965 that the Administration program was finally bringing about the long-sought balance between supply and demand.

Others were less hopeful that we had discovered the magic key. Russian wheat shortages had led Moscow to make heavy demands on the world's wheat reserves. India was experiencing the worst drought in a century and importing millions of additional tons of American wheat. These provided temporary rather than permanent relief from United States surpluses. Cotton stocks were reaching ominous all-time high levels. Farm output potential was increasing three times as fast as in 1935, according to Dr. Walter W. Wilcox of the Legislative Reference Service. An article in the highly respected *Journal of Farm Economics* in August, 1966, presented impressive evidence that production controls would remain essential for feed grains and cotton.[5] In general, however, optimism prevailed.

Secretary Freeman frequently observes that whereas 30 years years ago 300 members of the House of Representatives represented predominantly rural constituencies, and 135 represented urban areas, the situation is reversed today. Under these conditions, how long will an urban-oriented Congress countenance a farm program that costs a thumping $7 billion or more annually?

The answer is unknown, but several factors work to strengthen the farmer's claim on the federal treasury. Benefits that are enjoyed over a long period of time come to assume the position of

[5] W. E. Johnson and G. S. Tolley, "Future Cropland Requirements and Projection Sensitivity," pp. 597–611.

"vested rights" and are extremely difficult to dislodge. The American citizen, moreover, retains a sentimental attitude toward the farmer—the sturdy yeoman of the soil, the backbone of the nation, the rugged individualist, and so on—that is convertible into political capital. And if farm prices and income are hereafter supported primarily by massive federal purchases of foodstuffs to relieve famine abroad, this program will draw on the widely accepted premise that America should do what it can to feed the hungry—even if the cost is great. The American farmer is unlikely to suffer neglect despite his dwindling numbers. (Only about 6 percent of the population now live on farms—roughly 12 million persons.)

Surpluses in a Hungry World

One billion persons are reliably reported to suffer from "daily or recurrent crippling hunger." The Food and Agriculture Organization of the United Nations also estimates that 10,000 persons daily die of hunger; far more are so weakened from malnutrition that they are easy prey for various lethal diseases. In India alone, 5 million persons a year are believed to die directly or indirectly from malnutrition. The average life span in many food-deficient areas is only 30 years. As Senator George McGovern has put it, this is "not very long to live but a long time to be hungry." In East Pakistan, 50,000 infants are said to be blinded each year by Vitamin A deficiencies. These and similar tragic facts have long led many persons to ask: why should not American surpluses be used to feed a hungry world?

Unhappily, surplus disposal overseas does not represent an easy solution to the surplus problem. Sales at low or at giveaway prices often incur the displeasure of our free-world allies who find their own agricultural markets impaired—markets that are often crucial to their foreign exchange equilibrium. If food enters a food-deficient country in large amounts, moreover, it tends to depress the price of farm products for the native farmers, whose skimpy existence thus becomes skimpier still. Costs of transportation and storage are high; an efficient administrative apparatus is frequently lacking, so foods may wind up in the hands of profiteers instead of in the mouths of the hungry.

But although increasing our current volume of food assistance is a road heavily pocked with pitfalls, American efforts to accomplish this will continue. Currently, 40 million school children, including one out of four school-age children in Latin America, are being fed from United States programs; 35 million other children received food supplements. Sixteen million American children were also benefitting from the school lunch program, and 7 million more were receiving low-cost milk. Food was being used as a wage or a supplementary wage for some 5 million persons abroad while they built roads, schools, homes, public buildings, established irrigation systems, or settled new areas. Over all, the United States had shipped over $15 billion worth of food overseas between 1954 and 1965 through Food for Peace and related programs. Nearly 100 million persons in over 100 countries were being helped by American food contributions.

School lunches are an ideal vehicle for expanding food assistance, because they do not interfere with foreign exports, do not adversely affect native food markets to any appreciable degree, and put the United States in the most favorable international light while commanding public support at home.

It seems that every new administration comes forth with bold and inspiring statements about using our surpluses to feed the starving. Some progress is made, but the official attitude soon becomes one of stressing the difficulties of substantially enlarging the program.

The time may soon come when American imagination, ingenuity, and determination in this area will be tested more severely than ever before. In the opinion of Gunnar Myrdal, the famous Swedish economist, all of America's food-production potential will soon be needed to avert catastrophic famines abroad. With world population growing by 35 to 40 million a year, and much of this growth concentrated in food-shortage areas, Myrdal predicts that within a decade American agriculture will be presented with a "great opportunity to head off world calamity."[6] Southeast Asia, for example, has recently moved from a food surplus to a food paucity area. In Latin America, the

[6] From an address, "The American Farmer in the World Economic Revolution," delivered before the National Farmers Union Convention, Chicago, March 15, 1965.

population has risen 11 percent in five years while food production has climbed only 6 percent. Chester Bowles, United States ambassador to India, told a Senate subcommittee in 1965 that "the most colossal catastrophe in history impends unless major measures are taken." A spokesman for USDA agreed that experts are substantially less hopeful these days about the prospects of avoiding world famine.[7] The director-general of the UN's Food and Agriculture Organization declared, "We face a disaster of unprecedented magnitude."

The ultimate hope for balancing world food supplies with world needs may rest in family planning; President Johnson has stated that $5 billion invested in this area is worth $100 billion of economic aid. On this subject, however, the realists are almost all pessimists. Among the rural masses (which constitute 80 percent of the people in Asia and Africa), family planning is still a distant goal. Although there is growing agreement that our best efforts must be devoted to coping with the fecundity problem, a major speed-up in food production and distribution may prove essential if famine is not to reach frightful proportions in some lands. Secretary Freeman put it this way:

> The President's strategy in the war on world hunger has three elements: We will use our food to buy time, we will help those countries where food is sent to modernize their agriculture and move along the road of economic development, and we will assist those countries to undertake more intensive programs in family planning. All three are essential to each other.
>
> Let me emphasize that the tide we face is running swiftly. In the next 15 years the world must make room for another billion people, and fully three fourths of them will be living in the regions already short on food.[8]

The West is in a strong position to mitigate hunger in the next decade. Western Europe's food output is rising more rapidly than its population. About one seventh of America's tillable land

[7] Lester Brown, *World Population and Food Supplies, 1980, Current,* October, 1965, pp. 21–23.

[8] USDA press release 1483–66.

(until 1966) lay idle. The question is not, can we do the job? It is, *will* we? The cost would be great, not only in terms of increased federal purchases of food, but also in terms of assisting the transportation, storage, and distribution of food abroad. Greater expenditures will also be needed to build fertilizer plants abroad and to give other forms of aid that will bolster food production in the developing nations. Whether America and Europe are prepared to assume this burden rather than face the ugly prospect of preventable mass starvation may be one of the most solemn decisions that lies ahead. Given strong executive leadership, the instincts of the American people will probably be affirmative. If so, the American food surplus problem—at least for a time—will have passed away.

CHAPTER

◂ 4 ▸

EDUCATION:

What Role for Washington?

If ours can be called the Atomic Age or the Age of Outer Space or the Age of Science, it can also be called the Age of Education. Particularly in the Soviet Union and in the emergent nations education is seen as the key to national development, prestige, and power. In the United States the stress on higher education (or, should we say, on going to college?) is hardly less noteworthy, although less emphasis has been placed on education's significance to the nation than on its importance to the individual. Capable young people, especially in their later high school years, are usually well aware of the stakes involved in higher education. They know that most of the well-paying and prestigious jobs demand at least a bachelor's degree, frequently a master's, and often even more advanced training. (It is estimated that a person with only an eighth-grade education enjoys lifetime earnings of about $150,000; high school graduates earn about $275,000; and college graduates about $450,000.[1])

Finally, education has become "the thing." Aside from its national, cultural, and occupational value, going to college has become a "must" for socially ambitious youngsters. Denial of the opportunity to go to college, or flunking out once they arrive, is regarded as the supreme disaster to many young people because the college degree has become a status symbol of such importance.

The interest in college, heightened by Soviet scientific achievements as well as by technological imperatives and social snobbery, has also led to growing concern over the character and quality of education in the elementary and secondary schools. Following the launching of the Sputniks and prodded by Dr. James Bryant Conant's historic study, *The American High School Today,*[2] American education underwent perhaps the most intensive reappraisal in its history. A rash of meetings, speeches, reports, studies, investigations, and exposés focused on the question, "What goes on in our schools, anyway?" This ferment is generally conceded to have had a salutary effect on the American school system. The reappraisal has continued in a somewhat lower key ever since, and it has stimulated a crop of national issues as well.

Supporting our vast educational enterprise is an immensely costly business. About $35 billion is spent annually on education in accredited public and private schools at all levels; by general consent the sum should be enlarged. Not all children are able to go to school full-time; the number of teachers is inadequate; the quality of instruction often leaves much to be desired; and the educational performance is shockingly uneven in parts of the nation. Finally, the burden of paying for the schools has reached crisis levels in many communities, and forecasters are predicting heavy increases in educational costs during the coming decade.

[1] From a speech delivered by President Lyndon B. Johnson before the Committee on Economic Development, November 19, 1964. Quoted in *The Saturday Review,* January 9, 1965, pp. 28–29.

[2] *The American High School Today: A First Report to Interested Citizens,* New York, McGraw-Hill, 1959.

Where will the money come from? How can sufficient amounts be raised in the most equitable manner and spent to the greatest advantage? Should Washington give more aid or can state and local governments do the job adequately and with greater safety for our free institutions?

The prolonged debate over the desirability or danger of federal aid to education has been largely resolved by federal legislation in recent years. The question no longer is, Should we have federal aid? It is now, How much and for what purposes? It is imperative in understanding our future school-finance controversies, however, to be aware of the reasons why Americans were reluctant to give Washington a major educational role, the forces that nonetheless propelled Washington into that role, and the character of the decisions that have been made to date. The future grows out of and is ineluctably shaped by the past as well as by the changing requirements of the present. We do not construct legislation as if we were somehow a new society facing new problems without a history and without ingrained fears and predilections to guide us.

Federal aid to education is not a phenomenon singular to our times. Some form of federal aid extends back to our earliest history as an independent nation. For example, the central government assumed responsibility for giving instruction in mathematics to Washington's army. After the Revolutionary War, it provided financial support for the schools through the Northwest Ordinance of 1785, which set aside one section in each township for the establishment of schools. Federal land grants were made from time to time for the support of higher education (a federal land grant helped establish Miami University of Ohio in 1809, for example), culminating in the famous Morrill Act of 1862. This historic measure set aside areas in the several states for the creation and support of the great land-grant colleges that have played so important an educational role in the nation. This was followed in 1865 by further grants to finance agricultural experiment stations, which have received continuing federal subsidies ever since. In 1914, Congress passed the Smith-Lever Act providing matching funds to promote agricultural training in the public schools. And, in 1917, the Smith-Hughes Act offered grants-in-aid for the promotion of commercial, industrial, and domestic-science education in those schools.

During the Depression about $1 billion went into school construction through the Public Works Administration. The National Youth Administration also provided help for students needing financial aid for their college education. The war terminated these programs, but brought a new form of federal aid to education through the "defense impact program." In many areas the federal government purchased large tracts of land in connection with major defense programs attracting thousands of workers. With so much of the potentially taxable property no longer subject to local taxation, Washington was obliged to provide funds to help finance schools deprived of normal property-tax revenues. By the early 1960s about $3 billion had been expended for this purpose. Following World War II the federal government appropriated over $14 billion to help millions of veterans finance their college education. The money was available for attending the college of their choice (if it met certain minimum standards), whether the institution was public or private.[3]

After the Sputniks prompted reports that the Soviet Union was producing far more engineers than the United States, and perhaps as many technically trained personnel as Western Europe and America combined, Congress passed the National Defense Education Act in 1958. Under this act, hundreds of millions of dollars have been spent for a variety of purposes believed to be related to national defense. These include help to universities establishing or expanding graduate programs; scholarships for students doing graduate work in certain fields; aid to students planning to enter the teaching profession; loans to college students unable to privately finance their education (with preference for those in defense-related fields); and assistance in financing laboratory equipment and remodeling classrooms for the teaching of mathematics, science, and modern foreign languages.

Over 50 percent of college research is now federally financed, much of this emanating from the National Science Foundation. A number of major universities now receive over half of their

[3] It is roughly estimated that this educational investment will ultimately produce approximately $35 billion of additional tax yield.

income from federal grants. Medical research relies heavily on federal funds. The federal government has advanced hundreds of millions of dollars in low-interest loans to colleges for dormitory construction since 1950. Student exchange programs operate with federal subsidies, and the national government supports schools for the deaf and blind, as well as Howard University in Washington. The Pentagon supervises a far-flung educational program for children of servicemen stationed overseas. And the United States Department of Agriculture's Graduate School annually enrolls about 12,000 students.

Although the federal government has been actively interested in the cause of education for over 175 years, attempts to extend this aid from specific programs to aid of a more general nature have met with a long series of rebuffs in Congress. In 1948, a bill authorizing the federal government to spend $300 million a year for aid to schools was cosponsored by "Mr. Republican," Senator Robert A. Taft of Ohio. The bill cleared the Senate but died in the House when it became impaled on a rancorous controversy over aid to parochial schools. The bill permitted the states to decide whether money would be available for parochial schools, a concession that antiparochial school aid forces strongly opposed. In 1955, President Eisenhower recommended that the federal government authorize the purchase of $750 million of local school bonds (where this would prove helpful) plus $200 million in grants for school districts with demonstrated need and demonstrated lack of adequate local resources.

The following year he proposed that $1.25 billion be spent on a "crash program" to eliminate the classroom shortage. House Republicans, however, successfully supported an amendment by Negro Representative Adam Clayton Powell forbidding any grants to states defying the Supreme Court's 1954 school desegregation decision and then joined with Southern Democrats to kill the bill. Mr. Eisenhower tried again in 1957, calling for the same expenditure over a four-year period. The Powell Amendment was withheld by pressure from pro-federal-aid forces, and a bill tailored precisely according to Mr. Eisenhower's 1956 specifications narrowly failed of passage in the House by a vote of 208 to 203. Three of Mr. Eisenhower's key House lieutenants voted against the measure, leading responsible observers to declare that an appeal from the President could have carried the day.

In 1960, a major bill to help finance both public school construction and/or teacher salaries (at the discretion of the states) passed the Senate, and a bill authorizing aid for school construction only received a favorable vote in the House. The House Rules Committee, however, declined to permit a conference committee to iron out the differences, and the bill perished. Roughly comparable bills cleared the two houses in 1961, but although the House Rules Committee had been enlarged by three new appointees (believed sufficient to overcome the roadblock that Rules critics claimed the committee had become), the unwillingness of the President and Congress to support aid for parochial schools led a key member of the Rules Committee to oppose putting the measure before the House. In 1962, the President unsuccessfully included school aid in his legislative program, but groups favoring it were critical of what they regarded as the lukewarm efforts of Mr. Kennedy on behalf of his bill. The President tried a new tack in 1963, recommending an omnibus bill for aiding teacher salaries at the top and bottom of the salary scales, and school construction where needed to eliminate slum schools, firetraps, and double sessions in "impacted areas." More aid was also requested for vocational education and for the colleges. This time Congress responded by approving loans and grants to higher education of about $2 billion over a three-year period; vocational aid was almost quadrupled; a liberalized college-loan program was authorized, including National Defense Education Act loans for students in the humanities and social sciences; and substantial sums were voted for the construction of medical schools and for aid to medical students. Nonvocational aid for elementary and secondary schools, however, fell by the wayside once more. The following year Congress enacted its historic Poverty Program, involving Operation Head Start as well as a number of other educational features. Well over one half of the funds administered by the Office of Economic Opportunity were concerned with educational activities.

A broad-ranging breakthrough in financing elementary and

secondary education was finally achieved in 1965. With surprising ease, considering the prickly nature of the undertaking and previous congressional intransigence, Congress enacted what may have been the most significant educational bill in United States history. It appropriated $1.3 billion a year primarily to aid slum schools and impoverished school districts in rural areas. This was to be accomplished by requiring eligibility for these federal funds to be based on the number of school children in a district whose parents were on relief or were earning less than $2,000 per year. The federal government offered to add 50 percent to the per-pupil contribution being made by state and local governments for children in these categories. The money, thus, must be spent specifically for programs designed to correct educational deficiencies among the poor.

The act also provided funds for the purchase of textbooks and library books (for both public and parochial school pupils), so long as the books were not of a sectarian character. Money was similarly appropriated for the establishment of "supplementary education centers" in which a number of experimental approaches would be tried to seek more effective instruction for those with educational handicaps. These centers, primarily in crowded urban areas, would stress remedial education, experimental uses of educational television, improved vocational training, counseling and guidance programs, the provision of health services, and shared-time classes. In conjunction with Operation Head Start, the centers would hopefully enable some solid progress to be made in helping children from culturally deprived homes and neighborhoods to receive an education more like that available in typical suburban schools.

Congress also pushed through additional aid for higher education in 1965, establishing undergraduate scholarships on the basis of need for 140,000 students. Those in the upper half of their classes were to receive more generous aid than less academically proficient students.

A review of the debate that has taken place over federal aid to public schools will help clarify the issue, explain the intensity of feeling that existed on both sides, and provide a background for the evaluation of future questions of a related nature.

The Children's Crusade

Those who fought the battle for federal aid championed their cause as follows. There can be no questioning the inadequacy of either current school facilities or the general level of expenditure on education. The Office of Education, under both Democratic and Republican administrations, has repeatedly found a classroom shortage in excess of 120,000. Over half a million school children go to school on a part-time basis, because building limitations do not permit full-time instruction. Millions of youngsters who do obtain full-time instruction received it in overcrowded classrooms that militate against the best educational performance. More than 100,000 additional school teachers are needed, in addition to replacing or giving advanced training to the tens of thousands with temporary or emergency teaching certificates.

It is a disgrace for a nation as wealthy as ours, overflowing with television sets, two-car garages, and luxuries unknown to royalty in previous centuries, to permit educational deficiencies to continue in the magnitude that has existed since World War II. The nation has no greater moral obligation than that of insuring that each child in America, without regard to the accidents of birth or geography, has the best education the nation can provide. In democratic theory, at least, there is widespread assent to the proposition that equality of opportunity is the birthright of every American. This is a noble ideal, too noble to be reserved for lip service alone. In modern times, equality of opportunity must embrace the right of every child to discover his creative abilities and develop them to the fullest extent. This will not only enrich his private life and open wide many doors that would otherwise remain closed, but it will also enable him to make the most constructive contribution to his community and his country. No national goal has higher priority than the mobilization of the potential talents of our people, and nothing can bring this about as effectively as the improvement of educational excellence and the broadening of educational opportunity. A major federal effort is required if this is to be accomplished.

We have been forcibly reminded of the importance of an adequate educational system since World War II. Russian technical advances have made it soberingly clear that we cannot afford to allow potential mathematicians, physicists, engineers, and other technicians to become stunted because of insufficient local funds or insufficient local vision. To achieve the maximum rate of national growth and reduce hard-core unemployment to a minimum we need to train both our youth and many more adults in the skills that a nation with a rapidly developing technology requires. But because man does not live by bread alone, the quality of people's personal lives and of our collective civilization depends heavily on educational exposure to the richness and diversity and excitement of human aspiration and achievement in nontechnical realms.

There is general agreement that educational expenditures during the next decade will need to increase sharply. With so many school districts already strained to the limit, it is naive to expect state and local governments to bear this burden without federal aid on an imposing scale. Although the states, in many instances, have done a highly creditable job, the hard facts militate against their ability to provide equal educational benefits. Mississippi, for example, recently had a net income per child of less than $1,100, while Connecticut's net income per child approximated $8,000. Mississippi is obliged to spend 10 percent of her taxable income on education without meeting the quality standards Connecticut can achieve on an expenditure of 3.1 percent of her taxable income. The five poorest states spend less than half as much per pupil as the five richest. Differences in taxable wealth per pupil in given school districts may vary as much as 100 to 1, if one district is poor and rural and another is able to tax a wealthy corporation within its limits. Little wonder that Senator Robert A. Taft, a distinguished conservative but also a distinguished realist, explained his support for federal aid to the schools by saying that the federal government could not stand idly by and let a poor state do the best it could "if its best is not good enough."[4]

[4] Stewart L. Udall, "Our *Education* Budget Needs Balancing," *The Reporter,* June 25, 1959, p. 23.

Not only do many states lack the financial resources with which to do a satisfactory job, but some fairly prosperous states are reluctant to impose the tax levels needed to sufficiently support their educational systems lest their industries lose a competitive tax advantage or fall victim to a competitive disadvantage. Undue reliance on state action, therefore, tends to prevent ample support for education just as it once retarded the spread of state unemployment compensation and old-age pension systems.

A large number of states are hobbled by institutional weaknesses that yield only slowly to the reforms that are essential if the states are to fully assume their responsibilities. Representatives from rural areas have dominated state legislatures—representatives who made sure the state-aid school equalization formula was amply weighted toward rural areas but who were relatively indifferent to the massive school needs of urban and especially slum areas. Often convening every other year (and then for limited sessions, in some instances), badly underpaid, lacking the public prestige that attracts the best men, hampered by constitutional restrictions on borrowing and spending and taxing, beset by swarms of special-interest lobbyists, poorly covered by the state's press, the performance of state governments is deplored by every knowledgeable student. Some states have excellent government, others are doing surprisingly well considering their handicaps, but most states fall considerably short of doing their job as well as modern conditions require. Expecting all of them to acquire the vision, the resolution, and the capacity to meet the educational job ahead was expecting the impossible.

State taxing systems are too regressive, in any case, it is argued. The states rely overwhelmingly on sales, excise, and property taxes, adding up to a tax burden that substitutes the "most feathers for the least squawk" for the ability-to-pay principle. The federal government, on the other hand, derives most of its revenue from the progressive income tax and a heavy corporation tax, which reflect more faithfully the ability to pay.

The most unfortunate aspect of local school financing is the heavy reliance on the property tax. In the early 1960s, about 56 percent of school costs were met from the local property tax, with the states meeting about 40 percent and the federal government about 4 percent.[5] Yet the property tax is assailed by virtually all tax experts as costly to administer and often badly administered. Its burdens bear little relation to either total wealth or current income receipts. When 75 percent of our national wealth was in the form of real property, there was greater justification for substantial reliance on the property tax; now that only about 25 percent of our wealth is in this form, the obsolescence of the property tax is more glaringly apparent.

The Camel's Nose

Groups hostile to federal aid to education fought back as follows: Efforts to discredit state and local governments by pointing out how far they fall short of needed educational outlays ignore the remarkable achievements of recent years.

Bringing the figures up to 1964, anti-aid polemicist Roger Freeman observed that since 1947 school spending per pupil (discounting the effects of inflation) had increased 77 percent. From 1944, the spending for public schools increased from 1.4 percent of the national income to 4.5 percent. This was the result, almost entirely, of vigorous efforts on the state and local level.[6] Furthermore, the classroom shortage declined 24 percent since 1956, according to *U. S. News and World Report,* and the nation was continuing to build 70,000 classrooms a year. Schoolteachers' salaries increased 164 percent from 1946 to 1964 (averaging about $6,000 in 1963 to 1964). Finally, the number of pupils per teacher has steadily declined in this century, moving from 37 in 1900 to 29 in 1940 to about 26 today. Does this sound like a "failure" of state and local government? If existing funds were used more prudently, with fewer expenditures for frills and nonessentials, there would be no need for federal aid.

Granting, nonetheless, that additional funds might be needed, anti-federal-aid groups believed that the states and local school districts were best able to supply the need. Businessmen, especially, warned that federal expenditures were already at dizzy-

[5] The federal share rose to about 8 percent in 1965.

[6] "How to Railroad a School Bill," *The National Review,* May 18, 1965.

ing heights, that the national debt had reached astronomical levels with no end in sight, and that the federal government should keep future spending—above all, deficit spending—down to an irreducible minimum. A nation with a $320 billion national debt and an annual budget of well over $100 billion and 2.6 million federal employees behooves itself to exercise the utmost fiscal prudence and economy. National solvency and a responsible attitude toward spending the taxpayers' hard-earned money are prerequisites to a healthy society, and we have already gone far toward impairing both.

Of perhaps equal importance to our society is the protection of our federal system. To preserve strong state governments with sovereign spheres immune to national interference is to preserve one of the indispensable elements of the constitutional system that our Founding Fathers so wisely created. The Constitution set aside major governmental powers for exclusive state control and forbade the national government to exercise those powers. As long as the states guard their allotted sphere, a powerful safeguard against centralized tyranny exists.

In recent decades, however, we have witnessed an insidious erosion of the authority of the states, with the central government using one pretext after another for invading the reserved rights of the states. Through a strained construction of the commerce clause (leading to such abominations as forbidding a farmer to produce as much feed as he needs for his own livestock); through so-called grants-in-aid that dangle monetary bait before the states while concealing the hook of federal control (giving Washington control over innumerable welfare activities, for example); and through tax programs ostensibly designed to raise revenue but actually intended to impose regulatory controls over areas outside Washington's delegated powers—by all of these we have experienced the dwindling of a precious portion of our birthright of balanced powers. The trend has already gone far, much too far, and it is the responsibility of every freedom-loving American to prevent the further intrusion of Washington into the domain reserved to the states. Nowhere is this responsibility more compelling than in the realm of education.

Historically and logically, education has always been reserved to the jurisdiction of the states. Not a shred of constitutional authority can be found empowering the national government to control education, directly or indirectly. Yet, that control is certain to follow if the federal government begins making general grants to the states for educational purposes, grants containing those inevitable clauses "safeguarding" the proper expenditure of the taxpayers' money. The Supreme Court has ruled that the national government can legally attach conditions to the expenditure of its funds. As sure as night follows day, the national government will attach conditions to the receipt of federal monies in support of education, conditions that will deepen the federal inroads into state powers that have become ominously apparent since the early 1930s. But this time that erosion will be far more serious than anything the nation has witnessed before, because it will involve the one area that prudence demands should be kept free from centralized control—education. The practices of totalitarian regimes should be ample warnings to us, for their first instinct is to establish an iron central grip on the educational system. If they can control the approaches to the minds of the young, they know they have taken a long step toward insuring the obedience and loyalty of their people. Central control of education is as integral to a totalitarian regime as is the control of the communications system.

Of course Washington would not immediately desire nor seek to impose a straitjacket on American education. Rather, the controls would be mild and seemingly innocuous at first, but would gradually broaden and deepen as the people became accustomed to minor regulations and as the federal appetite for control sharpened. In the words of James Madison, "Since the general civilization of mankind, I believe there are more instances of the abridgment of the freedom of the people by gradual and silent encroachments of those in power than by violent and sudden usurpation." It is the *direction* of government policy that must be firmly guided if liberty is to endure. Legislative acts leading in the *direction* of federal control of education, no matter how innocent those first shy steps may seem, must be curbed at all costs. It is naive to expect the national government, once it has tasted the forbidden fruit of educational control, to overcome the temptation to take ever larger bites. The appetite for power is a concomitant of human nature, and the warnings of our forefathers and of wise men from time immemorial should not go unheeded. There is only one safe course, and that is to deny the federal government the opportunity to develop that taste at all in the domain of education. Woodrow Wilson's words will always be timely: "A concentration of government power is what precedes the death of human liberty."

Even Francis Keppel, head of the Office of Education under President Kennedy, admitted that federal aid would bring a certain amount of federal control. The National Defense Education Act of 1958 brought a loyalty oath for those seeking federal loans; it stimulated a new system of graduate schools that altered the evolution of higher education in America; and it encouraged a shift from liberal arts to scientific education.[7] Whether these are good or bad, they demonstrate clearly that federal aid will subtly reshape American education. (Federal money spent to upgrade slum schools prompted a rash of charges that Washington was seeking to unduly influence local education.[8]) Let's keep the camel's nose from getting any further into the tent—remember the Arab fable.

Aside from the threats to liberty involved in federal aid to education, there is also the related threat to the health of local government. In practice, the control of the schools has largely been left to local governments, and wisely so. Education vitally affects almost every American family. Because most parents are eager to give their children the best possible education, most of them can be relied on to take a lively interest in local educational matters. They may not come to uniform conclusions concerning the curriculum or the general principles on which the schools should operate, but this in itself is an element of strength. The diversity of local decision both reflects the rich and creative diversity of American life and helps perpetuate it. Nothing could have a more deadening effect on American education than

[7] Daniel P. Moynihan, "A Second Look at the School Panic," *The Reporter,* June 11, 1959, pp. 14, 19.

[8] See "A Federal Hand on Local Schools," *U. S. News and World Report,* November 8, 1965, pp. 54–56.

the imposition of a uniform educational system that either destroys or drastically reduces the opportunity to experiment, to incorporate the unique insights of particular school boards and principals, and to tailor educational practices to local needs and traditions.

Certainly it is unfortunate to encourage the people, whenever fiscal or other problems arise, to look to Washington for help and guidance. This is hardly the spirit of independence, self-reliance, and enterprise that has helped make America the greatest nation on earth. Nothing will sap the health of local self-government more speedily than the developing reflex inclination to "let Washington do it." If the lure of federal money is not waved so seductively before people by politicians more eager to woo votes than stand by fundamental principles, local communities will usually face their problems, roll up their sleeves, and do the job that needs to be done. It must never be forgotten that a strong, viable democrary must ultimately rest on strong, responsible local self-government. Undermine the latter and you have undermined the entire structure of popular government, leaving no real alternative to that centralized power that spells eventual tyranny.

It is sometimes well to remember that federal "aid" is something of a misnomer. The federal government cannot supply any funds that it has not first obtained from the people. The only "aid" it gives must first be taken from the people. Federal "aid," therefore, is not "free," as some are wont to think, but represents tax money lifted from one pocket and restored to another. Nor should it be forgotten that taxes en route to Washington and back have a disconcerting habit of shrinking as they pass through the hands of the mammoth bureaucratic structures entrenched in Washington. Bureaucracies are notoriously riddled with inefficiency and red tape, and these characteristics become more pronounced as size increases. It is far better that tax money should be raised by local officials familiar with local problems, under the surveillance of local people and responsible to the local electorate. Then the waste that occurs as taxes make the long trip to Washington and back can be avoided.

Some congressmen opposed federal aid on less ideological grounds. They observed that their states would be required to contribute far more toward federal aid to education than they would receive, because most distribution formulas incorporate criteria that directly or indirectly help the poorer states. Even if flat per-pupil grants were made, they ultimately would benefit the poorer states proportionately more because their per capita tax returns are less than in wealthier states. These congressmen, then, doubted that their constituents wanted them to vote for major tax programs that benefited other states proportionately more than their own.

Just how much will federal aid improve the quality of education, anyway? Education, in the last analysis, depends far more on the intelligence, dedication, and instructional ability of the teacher than on expensive buildings. It is most unlikely that Congress will ever appropriate the vast sums required to raise teachers' salaries to levels necessary to attract higher quality candidates in significant numbers. Small increases might be welcomed by the teachers, but they would make little if any difference to the quality of American education.

Senator Barry Goldwater has proposed that individual taxpayers be permitted to deduct from their federal tax obligations such proportion of locally paid school taxes as would be needed to reduce their federal tax burden by $3 or $4 billion. These savings would then be available for tapping by local school districts (where needed), without swelling the federal bureaucracy or endangering local control.[9]

Finally, one can agree with all that is said about equal educational opportunity and the importance of fully developing the nation's potential talent while concluding that this will best be done by continued reliance on the energies, ingenuity, and resolution of state and local governments. Federal aid proponents have no monopoly on idealism and no greater interest in the welfare of our children and of our nation than have their opponents. Either because of an inveterate bias for centralized government or an incorrigible propensity to seek big, showy—and seemingly easy—solutions to knotty problems, they have errone-

[9] Barry Goldwater, "*SR* is Wrong About Federal Aid," *The Saturday Review*, March 18, 1961, p. 44.

ously come to a conclusion that will create far more problems and dangers than it will ever solve. The state and local way may not be the spectacular answer to our educational needs, but it is the tested and tried method by which we can make the soundest progress without losing the democratic values we cherish.

The Closing Rounds

Federal-aid supporters welcomed the opportunity for rebuttal: The question is not, How much better are we doing than we did before? The question is, Are we doing as well as we can and as well as we should if we are to provide this generation with the best education we can? Virtually every study that has been made concludes that we are not, as indeed ordinary common-sense observation suggests. When we are over 100,000 classrooms short, we are not doing enough. When 500,000 children go to school on double shifts, we are not doing enough. When we fail to attract enough first-class people into the teaching field, we are not doing enough—whatever the percentages or the absolute figures may indicate.

Are the deficiencies being met? Federal-aid spokesmen denied that they were. In 1958, the classroom shortage was estimated by the Administration to be 140,000; in 1963, the Office of Education declared the shortage was still over 120,000. If, then, the school building boom that filled anti-federal-aid groups with such pride had failed to make a larger dent than this, it was time to recognize that a federal helping hand was needed. Certainly if a President so devoted to our federal system and so hostile to needless federal spending as Mr. Eisenhower believed federal aid was urgently required, this hardly suggests an inveterate propensity to spend federal money for spending's sake. One can sing hosannas to state and local governments until the heavens ring, but the stubborn fact remains of persistent, large-scale classroom shortage in the face of local inability or unwillingness to act. Even if the shortage were to be eliminated in ten years (a most improbable assumption), hundreds of thousands of children are getting inadequate educational opportunities *now*—and they only pass this way once. Why be indifferent to their misfortune?

Admittedly, we are getting a gratifying increase in the number of college students preparing to teach, but we are not yet over the hump. No one familiar with the products of our schools of education believes that these attract a satisfactory percentage of our most talented young people. Although many superior college students seek certification, reports repeatedly indicate that the academic potential of most enrollees falls below the college average. Furthermore, it is especially important to increase teacher salaries considerably in order to attract more good male teachers and to prevent them from drifting out of teaching and into administration once they have reached the low salary ceiling generally applied to teaching personnel. If the salary assistance heretofore proposed is insufficient, this argues for still larger federal aid rather than its abandonment.

If it is granted that the money currently available for public education might well be spent more advantageously, this can probably be said of all enterprises. If we are to extol local initiative and local control, moreover, our "marble palaces" are the product of precisely those conditions, and most of the educational impediments that have attached to the schools are the result of local pressures. There is no reason, however, why efforts to improve the spending of local moneys cannot go forward simultaneously with efforts to obtain the federal funds needed for improving the schools in other respects. As the Rockefeller Report noted, "All the problems of the schools lead us back sooner or later to one basic problem—financing."[10]

Can we afford to spend federal money to improve education? If the Congress were asked to spend billions more for defense, it would appropriate the funds without batting an eye. No one would say, "But we can't afford it!" If we can spend whatever is needed for defense, we can also spend whatever is needed for the education of our children. We are a rich nation. It is absurd to suggest that we cannot afford to educate our children well.

It is true that the federal balance has shifted somewhat since 1787 Although the states have exercised greater powers, federal activity has increased at an even more rapid pace. But this in

[10] *The Pursuit of Excellence*, Special Studies Report V, Rockefeller Foundation, Garden City, N.Y., Doubleday, 1958, p. 33.

itself need not cause apprehension. The gradual accretion of federal authority has reflected changing economic and social circumstances that have led the people to approve, and the Supreme Court to ratify, federal programs designed to deal with specific problems the states were unable or unwilling to handle. There is nothing sinister about this development, inasmuch as each step was taken after full public debate and with popular consent. Nor have any of our basic constitutional rights been impaired in the process. That a comparable trend toward greater centralization of power has taken place in every civilized industrialized nation in the world is cogent evidence that Washington has responded to the ineluctable pressures of our age. We should be proud that our system has the flexibility and adaptability to adjust to the imperatives of our time rather than bemoan the natural and orderly evolution of our system to one better suited to the governmental demands of the twentieth century. Nostalgia is a natural human sentiment, but it is not the stuff from which progress is made.

Has education always been a strictly local responsibility? Look back at the long list of national initiatives, going back to the Northwest Ordinance of 1785, in support of education. The Tenth Amendment did reserve to the states powers not granted to the national government, nor denied to the states nor reserved to the people, but the national government has certainly never lost the power to spend for the general welfare. In our early history many leading Americans believed that the power to spend for the general welfare was limited to expenditures needed to carry out its delegated powers, but the Supreme Court has rejected this view for the earlier Hamiltonian view that the spending power is not so limited. After 180 years of national support of education, it is a little late to be arguing that the national government is constitutionally precluded from giving fiscal aid to education. And if education is not embraced in the concept "the general welfare," pray tell what is?

Federal aid for education does not necessarily pave the way for federal control of education. The historical record sustains no such premise. Federal support for the agricultural experiment stations has not cost these stations their freedom. Aid to the "defense-impact" areas has not led to federal control, nor did the WPA school construction program produce this result. Aid to the colleges has not led to federal dictation of college policies. The record is consistent, convincing—and unsurprising. Washington, after all, acts in response to the pressures on it and avoids like the plague activities that predictably inflame the voters. Despite all the talk about federal aid to education "inevitably" leading to federal control, the plain truth is that federal aid inevitably will *not* lead to federal control unless the people desire those controls. On matters involving well-known, deeply rooted public convictions, neither congressman nor administrator will risk his future by challenging the public will. And if he misjudges, he will soon be set straight. Thus, although federal-aid bills usually specifically forbid the national government to exercise any controls over education in conjunction with the expenditure of the funds, such precautions are really unnecessary.

The fears so often expressed concerning the insatiable "lust for power" that politicians and bureaucrats allegedly hold are based on a serious misconception. A congressman has no power at all if he is not re-elected, and an administrator has no power if he loses his job. If they do "lust for power," they will be exceedingly careful not to offend the sovereign public by outraging its opinion where that is as well understood as is the public attachment to local control of the schools.

This is not to say that public opinion may not increasingly wish to use federal funds to influence the priorities of our educational system. Americans *wanted* to use federal money in 1958 to strengthen scientific education. And they *wanted* to stress and modernize vocational education in 1963. The point is, then, that whenever public opinion shifts and Americans want federal action to support changing educational goals, this can bring federal direction whether or not previous federal aid of that character existed. The will of the people will not be denied in the field of education any more than in any other field.

Yes, totalitarians do immediately seize control of the schools on assumption of power. But in many European democracies the central government subsidizes and controls the educational system without casting any totalitarian shadows and without imposing any rigid mold that stifles individual diversity, initiative, or experimentation. The establishment of *minimum* educational standards does not prevent local school systems from improving on those standards to the limit of their abilities.

Vigorous local governments are indeed essential cornerstones of healthy self-governing societies. But if they lack either the vigor or the capacity to solve problems adversely affecting the future of their children and of their country, why not have the federal government lend a hand? What is wrong with the partnership concept of federalism, whereby each layer in the federal structure gives assistance to the other where circumstances make this desirable? Is there any merit in having Washington, the states, and the local governments view each other with perpetual suspicion, each jealously guarding its precious prerogatives as if they were ends in themselves? The nation has been evolving toward a more cooperative relationship, with a characteristic American emphasis on solving problems rather than holding rigidly to abstract concepts viewed apart from living political realities. We should be grateful that our common sense and pragmatism enables us to escape from the sterilities of political dogmatism.

Advocates of federal aid sometimes challenge the sincerity of businessmen's devotion to the virtues of local self-government—a devotion said to underlie their opposition to federal aid. Is there any special reason, they ask, why the United States Chamber of Commerce, the National Association of Manufacturers, and their affiliates should be so uniquely appreciative of the merits of local government? Are they political philosophers whose profound knowledge of history and whose vast political experience has given them an extraordinarily perceptive grasp of the significance of local government in the cosmos of human liberty?

These cynics argue that the real reason business groups sing paeans to state and local governments is two-fold: (1) they can and do dominate these governments much more easily than they can dominate Washington; (2) the state and local tax system is based primarily on consumer and property taxes that touch business only lightly, whereas the federal tax system rests mostly on a heavy corporation tax and a graduated income tax that affect them deeply. Businessmen, it is said, have therefore acquired a generalized predilection for state and local governments, for quite understandable reasons. But these reasons have nothing to do with noble democratic principles of liberty.

Furthermore, if they were so opposed to federal spending because of its intrinsic dangers, they would less avidly seek federal appropriations for projects in their homes districts. The businessman's authentic attitude is said to be summed up by the action of the Spokane, Washington, Chamber of Commerce, which sent one letter to Washington asking for curbs on federal spending and another requesting $1.8 million for local expenditures on its Columbia River Basin project! Spending that means business prosperity, *Si!* Spending for education and help to unfortunate persons, *No!*

Finally, if local self-government is invested with such matchless virtues, state aid to and control of the schools should also be stoutly opposed. Why will federal aid corrupt our educational system, while state aid is universally accepted as desirable and beneficent? Far from limiting itself to fiscal aid, the states closely regulate local education systems in a variety of ways—all without any outcries that local self-government is withering and that democracy is imperiled.

A major shrinkage of tax money en route to Washington and back? Nonsense, federal-aid proponents scoff. The federal tax collection system is already established, however the money is spent. Because aid to education bills typically propose that a check be sent to each state in accordance with some formula involving the number of school-age children, per capita income, existing expenditure per school child, and the like, the administrative costs involved in making these computations and sending the checks would be insignificant. The impression so often given of money loaded on boxcars, with bureaucrats snatching at it as it wends its way to Washington and back, is a figment of the debater's imagination. Proof? Most federal assistance to the states comes under the grants-in-aid programs, and federal grants-in-aid are administered at a cost of only 1.8 cents on the dollar.

If congressmen choose to vote against federal aid because the formula requires the more prosperous states to help the less prosperous, that is their privilege. They may represent their people in so doing, but they also represent a parochial and myopic viewpoint. If the wealthier states have no obligation to help the poorer, even where something so fundamental as education is concerned, then presumably the wealthier counties have no obligation to help the poorer counties and state aid programs should be discontinued. Wealthier persons, then, would logically have no obligation to contribute more to the support of government than poorer persons, so the graduated income tax should be abandoned. This kind of reasoning exposes its own moral bankruptcy when carried to its logical conclusion.

Senator Goldwater's recommendation for aiding the schools will not survive close examination. The well-to-do states, which need little if any help, will be primarily benefited because their citizens pay high enough income taxes to gain the full benefits of tax forgiveness. Those who pay no income taxes, or a small amount, will derive proportionately slight benefits from the proposal. Instead of mitigating the disparity between the wealthier and poorer states, it would only widen it. And what assurance have we that the federal tax "savings" would lead to higher local property taxes in support of education?

Some proponents of federal aid have been less interested in general aid than in federal appropriations designed to correct specific deficiencies in public schools. The editors of *The New Republic*, for instance, have proposed that federal money be used to (1) stimulate research into the improvement of high school programs; (2) supplement the salaries of gifted high school mathematics and science teachers to prevent the raiding of their ranks by higher paying corporations; (3) offer teachers who have reached the top of their skimpy salary scales (usually around $9,000) the privilege of a two-year federal scholarship at a good university, with federal salary increments at the conclusion of this training that would enable them at the age of 50 to equal the salaries they could make in educational administrative work (thereby enabling good teachers to remain in the teaching field without undergoing financial sacrifices); (4) expand high school English departments sufficiently to enable them to require and properly evaluate at least one theme per pupil per week (as Dr. Conant recommended); (5) establish pilot schools in urban and rural slum areas to determine experimentally what can be done to improve unimaginative teaching and inadequate counseling in this area.[11]

How can Washington, in conjunction with state and local governments, stimulate the better teachers to accept employment in crowded slum schools where disciplinary problems are great, educational interest and performance are meager, parental concern is minimal, and the surroundings are ugly and depressing? It is natural that the most competent teachers prefer to spend their careers in comfortable, suburban communities, instructing clean, well-mannered (well—reasonably so!), more highly motivated students with interests and attitudes corresponding to their own. A spirit of dedication and self-sacrifice will divert some careers toward the slums, but heroes and heroines are never plentiful. Can a variety of financial or other incentives be established that will persuade promising young teachers, or older ones of demonstrated competence, to invest a part of their lives in the children who need them most?

Perhaps college loans could be offered to gifted young persons with teaching aspirations, loans partially or wholly forgiven for those who devote a portion of their careers to teaching in slum schools.[12] Can President Johnson, who combines acutely developed political sensitivities with an almost evangelical concern for education, help create an atmosphere that will attract able young people to slum schools as they are now attracted to the Peace Corps? His interest in establishing a federally financed Teachers Corps suggests that the nation will make a gradually expanding effort to deal with this serious national problem.

Although they are currently in a distinct minority, a growing, articulate and by no means insignificant group is favorably impressed with the potential fruitfulness of limited federal control. Few if any politicians would care to be identified with this unorganized group or its uncrystallized beliefs, but more and more

[11] "What Education Needs," *The New Republic,* November 27, 1961, p. 4.

[12] Courtesy of Bruce Palmer, Miami University (Ohio), class of 1966.

educators and some public figures are talking along these lines.

This school of thought considers diversity very fine, but says that the educational demands of our age are such that we can no longer afford the dismal standards that diversity sometimes brings. Admiral Hyman Rickover, for example, calls local control of schools "the greatest obstacle to school reform." Local school boards may represent grass-roots democracy at work, but they may also represent the kind of provincialism, backwardness, and sheer ignorance that will handicap products of the local school system for life.[13] All too rarely, it is said, are school boards composed of community figures with advanced views on educational developments and needs. Local board members are often eager to retain the traditional system associated with their own schooldays and fail to recognize the need for an educational program adapted to our current society—to say nothing of one adapted to the needs of the future.

But if the nation has an obligation to help give every child the best possible opportunity not only to compete in the national talent market, but to fully develop those talents that are necessary to national survival and to the advancement of civilization, perhaps it cannot afford such a chaotic educational system. Perhaps some national direction is needed.

Those who make these assumptions are anything but united on the course the nation should follow. Some believe the first step should be intensified fact-finding and information distribution by the United States Office of Education. Information programs that reveal the facts about our most glaring educational deficiencies and focus attention on the more promising educational innovations could have a salutary effect on the schools. Although this is being done on a small scale at present by both government and nongovernment groups, much remains to be done along these lines.

Some would not be adverse to establishing minimal curriculum standards throughout the nation in order to insure that proper attention is given to those areas educators regard as of

[13] Paul Pickrel, "New Nations and Old Problems," *Harper's Magazine*, November, 1963, p. 120. Also "Standards for Noah's Ark," *Time*, March 16, 1962, p. 50.

crucial importance. For example, a minimum number of years' work might be required in English, mathematics, science, and history for qualified students. Others would establish minimum national standards for teacher certification, with provisions for emergency certification until such time as was needed to bring a state's teachers up to the required level.

Educators and others who are thinking in this fashion often emphasize that the national government has a broader perspective than the local school districts, has a better knowledge of the technical and social skills that need to be developed, can draw more effectively on research that has been undertaken to improve education both here and abroad, and can better finance future research. Furthermore, because the federal government's proposals and actions are subject to the closest and most critical scrutiny by the nation's press and by the highest levels of interested groups, its recommendations would have to be defensible before they could meet the test of national and congressional opinion. As for the dangers of possible federal "thought control," these are dismissed with the observation that although Americans might conceivably approve federal legislation requiring the establishment of minimum standards, they would be united against any federal control of how courses should be taught, what opinions should be favored, and what interpretations should be placed on facts. So long as the nation believes in freedom, this situation will surely endure. Yet it is here, and only here, that federal control would really be a threat to democracy.

Those who would dissent from this opinion usually adhere to the same reasoning that is advanced in opposition to federal aid. They are fearful that a dangerous amount of federal control would come about through a series of nibbling actions, none of which was great enough to arouse public hostility but which in the aggregate would be a genuine menace. They strongly resist any federal tendency to introduce uniformity into the schools, feeling that this is a greater threat to a free and healthy educational system than the occasional weaknesses that may grow out of antiquated or myopic school board rulings. The latter is one of the prices to be paid for federalism, and for decentralized government, but it is a price they believe is well worth paying.

If curriculum standards need to be improved, and certification criteria tightened, it is better to leave this in the hands of the states. They already have well-developed educational departments that are not derelict in meeting their responsibilities.

The arguments pro and con do not adequately reveal why the nation finally decided to go ahead with federal aid to education on an imposing scale. A number of political forces seem to have been at work that pushed federal aid over the top.

The growing awareness of the massive educational task that lay ahead if the Negro Revolution were to avoid an explosive and destructive course helped prepare public opinion to accept major federal aid. Adequate educational opportunity was seen as absolutely imperative if the Negro were to maximize his chances for genuine equality; the likelihood of this being accomplished in the near future without decisive federal stimulus seemed dim. Fears that automation's surge would push more and more young people into unemployment, crime, dope addiction, and the relief rolls, unless the schools were better able to train them for newly developing employment patterns, also reduced resistance to federal aid.

The opponents of federal aid bore the formidable handicap of *appearing* to be against better education, whatever the realities may have been. Education is regarded as such an unchallengeably "good thing" that federal-aid critics were perpetually on the defensive, seemingly cast in the role of blocking progress. Unfair though this may have been, it undoubtedly played a part in reducing the effectiveness of these critics. Sheer familiarity with the idea of federal aid, an idea that was debated steadily for more than 15 years, also helped soften antagonism to it in a period during which people were becoming more and more accustomed to permitting the federal government to play an ever widening role in the life of the nation. (Some have referred to this as the triumph of "creeping liberalism.") The familiar is always less fearsome, and it seems to take societies time to get accustomed to a major proposal that represents, or appears to represent, a break with the past.

The assassination of John F. Kennedy had an intangible but nonetheless significant effect on the political mood of the nation.

Mr. Kennedy's "Prince Charming" image, his capacity to make public service attractive to bright American youth, his blend of wit and dignity, his vigor and courage and intelligence, and his vision of America's role at home and abroad—all were illumined and magnified when a stunned nation saw him cut down at the height of his career. The nation's political temper was never quite the same again. As if to make amends for the brutal and capricious slaughter of the man who symbolized a nobler American dream, the nation seemed more receptive to legislation that might make the dream come true.

Finally, the legislative acceptance of federal aid was facilitated by the nomination of Barry Goldwater on the Republican ticket in 1964, his smashing defeat at the polls, and the simultaneous election of a more liberal Congress. The Congress of 1965, responding to the forces we have been describing, as well as to Lyndon Johnson's skills in muting the parochial school issue, did not have to be coaxed into supporting massive federal aid.

Parochial School Aid: Yes

Whether wise or unwise, it seems clear that federal aid to education is here to stay. What then about public aid for parochial schools?[14]

The Catholic position on parochial aid has shifted somewhat in recent years. In 1949, Cardinal Spellman said the church was not asking for general support of religious schools; in 1955, Cardinal Cushing stated that he would "absolutely refuse" federal aid for parochial school construction lest it eventually bring about federal controls.[15] Church and lay leaders were in agreement in 1959 that direct federal aid was "out of the question" because the Supreme Court would rule such aid unconstitutional, because most state constitutions forbid aid to parochial schools, because the independence of Catholic education would be jeop-

[14] Currently 85 percent of school children are in public schools, 13 percent in Catholic schools, 1 percent in Protestant and Jewish schools, and 1 percent in independent schools.

[15] Neil McCluskey, *Catholic Viewpoint on Education*, Garden City, N.Y., Hanover House, 1959, p. 180.

ardized thereby, and because this aid would foment such bitter controversy that church interests would be imperiled.[16]

After the election of Mr. Kennedy, however, some church leaders appeared to adopt a different posture toward federal aid. The Archbishop of Cincinnati announced that public loans to private educational institutions were not only constitutional, but that it would be "discriminatory" to deny such loans if a general aid bill were enacted. President Kennedy's aid to education bill, omitting aid to parochial schools in accordance with a campaign pledge, was roundly attacked by members of the Catholic hierarchy for its "discriminatory" character. Some members of the hierarchy implied that unless appropriate aid was available to parochial schools, no expansion of public school aid should be voted by Congress. Other Catholic prelates, while agreeing to the need for and propriety of parochial school aid, deplored an intransigent attitude of opposing more aid to public schools unless it was accompanied by parochial school aid.

Why the shift? A number of factors seem to have been involved. Many Catholics have become uneasily aware, especially since World War II, that the quality of many Catholic schools leaves something to be desired. The eminent British writer Denis Brogan has observed that "in no Western society is the intellectual prestige of Catholicism lower than in the country where, in such respects as wealth, numbers and strength of organization, it is so powerful."[17] Monsignor John Tracy Ellis added that "no well-informed Catholic will attempt to challenge that statement."[18] Writing in *The New York Times Magazine* in 1965, John Leo decared that ". . . American Catholics are dramatically under-represented on the intellectual front. There are no great American Catholic scientists. . . . Neither are there Catholic philosophers, poets, theologians, and writers in any proportion to the Catholic population."[19]

[16] *Ibid.*, p. 168.

[17] Daniel P. Moynihan, "How Catholics Feel About Federal School Aid," *The Reporter*, May 25, 1961, p. 36.

[18] *Ibid.*

[19] "The American Catholic Is Changing," *The New York Times Magazine,* November 14, 1965, p. 141.

Many Catholic schools, it should be pointed out, are of superior quality. In Boston, for example, 54 percent of Catholic school tenth graders scored "able" in a nationally recognized test, whereas only 30 percent of their public school counterparts did as well.[20] In New York, 15 percent of the New York State Regents scholarships go to Catholic students. On the other hand, it is no secret that many Catholic schools are appallingly overcrowded, and the percentage of inadequately trained teachers is embarrassingly high. Only about half of the elementary school teachers have college degrees; 20 percent have had only one year of college or less.

Daniel Moynihan, a sympathetic observer, declares that, "In many areas Catholic schools are demonstrably superior to their counterparts. But by and large the local Catholic school is weaker than the local public school; the disparity in incomes makes this almost inevitable. In any event, the drain of resources into elementary and secondary schools has severely inhibited the quality of Catholic higher education."[21] Martin Mayer concurs: "By and large . . . the Catholic schools seem to be a depressed area in American education. By whatever objective measurements we can make, they rank well below the public schools of their areas. Less money is spent per pupil, class sizes are substantially larger, there are fewer teachers per thousand pupils and the teachers themselves are typically less well prepared. . . ."[22]

Heightened awareness of Catholic school deficiencies since World War II has led to considerable soul-searching among Catholic educators, but other factors played as great or a greater part in shaping Catholic attitudes toward public support for education. The postwar baby boom placed a severe financial burden on church schools already overfilled with students; and the rapid rise in public school teacher salaries during and since the 1950s further intensified the problem, because Catholics must

[20] Thomas J. Fleming, "The Crisis in Catholic Schools," *The Saturday Evening Post*, October 26, 1963, p. 21.

[21] Moynihan, *op. cit.*, p. 37.

[22] Daniel Callahan, ed., *Federal Aid and Catholic Schools*, Baltimore, Helicon, 1964, pp. 100–101.

hire a large number of lay teachers in competition with rising public school salary levels. (It costs between $650 and $1,250 for a nun's annual subsistence and allowances, whereas Catholic lay teachers were paid about $3,500 a year in 1964. Although nuns outnumbered lay teachers by 13 to 1 in 1949, this had shrunk to 3 to 1 in 1959 and is expected to reach a ratio of 1 to 2 by 1970.[23])

The teacher recruiting problem, particularly in the elementary schools, is also becoming acute because of what Dr. George N. Shuster calls "a waning attraction to the life of the teaching religious"; and finally, general school costs are rising as the demands on the schools for better science training and higher standards in general reflect the emphasis on adequate precollege preparation.

The Catholic Church places great stress on the importance of its school system, believing that it is an indispensable instrument for training its young people and keeping them in the fold. Whatever threatens the survival or well-being of those schools is regarded as a threat to the church and to the carrying out of its mission on earth. With financial strains reaching such a point that Dr. Shuster and others believe many elementary Catholic schools may have to be abandoned,[24] the church is of course prepared to fight for what it regards as fair play in the administration of federal educational funds.

Some Catholic scholars are not so convinced of the value of parochial schooling on the elementary or even the secondary level. They believe competent studies disprove the theory that Catholic schools promote better moral standards—or greater interest in religious questions.[25] Mary P. Ryan, in *Are Parochial Schools the Answer?* suggests that Catholic schools be abandoned

[23] Helen Shaffer, "Catholic Schools," *Editorial Research Reports,* August 5, 1964, p. 565; and Carl Degler, "Aid For Parochial Schools–A Question of Education, Not Religion," *The New York Times Magazine,* January 31, 1965, p. 11.

[24] George N. Shuster, "Schools at the Crossroads," *The Atlantic Monthly,* August, 1962, pp. 97–98. By 1965, 160 Catholic elementary schools had dropped some classes. Catholic schools once enrolled about half of all Catholic children; the figure had fallen to 42 percent by 1966.

[25] See Fleming, *op. cit.*

and that the funds used for their support be devoted to special programs to bring improved religious education for all Catholic youngsters including the 53 percent who now attend public schools. Herself a Catholic, Mrs. Ryan believes that Catholic schools promote a "ghetto mentality" and deprive Catholics of the opportunity to influence the development of public education. The views of Mrs. Ryan apparently represent a distinctly minority position with the church.[26]

It may be that the church regarded the inauguration of Mr. Kennedy as a propitious time to open a campaign for parochial school aid. Not that Kennedy's Catholicism could help their cause, for he was irrevocably committed to opposing general aid to parochial schools. But if a major federal aid bill were to pass under a Catholic President, involving large sums of money for public schools and none for parochial schools, the precedent might make it exceedingly difficult for parochial school funds to be obtained at any future date. If general federal aid to education were to become institutionalized as part of national policy, it was essential from the Catholic view that the groundwork include recognition of Catholic "rights" as the church conceived them. (The church later was encouraged by the fact that whereas public opinion polls disclosed that 57 percent of the people were aligned against federal aid to parochial schools in 1961, only 44 percent were opposed in 1963.)

Attitudes toward aid to parochial schools probably break down into four main divisions:

1. Those who think that parochial schools (which are principally Catholic) are necessary to the churches concerned and beneficial to society, that at least limited public aid is fully justified on grounds of equity, and that no serious dangers are involved in accepting such aid.
2. Those who think that parochial schools are necessary to the churches concerned and beneficial to society, but that the receipt of aid on a wider scale than that now enjoyed would jeopardize church control of these schools.
3. Those who prefer public to parochial schools, but believe that

[26] New York, Holt, Rinehart and Winston, 1964.

because parochial schools are here to stay, society would benefit more from the improved education public aid would bring than from the continuation of inferior parochial schools.

4. Those who are hostile to parochial schools, hope they will decline, and want to do nothing that will help strengthen or perpetuate them.

The arguments, legal and otherwise, that are used to sustain or oppose aid are probably selected because they lead to conclusions consistent with the debater's basic orientation toward the role of parochial schools in general and Catholic schools in particular.

The case for aid to parochial schools runs something as follows: Assistance to parochial schools of all denominations on an impartial basis is not a violation of the Constitution in the light either of history or of the plain wording of the Constitution. The latter forbids Congress to make any law "respecting the establishment of religion or denying the free exercise thereof." Insofar as the "establishment of religion" is concerned, James M. O'Neill states flatly, "There is not an item of dependable evidence" that the word "establishment" meant anything more than "a single church or religion enjoying formal, legal, official, monopolistic privilege through a union with the government of the state."[27] The eminent constitutional authority, Professor E. S. Corwin, agrees that "establishment" refers to a preferential church status, not to a rigid separation of church and state.[28] Professor Wilbur G. Katz, former dean of the University of Chicago Law School, and Professor Arthur E. Sutherland of the Harvard Law School concur.

When the Constitution was drawn up, nine of the 13 colonies had "established" churches, but sentiment in favor of "disestablishmentarianism" was gaining ground. The Founding Fathers wanted to insure that no church received a favored legal position from Congress and, therefore, incorporated this safeguard in the First Amendment. They also wanted to reassure states with

[27] Leonard Levy, "School Prayers and the Constitution," *Commentary*, September, 1962, p. 228. Dr. Levy, it should be pointed out, cites these opinions without agreeing with them.

[28] *Ibid.*, p. 226.

"established" churches that the federal government would not interfere with state "establishmentarianism"—a far cry from the current Supreme Court view that the Founding Fathers favored strict separation of church and state as a general political principle.[29] In some states, it should be added, tax money went to Christian churches impartially.

It is equally clear that aid to parochial schools did not run counter to the convictions of our early forefathers, because church schools received tax sustenance in most of the states throughout the first half century after the Constitution was adopted. Most of the early schools were established by church groups that were anxious to teach the Christian faith as well as provide a general education for their members. State support of these schools continued, for the most part, until the Know-Nothing period in the 1840s, during which many states began to include constitutional provisions forbidding state aid to parochial schools.[30] Thus, although the Supreme Court has taken a position that seems to preclude general parochial school aid, this represents a latter-day interpretation not borne out either by the literal wording of the Constitution or by earlier historical practice. As for parochial school aid "denying the free exercise" of religion, such aid would deny no one either the privilege of worshiping as he pleases or of propagating his faith.

Catholics pay their full share of taxes to support the public schools, even though about 6 million Catholic children do not attend these schools. (Almost one half of Catholic children are enrolled in Catholic schools.) To deny Catholic parents any share of tax funds because they choose to send their children to "God-centered" schools comes close to being a denial of "the free exercise of religion," because parents who are faithful to this aspect of their religious belief are discriminated against by public policy. The state says, in effect, follow your religious beliefs as you please, but if those beliefs obligate you to send your children to church schools, we will make it as difficult as possi-

[29] Neil McCluskey, "Federal Aid for Private and Parochial Schools? Yes," *Current History*, August, 1961, p. 73 (fn.). Also see Robert F. Drinan, "State and Federal Aid to Parochial Schools," *Vital* Speeches, July 1, 1964.

[30] Moynihan, *op. cit.*, pp. 35–36.

ble by withholding tax funds for those schools. In the words of Neil McCluskey, S.J., "If public benefits are so administered that citizens must do violence to their conscience in order to share in them, then the benefits are discriminatory."[31] Certainly the state is not required by the First Amendment to be hostile to religion—it is only required to be impartial. Impartial aid to all schools is *not* a violation of the First Amendment.

Parochial schools render a valuable public service by instructing millions of children in secular subjects, instruction that would have to be carried out by the state at great expense if the parochial schools disappeared. It is estimated that Catholic schools alone save the nation over $2.5 billion a year in operating costs, while public school construction expenditures would have to be raised by about $400 million per year but for Catholic schools. Surely it is not improper for the state to return a portion of tax revenues paid by Catholics in compensation for the public responsibilities they have assumed. And only a portion is asked, because neither the Catholic Church nor any other church wants public funds to finance the religious aspects of parochial instruction.

It is too late to contend that *all* aid to parochial schools or to religion is unconstitutional, because public policy has supported numerous measures that benefit the churches by indirection. Church property has always been exempt from taxation, a considerable indirect favor to the churches. Church contributions of up to 20 percent of one's income may be deducted from income tax obligations. This has undoubtedly encouraged millions of persons to give more generously to the church of their choice and has been a major financial boon to the churches. Public funds pay for the services of fire and police departments, yet these agencies provide protection for church buildings and church property. Nine states permit tax funds to be spent for secular textbooks to be used in parochial schools. In a number of states, free bus transportation is provided to parochial school students, with the Supreme Court's sanction. School lunches are provided to public and parochial schools alike in over half of

[31] McCluskey, "Federal Aid for Private and Parochial Schools? Yes," p. 72.

the states. The GI Bill of Rights helped veterans finance their college education irrespective of the college of their choice, a policy that was of substantial assistance to parochial colleges. In fact, some 2,000 rabbis, priests, and ministers received seminary training under its provisions. Under the National Defense Education Act of 1958, federal loans are available for the purchase of equipment for foreign language, math, and science instruction. Tax funds were also offered for classroom remodeling in parochial institutions to enable the installation of equipment needed to promote this instruction. Federal loans at low interest rates have been offered to parochial as well as public colleges for dormitory construction, and research grants make no distinction between public and private institutions. The Education Act of 1963 made federal funds available for public and parochial colleges, and the Elementary and Secondary Education Act of 1965 enabled the public purchase of textbooks which were then "loaned" to parochial school pupils. Teachers and counselors having special skills in dealing with children from poor homes are publicly hired and then may be sent, part-time, to do special and remedial work in parochial schools. Supplementary Education Centers serve public and parochial students alike. (The practice of extending aid to pupils, not institutions, has satisfied the constitutional doubts of many, but by no means all, citizens.)

The Public Health Service Act of 1948 appropriated funds for the construction of religiously operated hospitals as well as conventional community hospitals. These hospitals constitute an important part of the work of the Roman Catholic Church. Finally, separation of church and state purists overlook the fact that tax money pays for the services of chaplains in federal prisons and in the armed forces, as well as in the House and Senate.

In view of this imposing list of aids to religion, how can it be logically contended that the First Amendment forbids aid to parochial schools? The "wall of separation" has been penetrated in a host of ways with popular and Supreme Court consent, and any distinction drawn between these forms of assistance and aid for the secular aspects of parochial schools is a tortured one.

If it is important to mobilize the brains of the nation, as everyone theoretically agrees, is it less important to mobilize Catholic than non-Catholic brains? Well-educated Catholics are just as useful to the nation as well-educated non-Catholics. Their contributions to science, business, the professions, and the creative arts add as much to the quality of our civilization as do others. At a time when shortages of skilled persons exist on such a disturbing scale, it is highly imprudent to pretend that society at large has no concern with the educational welfare of over 6 million children.

If Congress feels it cannot obtain Supreme Court approval for general appropriations, it could at least provide tax deductions for tuition payments to parochial schools, as proposed by a former secretary of health, education, and welfare, Abraham Ribicoff.[32] If there are no constitutional objections to allowing tax deductions for direct contributions to churches, there can hardly be constitutional objections to deductions for tuition charges that largely support secular education. Congress could also offer grants for the purchase of laboratory equipment (instead of the loans now offered parochial schools when grants are given public schools), and loans could be made available for construction of buildings in which secular instruction is given. Catholic schools should enjoy the full benefits of such auxiliary educational benefits as free bus transportation, secular textbooks, and school health services.[33]

At the very least, additional expenditures to enlarge the laboratory and vocational-training facilities of public schools, so that these facilities could be used on a "shared-time" basis, is a reasonable request. Shared-time arrangements have worked well in a number of communities for over 20 years. Approximately 280 public schools now have a shared-time system, and the extension of this principle would improve the over-all educational system, as well as encourage more Catholic voters to support public school bond issues and tax levies.

Many Catholics suspect that the "issue" of parochial school aid would sharply diminish if non-Catholic schools were the major

[32] *The New York Times*, May 26, 1963, p. 9E.
[33] McCluskey, *Catholic Viewpoint on Education*, p. 181.

beneficiaries of that aid. They believe that anti-Catholicism is concealed behind the façade of the constitutional arguments, and question whether such attitudes should carry great weight in determining major constitutional questions. Many Catholics and non-Catholics believe antagonism to religion, per se, is also a potent factor. Naturally, such prejudice is skillfully disguised.

Parochial School Aid: No

The opposition to parochial school aid argues somewhat as follows: Although the historical record does provide evidence of direct tax aid for religious schools, this involved state and local aid, not federal. Until 1925, the First Amendment was held to be a limitation on the national government but was regarded as inapplicable to the states. The precedents cited for our early history, then, provide no support for the view that federal aid today would build on relevant precedents in our early history.

The Constitution is what the Supreme Court says it is. We have no other authoritative basis for interpreting its meaning, and the dictum of the Supreme Court in the Everson case was so sweeping as to leave no grounds for reasonable doubt concerning the unconstitutionality of general federal aid to parochial schools. In a widely quoted paragraph, the Supreme Court declared:

> Neither a state nor the Federal Government can set up a church. Neither can pass laws that aid one religion, aid all religions, or prefer one religion over another. Neither can force nor influence a person to go to or to remain away from church . . . or force him to profess a belief or a disbelief in any religion. . . . No tax in any amount, large or small, can be levied to support any religious activities or institutions, whatever they may be called, or whatever form they may adopt to teach or practice religion . . . in the words of Jefferson, the clause against establishment of religion by law was intended to erect "a wall of separation between Church and State."[34]

The court, moreover, was fully aware of all the historical precedents and gave them due weight in coming to this conclusion.

[34] *Everson* v. *Board of Education,* 330 U.S. 1 (1947), pp. 137–138.

Among other things the court took cognizance of the fact that the six states that had "established" churches in 1791 gave impartial aid to "multiple" establishments—that is, aid was given to all Protestant churches in three states and to all Christian churches in the other. Thus, the Fathers were familiar with the concept of impartial aid to all churches but forbade this form of aid when they required that Congress make "no law respecting the establishment of religion."[35]

The court is, therefore, unequivocally on record as opposed to tax aid to religion on the smallest scale even if it is administered impartially. And although the Everson case was a 5-to-4 decision, the four-man minority opposed the use of tax money even to provide transportation for parochial school students. The majority found this permissible, declaring that the funds provided for the safety of the children rather than for aid to religion. Since then, it might be added, Justice Douglas has indicated that his original affirmative vote for state-financed parochial school transportation was a mistake, further suggesting the direction in which the court is moving.

As for tax funds for secular textbooks to be used in parochial schools, this has not been tested since the Supreme Court put the states squarely under the provisions of the First Amendment.

James Madison, who qualifies most nearly for the honor of being the Father of the Constitution, did not hold to the view that the term "establishment of religion" referred only to a state church. In his famous "Memorial and Remonstrance Against Religious Assessments" in 1785, he interpreted this controversial phrase to apply to religion in general and opposed the use of tax funds on even an impartial basis for religious purposes. He later declared that the appointment of chaplains to the two houses of Congress was unconstitutional, as well as the provision for chaplains in the Army and Navy, and argued for a "perfect separation" of church and state.[36] Whether or not this is

[35] C. Herman Pritchett, "Prayers and Politics: The Supreme Court—1961–1962," Jack W. Peltason, ed., *1963–1964 American Government Annual,* New York, Holt, Rinehart & Winston, 1963, p. 24.

[36] Irving Brant, "Madison and the Prayer Case," *The New Republic,* July 30, 1962, p. 20.

conclusive evidence of the intent of the First Amendment, it surely gives the court grounds for holding that "the establishment of religion" refers to more than the conferring of special privileges on a particular church.

It is a sophistry to contend that unless parochial schools receive their "share" of tax funds, certain parents are being discriminated against, and that the state is going out of its way to make it hard for them to carry out the requirements of their faith. Free public schools are available to the parents of all religious denominations. If some parents are not content with the type of school that the state conducts, they should expect to pay for the establishment and operation of separate schools. The state is protecting religious freedom when it grants churches the right to operate parochial schools, but the state is certainly under no obligation to finance any part of these schools. They exist for the purpose of giving children a religiously oriented education and of strengthening the loyalty and devotion of its members. Unless the churches felt that, as religious organizations, they had a tremendous stake in the maintenance of church schools, they would never endure the financial sacrifices that church schools entail. Thus, whatever tax funds sustain any part of parochial school education are sustaining one of the most important activities of the church. Viewed in its broader and most meaningful sense, it is unconstitutional to compel a taxpayer to support religion directly or indirectly, and surely it is unconstitutional to compel him to help finance a religion in which he does not believe.

Despite all the talk about the impartial support of parochial schools, federal (or state) tax support would accrue almost exclusively to the Roman Catholic Church. The Protestant churches and Jewish temples that sponsor schools have mostly opposed tax support, and many of them have stated flatly that they would not accept such support. Thus, public funds, in practice, would be siphoned to the coffers of a particular church, and the "impartial" aspect would be verbal only.

Let us suppose, however, that the non-Catholic churches changed their minds, and decided to accept tax support. With public funds now available to make parochial schools more financially feasible, it is possible that more and more churches will start their own systems of church schools, leading to the steady erosion of public schools and their replacement by parochial education. In the Netherlands, public tax support for parochial schools transformed the nation's school system from one in which two thirds of the schools were public and one third were private to a reversed proportion. Is this a development to be desired? Even if it did not bring about the proliferation of non-Catholic parochial schools, it might lead to the expansion of the Catholic school system. This would be an inappropriate and an unconstitutional use of the taxpayers' money.

Whatever weakens the public school system inevitably weakens the values that public schools uniquely encourage. Public schools foster the spirit of tolerance and understanding between members of different religious faiths. Children come to recognize that those with different religious backgrounds are essentially similar to themselves in their moral outlook, in their interests, ambitions, fears, and general behavior. And they learn, perhaps to their surprise, that students who are associated with no church whatever still share the general moral values of the community at large.

Furthermore, many students will be motivated, as the result of their public school experience, to re-examine their own religious inheritance in the light of a broader perspective and eventually to arrive at religious conceptions that are their own rather than the hand-me-downs of the family religious tradition.

It is perhaps especially valuable for Protestant children to go to school with Catholic children, so that the remaining elements of Know-Nothing hostility to Catholics can be eliminated. The fear of Catholics in high places, which was still surprisingly apparent in the 1960 presidential election, can best be reduced by fraternal experiences in public schools, just as the fear of Negroes is best dissipated by sharing a common school experience.

In sum, the public schools make an invaluable contribution to national unity by wearing off the abrasive edges of divisions that can be fruitful under certain circumstances, but that can create needless friction, discord, and hostility where groups turn inward and acquire the suspicions and misunderstandings that are the natural product of a communications shrinkage with other groups.

Thus, although it can be argued that the moral training a child receives in parochial school helps undergird the moral health and stability of a nation, it can be argued even more persuasively that public schools contribute experiences and heighten values that are indispensable to a democracy resting on an astonishing diversity of religions, races, nationality backgrounds, and economic and social strata.[37]

Public school partisans fear that the strengthening of parochial schools will aggravate a troublesome condition that grows out of the existence of those schools. Parochial school superintendents customarily expel their "trouble-makers" and often find ways of shucking off other unpromising students. These, then, drift to the public schools to aggravate their problems and weaken their performance. Agnes Meyer says, "If the federal government should yield to the pressures . . . for the support of private schools, the public schools would become pauper schools in our large cities, attended only by Negroes and poor whites."[38] Furthermore, if an increasing number of Catholic parents send their children to Catholic schools, will they be as willing to vote for public school bond issues? The ramifying results of parochial school aid are thus believed to cast an ominous shadow on the future of public education.

(Paradoxically, some persons would argue that federal aid to parochial schools has more symbolic than practical importance. They doubt that the amount of money likely to be appropriated by Congress would be sufficient to rescue parochial schools from their truly severe financial plight. They foresee an inevitable cutback in parochial schools whether public aid is or is not given.)

Focusing more specifically on the argument that aid could be given to secular aspects of church school education, critics point out that this is easier to handle in theory than in practice. Those

[37] Some who favor "shared-time" arrangements, with Catholic students attending their own schools in the morning and public school laboratory and shop sessions in the afternoon, think this would serve as a bridge between members of different religious faiths.

[38] "Slums and Schools," *The Atlantic Monthly,* February, 1962, p. 79.

familiar with Catholic schools insist that many (although not all) Catholic teachers interweave their theological views into their secular courses. Wherever scientific or historical evidence can be found to bulwark a church belief, it is regarded as altogether fitting and proper to make reference to that evidence. Some even regard themselves as remiss in their duties—for their first duty is to strengthen the roots of faith—if they fail to do this. We can hardly expect the non-Catholic taxpayer to finance the blend of religious and secular education that permeates so many Catholic classrooms. Because the church does not want the state to tell it how to run its schools, is it willing to voluntarily reshape its secular teaching practices?[39] Is it willing to use only state-approved textbooks in its secular courses and to eliminate all instructional comments of a theological nature in secular courses? Can this be done in the light of Catholic teachings that religion cannot be extracted from the whole of life and compartmentalized without doing violence to its true character and impairing its central message?

Permitting parents of parochial school students to deduct all or part of their tuition from their tax obligations would in effect subsidize parochial schools (though in an indirect way). Even though an element of comparability exists so far as church *contributions* are concerned, one could obviously press this precedent to the point of demanding full tax support for churches in general. Precedents are useful in a democracy only insofar as they lead toward programs and results of which a people approve or away from programs and results of which they disapprove.

If private church schools are to enjoy public subsidization, it would then become constitutional for other private schools to receive such aid also. And if churches are free to exclude non-church members from their parochial schools (or accept them at their discretion), why could not private Southern schools exclude nonwhites from their schools and still qualify for public aid? Is discrimination on grounds of religious affiliation any less repugnant to the Constitution than discrimination on grounds of race?

[39] *The New Republic* suggests that the nation find out if the Catholic church will accept certain minimal control. See editorials, March 2, 23, 1963.

Conversely, it could be argued that equal protection of the laws would require that publicly supported parochial schools be opened to all applicants impartially. The Hill-Burton Act, it must be remembered, gives aid to all hospitals only if they agree to an open admissions policy. Are churches prepared to accept this limitation on their right to control admission?

Let it be admitted that a considerable amount of antiparochial aid sentiment springs from remnants of Know-Nothing attitudes on the part of certain elements in America. This does not, however, affect the validity of the con position, which must be evaluated on its merits rather than on the basis of the prejudices held by some of its adherents. It should be further noted, however, that a significant portion of the opposition to parochial school aid comes from those who are unfriendly to the entire concept of the parochial school. Many critics will unquestioningly concede the right of the parochial school to exist but will implacably oppose any public action that strengthens their relative position in the American educational system. Why? These critics believe the parochial school exists primarily to indoctrinate rather than to educate. To them, education means above all the development of intellectual curiosity, intellectual humility, and intellectual integrity. Education should foster a free and adventurous mind that is not confined by the doctrinal rigidities that limit the spirit of dissent or that inhibit the freedom of the mind to seek truth wherever it can be found in accordance with the scientific spirit. The well educated, it is held, are likely to become so only in institutions in which academic freedom is cherished.

Thus, it is all very well to talk about mobilizing *all* the brains of the nation, but is the over-all objective served if the nation strengthens schools that by their very nature are inhibited from developing those intellectual qualities most valuable to the nation? Surely we ought not to extend additional aid to parochial schools until the public schools have received the aid they need. The latter should have first priority—and we have a long way to go before they will be adequately supported.

If we are to accept the most up-to-date Catholic evaluation of their own schools, we would question the need for public aid. *Catholic Schools in Action*—reporting on a study, supervised by scholars at the U. of Notre Dame, of nearly 90 percent of Catholic schools—proudly declared that more than 80 percent of their students scored above the national average in scholarship tests (*Washington Post,* August 26, 1966). Although the results may well reflect the church's selective admission policies, they sharply dispute the view that Catholic schools need public aid to put them on an educational par with public schools.

Finally, the granting of parochial school aid would divide the nation into bitterly contending camps. Nothing could do more to inflame public opinion and to initiate a prolonged period of acrimonious national debate. The hostility toward Catholics that has been ebbing away for generations would be revived, and the Catholic Church would suffer most from the poisonous atmosphere that would mark the debate. We know all too well from European experience how nations can be shaken to their roots by parochial school aid questions, and that the wounds incurred continue to fester for decades. Are pro-federal aid Roman Catholics doing their church a service by demanding a public policy that can only precipitate bitterness and turmoil on such a scale?

The parochial school proponents are prepared to fight back on many fronts. The Constitution may be what the Supreme Court says it is, but the Supreme Court has changed its mind on many, many occasions in this century. Two of its most important decisions—on school desegregation and on legislative reapportionment—involved reversals of earlier findings. American experience certainly sanctions the practice of challenging the wisdom of Supreme Court decisions (while accepting their current legal force). Because the court ultimately tends to reflect shifts in national sentiment, an appeal to national sentiment on behalf of what groups regard as a more defensible constitutional interpretation is standard American practice.

Because the negative chose to quote Madison on the Constitution, it might be noted that Madison once recommended that a state university building be used for religious services—which is hardly consistent with the strict wall of separation advocated by him on other occasions. He also served on a joint committee to appoint chaplains to Congress, approving funds for their support in addition to funds for the religious education of Indians. Like Jefferson, Madison can be cited in support of various positions.[40]

If other parochial school systems choose not to accept public aid, that is their privilege. The state, however, has met its obligations when it makes funds impartially available to all. The difficulties of applying tax aid to strictly secular subjects are not as great as critics would make it appear. In mathematics, foreign languages, and the physical sciences, for example, there is no appreciable blending of religion and the secular subject matter. It is true that illustrations may sometimes have a religious note, but "the law is not concerned with trifles." This is more of a trumped-up objection than a serious argument.

The fear that American public education might give way to a badly "splintered" system of parochial and other private schools is also something of a bogy. Operating a school is an extremely costly business. The relatively small amounts of aid the federal government might offer, although helpful to existing parochial school systems, would not be enough to make a major enlargement of private schools financially feasible.

Would aid for parochial schools compel persons involuntarily to support a religion in which they disbelieve, and thus violate their rights of conscience? We compel pacifists to pay taxes in support of war preparations or activities in which they disbelieve. The Amish must pay Social Security taxes despite their conscientious objections. And some persons may in principle oppose federal aid for school lunches in parochial schools, or free textbooks, or aids to Catholic hospitals. If appropriations are made for what Congress regards as a valid public purpose—which secular school training represents—there can be no valid complaint on grounds of conscience. (Rejoinder: Because compromises are sometimes made in difficult areas, this is no reason to ignore conscientious objections where a principle more clearly applies.)

It will be heatedly denied that parochial schools do not enjoy

[40] Letter to *The New York Times,* July 21, 1963, p. 8E.

substantial academic freedom. Because one is committed to a certain religious outlook, this does not mean that one lacks intellectual integrity or the readiness to face all relevant facts and come to an uncoerced conclusion. Cannot free inquiry lead to convictions that survive the tests of rigorous analysis? All teachers have intellectual commitments of one kind or another—if not religious commitments, then commitments concerning democracy, or academic freedom, or something else. Does this mean that their classrooms are vehicles for indoctrination and that the free mind faces a hostile environment there? Of course some indoctrination takes place in all schools, but it is insulting to advance the notion that Catholic schools are peculiarly indifferent to the values of intellectual freedom and are only interested in brainwashing.

Studies released in 1965 by the National Opinion Research Council, based on adequate samples of Catholics aged 23 to 57, challenge the belief that Catholic schools have the "parochial" effects their critics charge. The NORC found that Catholics who attended church schools had as many non-Catholic friends, belonged to as many non-Catholic organizations, and had as much sense of civic responsibility as Catholics who attended public schools. The authors of the report concluded that there was "no evidence that the schools themselves contribute to . . . divisiveness in any special way."[41]

Even if Catholic school performance is better than was once believed, this does not affect that case for equity and justice. Furthermore, smaller classes, better trained teachers, and more adequate libraries and physical facilities would improve the quality of instruction, whatever it may now be.

Arguments that parochial school aid would inflame the nation are unconvincing. Aid to parochial schools has been established in Great Britain and Canada with a minimum of friction. At any rate, if issues that sharply divide a people are to be smothered in the interests of national unity, the abolitionists performed a great disservice in the pre-Civil War period. Raising the slavery issue exasperated the South—as well as many Northerners—and

[41] *Carnegie Corporation of New York Quarterly,* April, 1965, pp. 2–3.

the abolitionists were certainly a divisive influence on the nation. There are issues that are best shunted aside in the interests of amity, but there are others involving such basic moral questions that they are best faced openly, even if social conflict results. Struggle is often the essential matrix of progress, as history abundantly testifies.

Parochial schools are here to stay, and their continued existence on the high school level, at the very least, is not subject to question. Because they will continue to survive, would the use of public funds to strengthen the teaching of secular subjects fail to be in the national interest? Surely good parochial schools are to be preferred to poor ones. In facing realities, then, would not the entire nation benefit from the judicious addition of public funds to strengthen the teaching of secular courses?

Martin Mayer believes that if public funds are to be spent for Catholic schools, they should go toward improving education for the existing parochial schools but not for expanding those schools. "What the church should request is money to reduce class size, to hire additional teachers, to improve facilities, to introduce the new materials and methods now being developed." This, he thinks, could bring tax money "into private schools for the public good."[42] Historian Carl Degler, conceding that private schools have no right to public aid, thinks perhaps they should have it anyway—by grants to increase the salaries of teachers of secular courses, for laboratories and laboratory equipment, for books and new secular classroom construction.[43] Walter Lippmann, James Reston, and Robert Maynard Hutchins also have spoken out for some form of public aid.

But the thorny questions remain: Is it proper to use tax money to support the admixture of religious and secular education that prevails in many Catholic classrooms? Even if we already assist churches in certain ways, do we wish to go further along this road? At what point can concern for the education of all our children find common ground with our concern for separation of

[42] "Aid–with Strong Strings," in Daniel Callahan, ed., *Federal Aid and Catholic Schools,* Baltimore, Helicon, 1964, pp. 101–102.

[43] "Aid for Parochial Schools–a Question of Education, Not Religion," *The New York Times Magazine,* January 31, 1965, p. 49.

church and state—ground not entirely satisfactory to anyone but reluctantly acceptable to the major groups concerned?

What about aid to religiously affiliated colleges? Certain assistance has already been extended to colleges, such as loans for building classrooms, dormitories, and dining halls. The muted tone of the debate over such legislation reflects the fact that a large percentage of American colleges has some form of church relationship. In some cases, church control and influence are almost nonexistent, with the control shading in more strongly, but by almost imperceptible degrees, from one school to another until it reaches a point of total church domination of many colleges. Drawing a clear-cut line between those eligible for aid and those ineligible has proved an impossible task for legislators or administrators.

With the national mood currently disposed to finding more pragmatic and less doctrinaire answers to the parochial education problem, current and future experimental approaches may oblige the Supreme Court to reconsider its constitutional guidelines. The court cannot "settle" a question of this nature, but it can alter the shape and character of the debate and of the future steps we take.

CHAPTER

◂ 5 ▸

MEDICARE NOW:
Socialized Medicine Next?

The long struggle over Medicare has ended, but the controversy over public health insurance is far from over. The experience of other countries suggests that the United States will move through a series of legislative stages in its effort to deal with the financial burdens of rapidly rising medical costs. The desirability or folly of extending Medicare to cover other segments of the population may be a dormant national issue for a few years while America seeks to observe and digest the effects and problems of the new law. Still, it seems inevitable that the nation will soon resume the debate over public health insurance that has engrossed the nation's attention intermittently since the early part of this century.

Although Medicare is now embodied in law, the debate that swirled about it can be profitably reviewed. Many of the arguments will have a familiar ring when the next stage in the chronicle of American health insurance is reached. A close student of the controversy will be able to develop a growing sophistication in his evaluation of the often superheated claims of the antagonists in this arena. It will be instructive to observe whether Medicare, in operation, bears out the hopes of its sponsors, the apprehensions of its critics, or a combination of both.

Although Bismarck introduced the first national health insurance program in Germany in 1883, American interest in health insurance was minimal until David Lloyd George, then chancellor of the exchequer, pushed through his famous National Insurance Act of 1911 in Britain. This legislation provided compulsory sickness insurance for most British workers, assuring them of doctor's services and hospital care financed by workers, employers, and the general tax-paying public. The bill precipitated a tremendous furor in Britain, with doctors threatening to go on strike. Americans looked on with interest and at least a measure of sympathy for the act. A few years later a Social Insurance Committee of the American Medical Association (AMA) undertook a study of national health insurance. Although the committee made an affirmative recommendation, no supporting action was taken by the AMA's House of Delegates.[1] During the war the question was set aside, and opponents of health insurance were apparently able to make some headway with charges that health insurance had originated with the hated Germans under Bismarck, was further developed in Germany than elsewhere, and was a typical "Hun" measure. At any rate, interest in health insurance faded, and little was heard of it in America for the next 20 years.

During the formulation of the Social Security Act of 1935, serious consideration was given to including medical costs among the financial hazards to be insured by the act. The president's Committee on Economic Security recommended that compulsory health insurance be incorporated into the Social Security program. The proposal was set aside until the passage of the

[1] "The Time Has Not Yet Come," *The New Republic,* November 9, 1963, p. 26.

Social Security bill, however, lest its controversial character jeopardize the chances of that bill.

Interest in health insurance was renewed during World War II, spurred on by Lord William Beveridge's famous report outlining a sweepingly comprehensive plan for "welfare state" legislation to protect Britons against most of the fiscal hazards that lead to destitution. The Beveridge Plan was warmly received in Britain, partly because the depression had caused the most acute distress among the working classes, and partly because the wartime mood made Britons more responsive to collective measures seemingly related to the national welfare. Winston Churchill's Conservative government (which included members of the other major parties) issued a White Paper promising to adopt a full-fledged system of health insurance after the war, a proposal agreed to by the dwindling Liberal party and long advocated by the Labour party. The National Health Service Act of 1948, put into operation by the Labour party, insured the entire nation against the costs of doctors' bills, hospitalization, medicines, eyeglasses, special appliances, and dental services. (See "The British Plan: Success or Disaster?" below.)

In effect endorsing the Wagner-Murray-Dingell bill of 1943, President Harry S Truman proposed in 1949 that a system of compulsory national health insurance be established in the United States.[2] Mr. Truman's plan, following up a similar proposal in 1945, called for the insuring of surgical and hospitalization costs plus laboratory fees, dental care, and home nursing care, to be financed by a payroll income tax of 1.5 percent for employer and employee. As in Britain, doctors would be free to enter or stay outside the system. If they chose to be included, however, they were to have a choice of payment by salary (to attract doctors into "underdoctored areas" where population was sparse and income prospects bleak) or by a fee-for-service arrangement (earnings to be dependent on the amount and kind of doctors' services provided) or by a panel system. Under the last, doctors would be paid in proportion to the number of persons who agreed to select a given physician as their "family

[2] Message to Congress, *The New York Times*, April 23, 1949, p. 62.

doctor." Persons would be free to select the doctor of their choice and free to change doctors when they wished. Doctors who wished to carry on a private practice on the side, or a private practice altogether, would be permitted to do so; the percentage who would have found a completely private practice profitable would probably have been small, however.

A Gallup poll had earlier showed that about 70 percent of the American people indicated an affirmative attitude toward the general principle of national health insurance. Mr. Truman's proposal nevertheless ignited one of the most crackling political battles of the century. The American Medical Association violently opposed the plan, and it mustered a formidable group of allies. Enlisting the services of a famous public relations team, Whitaker & Baxter, the AMA carried out one of the most massive —and successful—campaigns of public persuasion in the nation's history.[3] Truman's plan failed to emerge from committee, and its reputation became so tarnished that even Adlai Stevenson, though sympathetic with the health insurance principle, declined to endorse it in his 1952 and 1956 campaigns. Instead, he contented himself with vague, general statements about the need to study more effective means for dealing with health costs.

As medical and especially hospital costs continued to rise, however, both political parties began to show a tentative interest in the problem. In 1954 President Eisenhower recommended a "reinsurance" plan, which, for the first time, placed the Republican party on record as favoring national legislative action to promote more effective medical insurance.[4] Mr. Eisenhower wanted the national government to support the efforts of private insurance companies to experiment with more comprehensive insurance policies. These companies had been somewhat hesitant about deleting certain "escape clauses" in their policies because of the difficulties of knowing what unforeseen costs might arise

[3] Irwin Ross, "The Supersalesmen of California Politics: Whitaker & Baxter," *Harper's Magazine*, July, 1959, pp. 55–61. Also see Bernard De Voto, "Letter to a Family Doctor," *Harper's Magazine*, January, 1951. For an account of a more recent AMA campaign against health insurance, see Gilbert Harrison, "Ward-Healers of the AMA," *The New Republic*, April 17, 1961, pp. 13–16.

[4] "The President's Health Reinsurance Proposal," *The Congressional Digest*, March, 1955.

in an area where actuarial data was skimpy. Eisenhower felt that if the federal government reinsured these companies against possible loss sustained from experimenting with bolder and more inclusive policies, private insurance might be encouraged to do a better job, thus reducing the pressure for public insurance. The bill was killed, however, partly because many congressmen wanted to keep the government out of this area altogether, while others felt the bill was too insubstantial to merit passage.

The percentage of the population in the over-65 bracket was increasing steadily; by 1960, it had reached about 16 million persons. Hospital costs, responding to costly technological advances, increased 300 percent in 15 years. The price of a private hospital bed per day zoomed from $9.39 in 1946 to $15.26 in 1950 to $23.12 in 1955 and to $32.38 in 1960. Since 1960, hospital costs have risen 7–8 percent each year. Meanwhile, although surgical costs had not increased as drastically, the cost of physicians' services and drugs was rising rapidly. As longevity increased and the retirement age dropped, there were bound to be demands for more effective methods of meeting medical costs, especially for the elderly. As a consequence of these developments, serious attention was given in the late 1950s to the so-called Forand bill.[5] In 1957, Representative Aimé Forand of Rhode Island proposed an increase in Social Security taxes to finance hospital and surgical care for Social Security beneficiaries over 65 years of age. Although the measure did not come up for a vote, there appeared to be considerable and growing congressional sentiment on its behalf. With interest in the problem of meeting the medical costs for the elderly obviously increasing, President Eisenhower proposed that the federal government and those states choosing to participate should pay part of the medical costs incurred by the aged—or that Washington should assist cooperating states by paying part of the private health insurance policies of elderly persons desiring the aid.

This recommendation also failed to reach the floor of Congress, but in the postconvention congressional session of 1960, the Senate rejected by 51 to 44 a bill sponsored by Senator John Ken-

[5] "Adding Medical Aid to the OASI Program," *The Congressional Digest*, March, 1960.

nedy to provide up to 90 days' hospitalization, or 180 days in a nursing home, for those over 65 who were covered by Social Security. Congress elected instead to pass the Kerr-Mills bill, which provided for federal grants to the states to help pay the medical costs for *indigent* aged persons. The states were privileged to spell out the criteria for indigence, to prescribe the amount of payments to be made and the period for which these payments would extend, or to pass up the program if they so desired.

After becoming President, Mr. Kennedy continued to press for passage of his Social-Security-financed "Medicare" program.[6] The bill was blocked in the House Ways and Means Committee, however, and lost a Senate vote in 1962 by a two-vote margin. A modified bill, including coverage for those outside the Social Security system, received congressional attention in 1964.

Early in 1965, fearing defeat, the AMA launched a major campaign to persuade Congress and the nation of the superior merits of its "Eldercare" program. Under "Eldercare," the various states (assisted by federal subsidies) would contract with private insurance companies to provide hospital and medical cost protection for those over 65. Those receiving less than a given income (at a level to be established by the separate states) would receive insurance without cost, others would pay on an ascending scale in an inverse proportion to their income, while those above a ceiling level would be ineligible for participation. To apply, the elderly would submit a simple statement of annual income; no means test would be given.

The heavily Democratic Congress, however, led by a President strongly committed to public health insurance for the elderly, made the somewhat surprising move of adding the substance of "Eldercare" to Medicare, producing a bill broadened well beyond that for which sponsors of Medicare had originally hoped. Passing both houses of Congress by fat margins, the Health Insurance for the Aged Act provides the following coverage: All Americans over 65 (some 19 million were initially involved) are

[6] "The Controversy over the Administration's New Medicare Plan for the Aged," *The Congressional Digest,* January, 1962.

insured for 60 days of hospitalization for each "spell of sickness." The patient, however, must pay the first $40, plus $10 for each day over 60 days. All hospital benefits end after 90 days. The patient is further eligible for up to 100 days' care in an approved nursing home, although he must pay $5 a day after the first 20 days. As an alternative, he qualifies for payment for up to 100 home visits by a nurse or therapist. Doctor bills are excluded from this mandatory portion of the bill.

The elderly are also eligible for federal assistance for the payment of doctor bills if they choose to match Washington's $3 per month contribution for the payment of premiums on private insurance policies. The patient pays the first $50 of these annual costs and 20 percent of the remainder. Social Security taxes initially rose 0.7 percent (half of this borne by the employer) and apply to the first $6,600 of annual income, instead of $4,800, as before. Medicare was expected to cost about $3 billion in its first year of operation, with the figure rising annually. (The nation's total spending for health purposes has been about $45 billion a year.)

The Row over Medicare

The advocates of Medicare argued their case as follows:[7] The aged have hospitalization bills running two or three times as high

[7] For a complete discussion of the history of and controversy over Medicare, see Richard Harris, *A Sacred Trust,* New York, New American Library, 1966 (an expanded and revised version of four articles, "Annals of Legislation: Medicare," *The New Yorker,* July 2, 9, 16, 23, 1966). Also see *Newsweek,* April 2, 1962, p. 51; Wilbur Cohen, "Medical Care for the Aged," *Current History,* August, 1963, p. 98; "Medical Care for the Aged: A History of Current and Past Proposals and Pro and Con Argument," Library of Congress, Legislative Reference Service, March 15, 1963, pp. 17–22; Roland Berg, "The Battle for Your Health Dollar," *Look,* April 11, 1961, p. 21; Marion Folsom, "How to Pay the Hospital," *The Atlantic Monthly,* June, 1963, p. 80; George M. Fister, "The Case Against Federalized Medicine," *The Saturday Evening Post,* February 23, 1963, p. 8; Joseph R. Mallory, "A Family Doctor's Fight Against Socialized Medicine," *Look,* May 23, 1961, p. 80; Thomas B. Curtis, "What Price Medical Care for the Aged?" *The Reader's Digest,* June, 1962, p. 95; "Your Doctor Reports," *Today's Health,* June, 1962, p. 72A; "The Case Against Socialized Medicine," *Human Events,* Special Supplement, 1963 ed., p. 2; Edward T. Chase, "Politics and Medicine," *Vital Speeches,* April 1, 1961, p. 377.

as younger age groups, and these bills come when they can be least afforded. The median savings of the aged are about $1,600; almost half have annual incomes of $1,000 or less. Under these circumstances, a major illness is also a major economic catastrophe. Their earnings are insufficient to enable the aged to buy private hospitalization insurance at the high rates necessarily required if private firms are to make even a modest profit from this illness-prone group. Moreover, private policies are riddled with loopholes and escape clauses, thus providing considerably less protection than the aged think they are receiving.

Although the aged often have only modest savings, these are of incalculable psychological value to them. They represent dignity, self-respect, and at least a measure of economic security. Medicare stretches out these savings and prevents premature destitution, where Kerr-Mills merely says, "Become a virtual pauper and then we will give you a hand." It is a humane, decent, and compassionate thing to stave off the bitter day when old persons must taste the tragedy of dependence on their county or on their children.

Social insurance has worked well in protecting the people from loss of earnings in old age, from disability, from unemployment, and from injury on the job. Why should it not be used to protect the aged against another unpredictable hazard—that of costly illness?

Under Medicare, every worker contributes to the Social Security fund, and eventually earns the protection he receives. Under Kerr-Mills, however, irresponsible persons might not bother to buy private hospital insurance, knowing that they can fall back on taxpayer help in case of an emergency in old age. Thus, Kerr-Mills perpetuates a "something-for-nothing" system while Medicare gradually phases it out. Shouldn't everyone who works pay his fair share of medical costs for the aged?

Social Security administration of health insurance is a considerably more efficient operation than private insurance. For example, Blue Cross carries administrative costs of 6 percent of its receipts; Blue Shield (covering surgical expenses) involves administrative costs of about 11 percent; commercial companies that sell group policies have a profit and cost overhead averaging

9.3 percent, while commercial companies selling individual policies have profits and costs that consume 43 percent of the policyholder's dollar. Because Social Security applies to almost the entire aged population, thus keeping collection costs at a minimum, it can handle Medicare at not more than 3 cents on the dollar. There are few commercial operations in which the government is more efficient than private enterprise, but social insurance is one exception.

Medicare will make it easier for many of the aged to buy surgical insurance because the costs of hospitalization will already have been met. It will also be a boon to hospitals, which now must handle charity cases with little or no remuneration from the state, and which must charge paying patients more to compensate for nonpayment by the indigent. Finally, Medicare promotes greater labor mobility, because a worker need not feel frozen to a company in which he has earned (as a fringe benefit) hospitalization insurance after retirement. This mobility is beneficial to both the worker and to the economy.

The opponents of Medicare insisted that Medicare was unnecessary because more than 50 percent of the aged have hospital insurance and the number is growing. Private insurance companies were offering superior policies as experimentation goes forward along this front. Considering the excellent job private insurance was doing, we should avoid government competition with, or displacement of, this form of private enterprise.

Are the aged really as poor as Medicare partisans allege? They owe few medical bills, they have less general indebtedness than other groups, and they often own their own homes. They usually enjoy Social Security benefits and often receive private pensions. In any case, why pay the hospital costs of those aged who are perfectly able to take care of their own bills? Should their bills be paid by taxpayers who are often in worse financial straits than the well-to-do segment of the aged?

Because Kerr-Mills provides help for those who really need it, isn't the cry for Medicare really the product of politicians looking for votes by dangling a superficially attractive plum before the voters? Of course Kerr-Mills requires a means test, but a means test is a sensible and essential way of separating the truly needy from the merely greedy. Because Kerr-Mills is locally administered, in accordance with state criteria rather than the iron rigidities of a centralized government, that administration is tailored to meet the needs of each individual state as modified by its fiscal resources. Local administration assures that help is limited to those with legitimate cases, while local concern insures that aid is not denied this group.

Medicare incorporates a regressive tax because it imposes an ungraduated tax on all earnings up to $6,600, while exempting income above that level. Kerr-Mills, on the other hand, is financed from general treasury receipts, thus reflecting more faithfully the "ability-to-pay" principle.

Medicare will lead to the overloading of hospitals, as people seek to take advantage of "something for nothing." This, in turn, will produce the heavily inflated costs that are sure to accompany such a program. As the government seeks to reduce these costs by ever tighter regulations, the hospitals will come under a widening network of political controls. Bureaucratic management of American hospitals does not pose a pretty prospect; nor does the certainty of bureaucratic decisions involving matters that should be left to the professional judgment of doctors and hospitals.

The fierce opposition of the American Medical Association to Medicare should warn us of the dangers that lie ahead. AMA members devote their lives to medicine and the health of the nation—shouldn't their judgment be deeply respected? Who else is better qualified to assess legislation affecting the nation's health? Should we rely on their expert opinion, uncorrupted by political considerations, or should we allow vote-hungry politicians to override them and introduce a system inevitably imperiling the quality of American medicine?

Freedom is not an abstraction; it involves concrete and specific situations. Above all, freedom means the liberty to choose from among the various alternatives in life, and the larger the range of choice, the greater the freedom. Yet Medicare demands that every worker in the nation, regardless of his preference, toe the line and submit. Freedom is much too important to be cast aside so cavalierly.

We should also reckon with the near certainty that Medicare is but one in a succession of steps leading to fully socialized medicine. Thus, the entire future of American medicine is at stake: Are we to have a system of free enterprise, individual initiative, and quality medicine? Shall we move toward a socialistic scheme of dictated state medicine that will destroy one of the most admirable aspects of the American system?

The friends of Medicare fought back. Voluntary health insurance is fine, they said, but it primarily helps those who need it least—the more affluent aged—while bypassing those who need it most. If it is wrong to displace private enterprise in this area, it must have been equally wrong to initiate Social Security, unemployment compensation, and workmen's compensation. All of these replaced private insurance to a certain extent (although Social Security eventually stimulated the buying of private insurance, as insurance men now concede).

Because states were obliged to match federal funds supporting Kerr-Mills, many of them never took advantage of the system; when they did, they often provided pitifully meager benefits. At best, Kerr-Mills helped the hospitals rather than the patients, because the indigent always received medical treatment, even before Kerr-Mills appeared.

The Social Security tax system is somewhat regressive, but this is unavoidable if we are to adhere primarily to contributory rather than general revenue financing. Contributory financing maintains the important principle that specific benefits follow specific deductions. It insures proper financing, places a brake on pressures for overgenerous benefits, and gives beneficiaries the satisfactions of receiving paid-for benefits rather than charity.

True, Medicare helps some who do not need it, but so do Social Security, unemployment compensation, and workmen's compensation. Are these to be condemned, likewise? Lest we forget, they too are compulsory programs. The AMA seems to overlook the fact that it takes compulsory taxes to support Kerr-Mills. Isn't it better to compel all workers to pay for possible hospitalization costs applying to all of the aged rather than compel all taxpayers to pay for Kerr-Mills benefits applying to only a limited number of aged persons?

Overuse of the hospitals? No one goes into a hospital without a doctor's order. Why should doctors unnecessarily send patients to the hospital just because they have Medicare protection? Do they do this when patients have Blue Cross coverage?

An incidental but important byproduct of Medicare may be more vigorous public and private efforts to reduce the 300,000-bed shortage in nursing homes. If this should occur, the nation can give thanks. Moreover, the increased emphasis on nursing home care should be a net gain for the hospitals. Probably more than 15 percent of hospital patients do not really require bed care but are kept in hospitals because there is no other place for them. Hospitals should not be burdened with people who do not need to be there.

The government has no intention of replacing the professional judgment of hospitals and doctors with "bureaucratic" judgment. The law, in fact, flatly forbids government interference in hospital management. Medicare will, however, lead to the upgrading of numerous substandard hospitals and nursing homes. To qualify for government contracts enabling them to participate in the program, hundreds of unaccredited hospitals will be obliged to establish higher standards of safety and hygiene, to have regular staff meetings, to set up tissue committees, and to improve their operating rooms. Of 700,000 nursing home beds, only 250,000 met minimum standards in 1965. The major efforts required to modernize these health facilities will be all to the good. And though minimum standards must be met and maintained, Washington will have no control over day-to-day operational activities. True, hospitals must periodically review the necessity for the continued hospitalization of patients, but the final judgment remains in the hands of professionals. Even the American Hospital Association agreed to the desirability of this kind of review.

The government finances medical research, but it does not interfere with the conduct of such research. It helps finance the construction of many hospitals through the Hill-Burton Act, but it does not try to run those hospitals. Because the overwhelming majority of Americans do not want the government to manage the hospitals, this is ample assurance that it will not be done. Ours is a democracy, and the government of a democracy does not do that which the people clearly do not want done.

The American Medical Association: Attack and Counterattack

The AMA's views on health insurance certainly merit respectful consideration, just as the views of any pressure group affected by proposed legislation deserve respect. But before abandoning independent judgment in the face of AMA opposition, two facts should be weighed. First, we do not conclude that because labor unions are most vitally affected by proposed labor legislation that the official views of the AFL-CIO should be accepted as an authoritative expression of the public's interest in that legislation. Nor do we assume that the views of the NAM should be regarded as the conclusive factor in legislation affecting monopoly or monopolistic or unfair trade practices. All pressure groups tend to have a biased view on legislation affecting them, and this is so well understood that it is surprising to hear the suggestion that the AMA is mysteriously free of the self-interested tendencies of other pressure groups.

Second, although the views of the AMA on the actual practice of medicine would not be challenged by any responsible person, doctors have no special professional knowledge concerning the payment of medical bills. This is a matter of economics and administration, not of medicine *per se.* Nor do doctors have insights into politics, government, and democracy that are denied others. In fact, they are probably less well read and more politically unsophisticated than other professional groups.

Third, the record of the AMA is not one that promotes extravagant confidence in the political judgment of that organization or its spokemen. For example, the *Journal of the American Medical Association* (*JAMA*) has a long and dismal record of labeling public proposals or practices as "communistic" or "socialistic" whenever it finds them unpalatable. Its spokesmen called the Social Security tax "a compulsory socialist tax" in 1936, following this up with a later statement that Social Security and unemployment compensation were definite steps "toward either Communism or socialism."[8] The AMA said that the extension of Social Security benefits to cover the disabled was not only a "serious threat to American medicine" but another step toward "socialization." Federal aid to state health organizations for maternal and child welfare care was once branded as "wasteful and extravagant, unproductive of results and tending to promote communism."[9] The editor of the *JAMA* said group medical practice (now a well-established institution) "savors of communism" and was the equivalent of "medical soviets."[10] And the *JAMA* also accused voluntary health insurance of being "socialism and communism" when a distinguished committee in 1932 recommended the promotion of voluntary prepayment plans.[11] The latter were labeled an "incitement to revolution" by the editor of *JAMA*. So if knowledgeable persons take some of the current AMA talk about socialism with a little salt, they can hardly be blamed.

Not only is the AMA inexcusably careless in its use of such expletives, but its record of opposition to a long string of useful federal initiatives in the field of medicine lends little luster to its record. In addition to calling voluntary health insurance "socialism and communism," the AMA did "almost everything possible to prevent its development"[12] in the 1930s and early 1940s, in the words of Dr. James Howard Means, chief of medical services at Massachusetts General Hospital for many years. Its opposition to group medical practice finally had to be broken by an antitrust suit successfully charging a conspiracy in restraint of trade.

The AMA also has the dubious distinction of having opposed the American Red Cross blood bank, federal aid to medical

[8] Speech by Representative Cecil R. King, House of Representatives, March 5, 1962 (reprint), p. 1.

[9] *Ibid.*

[10] Milton Mayer, "The Dogged Retreat of the Doctors," *Harper's Magazine*, December, 1949, p. 29.

[11] James H. Means, "The Doctors' Lobby," *The Atlantic Monthly*, October, 1950, p. 57.

[12] Toledo *Blade*, May 31, 1962; also see statement from *Journal of American Hospital Association* in speech by Representative King, *op. cit.*, p. 1.

schools, public venereal disease clinics, free diagnostic clinics for tuberculosis and cancer, public school health services, and federal aid to state public health agencies.[13] And as late as 1959, the AMA was saying that no federal action was needed to help the aged with their medical bills—just before it embraced Kerr-Mills as the logical solution to the problem! Some day, judging by the experience of the past, the AMA will be lauding Medicare as part of the American Way, while attacking the next step as a dire threat to the entire fabric of American medicine.

Considering this almost unblemished record of opposition to national legislative advances affecting the public health, perhaps the opposition of the AMA serves as the best possible endorsement for a proposal in this field. (The American Nurses Association and the American Public Health Association favored the Medicare principle.)

How can one explain the intransigence of the AMA in the face of almost every new proposal for improving the public health by government action? A number of answers have been offered. The hierarchs of the AMA are highly paid specialists, for the most part, who fear that a federal insurance program might eventually extend its boundaries to include surgical work, for which maximum charges would be prescribed that could reduce their income levels. Apprehensive over this prospect, the AMA leaders have carried on a program of unremitting propaganda against health insurance[14] and against the accumulation of power in Washington. *JAMA* editorials inveigh regularly against public health insurance, both as proposed for the United States and as practiced in other countries, but objective or favorable descriptions are normally screened out of the *Journal.* For many years letters to the editor of the *JAMA* that were friendly to health insurance were not printed.[15] The typical doctor, critics allege, has thus never had an opportunity to obtain a rounded

[13] Toledo *Blade,* May 31, 1962.

[14] Speech by Representative King, *op. cit.,* p. 1.

[15] David Hyde and Payson Wolff, "The AMA: Power, Purpose, and Politics in Organized Medicine," *Yale Law Journal,* May, 1954, pp. 1010–1011. Also see Edward T. Chase, "The Politics of Medicine," *Harper's Magazine,* October, 1960.

or reasonably objective picture of the case for public health insurance. Endlessly brainwashed by AMA chieftains, he has tended to accept their evaluation. He is usually unaware that America's better magazines and leading newspapers have carried generally favorable accounts of, say, British socialized medicine, whereas the *JAMA* has treated the system as an almost unmitigated failure. Two other factors are said to influence the AMA position. Any powerful interest group is reluctant to lose power it currently possesses, whether the loss is to other interest groups or to representatives of the general public. Finally, fear of the unknown acts as a conservative social force in circumstances such as those confronting the AMA.

Will Medicare lead to socialized medicine? Medicare proponents deny this charge, alleging that the AMA systematically distorts the meaning of the term. Britain has "socialized medicine" because the government owns and operates the hospitals, and doctors receive most of their income from the state. But there is little support among Medicare partisans for the introduction of such a plan in the United States. Government ownership of hospitals seems quite unnecessary to the attainment of the goals of social insurance in this country, even if those goals are enlarged beyond their current dimensions. Furthermore, the future of social insurance will depend largely on the success that Medicare enjoys in practice. If it is a failure, as its foes predict, neither Congress nor the American people would be disposed to enlarge its scope. If it is a success, on the other hand, and the American people should conclude that it could profitably be extended to include hospitalization for other groups or compulsory surgical insurance or major medical insurance for all, these are choices the people have a right to make.

Lenin's views are irrelevant to any reasoned consideration of health payment problems. Medicare is not "nationalized medicine," nor anything approaching it. Even if it were, nationalized medicine should be debated on its own merits, not decided by appeals to authority or associations with "devils." Karl Marx called for free public schools, equal rights for women, and a progressive income tax, but that does not make these either communistic or evil. A program is good or bad depending on its principles and effects; the labels applied are useful for propaganda purposes but substantively immaterial.

The opponents of Medicare are by no means prepared to lay down their arms. They question the validity of comparing voluntary health insurance experience in Europe with that in the United States, because income levels in the latter tend to be so much higher. They say it can be expected, therefore, that a larger percentage of American aged will be able to buy private policies once they are fully aware of the benefits available, while the remainder will find protection under Kerr-Mills. Kerr-Mills has not worked perfectly, but neither has it been tried long enough to give it a fair chance. If the states do not have identical provisions, this should be a source of satisfaction rather than of distress. The various states have different income levels, different tax resources, different views concerning prudent public policy. The diversity of American federalism, reflecting local judgment and conditions, is one of the great elements of strength in our nation. The statists may bewail this diversity, but the Founding Fathers built wisely when they established our federal system.

Although it is true that we have established a number of "social insurance" systems on a compulsory basis—and these are now generally accepted—that is hardly justification for enlarging the boundaries of compulsion where this can be avoided. If individual choice has been diminished in other areas, this is all the more justification for keeping it intact in as many other fields as possible. Freedom is our most precious heritage, and we should not be indifferent to its diminution from whatever quarter.

Federal aid for construction and research is one thing, but payment for the rendering of medical services is another. It is much easier for the government to play a minimal role in the former, but the compulsion to reduce the cost of services will generate persistent pressures to increase federal supervision of hospitals. The result can only be bureaucratic controls and red tape, with the consumer of medical services as the ultimate victim of this meddling.

The criticism leveled against the AMA, which is one of the

most respected and distinguished organizations in the United States, grows out of a shocking distortion of the AMA's over-all record. An editorial in the *AMA News* makes its position clear:

"Why does the American Medical Association oppose so many things?" Every now and then someone asks this question which indicates it isn't always easy to discern between negative and positive action. It further points up the difficulty the more conservative organizations have had in recent years in presenting a positive posture in face of the continuous trend toward more government intervention.

Someone has likened the role of the conservative in this period to a man trying to stop a runaway horse. In that situation which provides the positive force—the man or the horse? To the innocent bystander the horse looks much more positive than the man chasing it.

For more than 112 years the AMA has been dedicated to the promotion of "the science and art of medicine and the betterment of public health." This, the record shows, it has done. And the spectacular and dramatic medical progress in the last decade alone, in which the AMA has played an important role, should provide the positive answer to the Association's record of achievement.

Consistent with its statement of purpose, the AMA has supported legislation which promised real benefit to the public. It has opposed—sometimes vigorously—bad legislation which would have resulted in bad medicine. In opposing the latter, the Association has been tagged as being against the proposals. Actually, it has been *for* protecting the public health and preserving the high quality of medical care.

But apparently it is difficult to translate this conservative approach into terms that are clearly positive. Being *for* what is in the best public interest often means being *against* creeping or wholesale government intervention in the health field.

To be for health, one must be against disease. Yet, being against disease is positive action.

AMA's effort to guard the nation's health means engaging in a continuous effort of preserving what is good and at the same time advocating improvement where reform is needed. It means practicing gradualism—looking before you leap. While this approach has proved to be sound, it may not be dramatic.

On the other hand, it has been relatively easy for those pushing for more government intervention to wear the cloak of positiveness. For it is the revolutionary change, the radical departure from basic fundamentals that makes the headlines.

Physicians, by the very nature of their profession, are trained to be prudent, ethical, and to carefully analyze all the facts. They shun expediency in legislation as they do in the practice of medicine.
But all through the years the AMA has been forward looking and has initiated scores of advancements.
As early as 1847, the AMA took action supporting a uniform and elevated standard of requirements for the degree of M.D. More than 100 years ago it recommended adoption by state governments of measures for procuring a registration of births, marriages, and deaths; supported establishment of schools of pharmacy and a board to analyze quack remedies and nostrums and to inform the public of their dangerous tendencies.
In 1902, the AMA surveyed the field and set up an "ideal standard" for medical schools. Three years later it began to analyze drugs and to publish the results. Then came the establishment of the Chemical Laboratory and Bureau of Investigation, followed by the Advertising Bureau to "assist journals in maintaining standards and in securing honest advertising."
This leadership has continued through the years. In fact, since its organization there has been no major public health problem in the United States in which the AMA has not played a significant role. . . .[16]

The British Plan: Success or Disaster?

It is interesting—and amusing—that both those who favor a national health insurance program and those who oppose it use the British health system to illustrate their respective contentions that national insurance works well or disastrously.

When the preliminary National Insurance Act system went into effect in Britain in 1911, it encountered violent opposition from the British Medical Association. At one point, the doctors even threatened to go on strike against the program. Initially, all manual workers (under contract) and others earning $1,250 per year or less were included. The program was financed by joint contributions from workers and employers, with the government contributing roughly 20 percent of the total cost. Cash benefits in the event of sickness were also provided to compen-

[16] "The Positive Approach," *The AMA News*, May 18, 1959. By permission of *AMA News*, published by the American Medical Association.

sate workers for income loss as well as the costs of illness. Workers chose their own doctors, and doctors received a flat annual payment of $3.25 for each worker registered on their "panels." Apparently the British doctors thought better of the plan after considerable experience with it, because the British Medical Association (BMA) praised the results of the plan when asked to testify before the Royal Commission on National Health Insurance in 1925. Five years later the BMA recommended that the plan be expanded to cover dependents of workers and to include the services of specialists. By 1942, the BMA was proposing that national health insurance should cover all but the richest 10 percent of the population, and in 1944 the results of a questionnaire sent out to all British doctors by the BMA disclosed that 60 percent of them favored public insurance for the entire population.

The National Health Service, which went into effect July 5, 1948, is undeniably socialized medicine: the government took title to most of the nation's hospitals, and doctors, for the most part, were placed on the state payroll. The plan provides for comprehensive health insurance, including hospitalization, surgical bills, the services of specialists, mental hospital care, maternity care, convalescence, rehabilitation and home nursing care, ambulance services, dental care and laboratory services, as well as free dentures, drugs and eyeglasses. The program is largely financed from general tax receipts (74 percent), with workers and employers contributing about 17 percent and the balance supplied by patients through small fees, such as 28 cents per prescription filled. Everyone is granted a free choice of doctor, and doctors are paid a flat rate per patient on their "panels," with a maximum of 3,500 patients permitted per doctor. (The average turns out to be about 2,300.) Doctors who choose to stay out of the system entirely are privileged to do so (less than 5 percent are in this category), while those in the system are permitted to serve private paying patients in addition to those on their panels. Doctors are forbidden to commence a practice in certain designated "overdoctored" areas and are given special incentive payments for entering "underdoctored" areas. In addition, specialists are paid on a fee basis, with rates graduated in accordance with experience and training, while special "distinction grants" are made available to particularly outstanding doctors.

How has the program worked out? The AMA and many conservative groups in America claim it has worked badly and has brought about a decline in the quality of medical care and a deep dissatisfaction on the part of the doctors. Many other observers contend that the program has been a signal success.

The AMA and other critics draw up the following indictment:[17]

The cost of the British National Health Service (NHS) has been far greater than was originally projected. An annual cost of 170 million pounds was anticipated, but by 1958 the bill was 705 million pounds and still rising. Chancellor of the Exchequer Derick Heathcoat Amory told Parliament in 1958 that the "free health service, whatever it may be doing for the health of Britons, is leaving the Treasury gasping." Today the cost is far higher. Nor should this be surprising, because hypochondriacs and "something-for-nothing" addicts will always rush to take advantage of a "free" service of this nature. What is the impact of the program on the quality of medicine?

Let's see how the average patient fares under NHS. Put yourself in the shoes of the patient. You've been feeling under the weather lately and you've got an unexplainable pain. You're not seriously ill but you figure you've paid your taxes and you're entitled to free care. So you go to your doctor's office the next day.

Appointment? No such thing. You "queue up" with the rest of the folks waiting to see the doctor. Since NHS was established doctors have been besieged by hordes of people who aren't really sick, who run to the doctor for minor aches and pains, for free prescriptions, free glasses, free hearing aids, even free wigs. So there are a lot of other people in the waiting room ahead of you.

Your doctor is a conscientious man, but he has dozens of patients to

[17] Most of the indictment is drawn from *The Pill That Could Change America*, Chicago, American Medical Association, 1959. Whether or not it faithfully reproduces current AMA thinking, it embodies viewpoints widely held within and outside the AMA.

see today. Figure out for yourself the amount of time he can allot to you—when after waiting a couple of hours you finally get into his consultation room. You are Patient Number 43—he has 67 other people yet to see. Your share of his day comes to approximately three minutes. During 180 seconds he must diagnose your ailment, prescribe a treatment, and fill out up to 16 different certificates and forms.
In those three minutes there's hardly time for a question or two about your symptoms. Most physical examinations must be confined to such superficial procedures as shoving a stethoscope down your shirt or blouse (no time to undress), looking at your tongue, or evaluating other obvious signs of illness. A conscientious doctor who hesitates to make such a snap diagnosis on the basis of such superficial examination probably will route you to a hospital for consultation with a specialist. Medical records? No time for keeping detailed case histories. . . . And hospital beds are hard to get. If you need a tonsillectomy you probably will wait from 18 months to two or three years for a bed. . . . In 1958, half a million people were on hospital admission waiting lists. And only in the British Isles are women advised to "apply 12 months in advance" for a bed in a maternity ward!

Socialized medicine is "state medicine" and "state medicine" in Britain, as elsewhere, brings certain preordained consequences. With the central government in charge, controlling the rates of pay and incomes of doctors and constantly prowling about to eliminate and prevent "abuses" in hospitalization and medical care, this search inexorably leads to the proliferation of bureaucratic personnel as well as of rules and regulations and paper work.

Ten years after the Service was established, 400,000 Britons were said to be employed by the Ministry of Health—two and one-half clerks for each British doctor. (The AMA estimated that a similar system in the United States would require the hiring of 1,740,000 clerks.) The AMA adds that "Privacy and individual attention just aren't in the cards when medical care necessarily must be dispensed on an assembly-line basis." In short, state medicine soon reduces a previously free system to one of sorry disarray and decay. Government has its place, but that place most assuredly is not that of board of trustees and general manager of medical systems.

Enoch Powell, former minister of health for the British National Health Service, himself declared that "The great machine is bound to have a one-track mind, to be cumbrous and unresponsive, to abhor variations, to be insensitive to the world around it. . . . [NHS] has swollen to unhealthy proportions."[18]

The British doctor fares badly under socialized medicine. The general practitioner makes only about $8,000 a year, compared to about $18,000 for the g.p. in the United States.[19] But salary aside, he is disheartened by the limitations and controls of "political medicine," by state dictation of where he may and may not practice, by the steady increase of patients seeking to capitalize on "free" medicine, and by form-filling ad infinitum. A writer for *Human Events* estimated that "where the government pays the bill, the doctor must spend 25 percent of his time filling out the forms required by the Government."[20]

No wonder an alarming number of doctors are emigrating from Britain. Dr. John Reckless of Duke University recently wrote that 3,530 British doctors emigrated from 1956 to 1960, equivalent to one third of all those who graduated from British medical schools during that period.[21] What more cogent evidence is needed that socialized medicine has destructive effects on the very persons who bear the responsibility of making the system work? (Americans should let this point sink home, the AMA would urge. If state medicine in the United States were to confront potential doctors with such a bleak prospect that the already dwindling supply of applicants for medical school training dried up still further, nothing could be more disastrous to the long-run health prospects of the nation. Young people will not make the sacrifices and exertions required by medical training if their only reward is to be the privilege of entering a field in

[18] John Reckless, "Weaknesses of the National Health Service," *Current History*, July, 1963, p. 35. Also see John and Sylvia Jewkes, "A Simple Error in Logic," *Fortune*, October, 1961.

[19] The median income for *all* American physicians in 1965 was $28,380. *Time*, May 13, 1966, p. 46.

[20] "The Case Against Socialized Medicine," *Human Events*, Special Supplement, March, 1963, p. 1.

[21] Reckless, *op. cit.*, p. 37.

which both financial and nonmaterial incentives have eroded away.)

In addition to the developing doctor shortage, there is already a severe scarcity of nurses and other hospital staff. Meanwhile the shortage of beds has long been a national disgrace. Not a single new hospital was built during the first 10 years of the National Health Service. Since 1948, the waiting list of persons seeking admission to hospitals has always been several hundred thousand.

British health has paid a price for enduring NHS. The AMA observed in the late 1950s that since 1900 American longevity has increased beyond that experienced by British citizens. Tuberculosis was said to be a serious British problem, partly because "doctors must diagnose in a matter of minutes and are required by the government to use X-rays sparingly." Only about half of British mothers delivered their babies in hospitals. Partly because of this, an estimated 25,000 British babies were stillborn or died within their first week. As for dental care, the chairman of the council of the British Dental Association "disclosed that the whole picture of the dental health of school children is a national scandal." School dental examinations were grossly inadequate, and the number of dentists should have been doubled. Preventive medicine, supposed to be encouraged by the NHS, has also proved a disappointment.

Medical research has fallen well below the U. S. performance, as even friends of NHS confess. As one evidence, Britain had three Nobel Prize winners during the decade before NHS, whereas the United States had four. From 1948 to 1962, four British doctors won this coveted award, compared to 19 for the United States.[22]

Damning evidence of the disillusionment that has accompanied NHS is found in the recent growth of voluntary health insurance programs. To be able to jump the hospital waiting lists and obtain private hospital rooms, about a million Britons have purchased private health insurance policies. This trend

[22] "The Case Against Socialized Medicine," *op. cit.*, p. 6.

can be expected to grow as the built-in defects of state medicine become ever more apparent. Assembly-line medicine cannot be quality medicine, and only the naive believe it can.

Friends of the NHS charge that this entire picture represents a wholesale distortion of the truth, a caricature so far removed from reality that it is shameful for the AMA to seek to delude its members and the American people in this manner. They insist that there has not been a single objective study of British socialized medicine that has emerged with an unfavorable verdict.

Costs are up well beyond what was expected, but the AMA explanations overlook the most important reasons. In part, increased costs show how far short the previous system fell of meeting the health needs of the people. Partly, increased costs represent the growing population and the skyrocketing costs of hospitalization and medical care that have taken place in every country, not least in the United States. Even allowing for differences in the cost of living, the traditional practice of employing midwives in Britain (which accounts for the larger percentage of babies born at home), and a tradition of voluntary service in carrying out certain administrative functions, British health costs remain lower per capita than in the United States.

Long waiting lines and hospital bed shortages? True, but this situation existed before NHS ever started. There was an estimated 100,000-bed shortage in 1948, with 30,000 persons in London alone awaiting admission to hospitals. The government has not eliminated the shortage (although waiting lists are currently shrinking), but it is unfair to disregard the problem the NHS *inherited*. After having given priority to the construction of badly needed schools and private housing (bombed out during the war) for many years after World War II, the government is now embarking on a vast building program—90 new hospitals are to be constructed by 1972 and 134 are to be remodeled. This represents progressive planning, even if belated, on a scale private enterprise could not hope to match.

The talk about assembly-line medicine has a familiar ring to

American patients. A *Time* magazine essay on American medicine in 1966 observed: "Patients complain of having to wait long periods in the doctor's ante-room even when they are on time for an appointment, then of being put on an assembly line—stripping, weighing, etc.—from which they emerge for only the briefest visit with the great man himself."[23] Capitalist medicine is pretty terrible also, isn't it?

A wealth of evidence challenges the assertion that socialized medicine has led patients to seriously exploit a "free" service. Nine months after NHS began, *Time* reported that "Contrary to dire predictions before the plan went into effect, doctors are free of at least one worry: there have been relatively few hypochondriacs."[24] Ten years later Dr. Harry Eckstein reported in a scholarly work, *The English Health Service,* that "There is precious little evidence to suggest that patients have abused the service by making inordinate demands on the practitioners."[25] And, in 1963, Dr. Osler Peterson of the Harvard University medical staff announced after extensive studies that Americans visit their doctors more often than do the British![26] He further reported that the hospitalization rate for Americans is 125 per 100,000 persons per year compared to 86 per 100,000 in Britain.

Dr. Richard M. Titmuss, head of the department of social science and administration at the London School of Economics, wrote in *Harper's* in 1963 that there was "no evidence of inordinate demands on the family doctor since 1948."[27] Kenneth Robinson, British M.P., confirmed this in an article for *The New York Times Magazine:* "There is little evidence to show that the problem is any more acute in Britain than elsewhere."[28] Don

[23] "Rx from the Patient: Physician, Heal Thyself," *Time,* May 13, 1966, p. 46.

[24] "Medicine Man," *Time,* March 21, 1949, p. 33.

[25] *The English Health Service: Its Origins, Structure and Achievements,* Cambridge, Harvard University Press, 1958, p. 222.

[26] "Medical Care in the U.S.," *Scientific American,* August, 1963, p. 22. Dr. Peterson reported Americans see their doctors 5.3 times a year versus 4.7 for the average Briton and 2.5 for the average Swede.

[27] "What British Doctors Really Think About Socialized Medicine," *Harper's Magazine,* February, 1963, p. 24.

[28] "The Case for Britain's Health Service," *The New York Times Magazine,* November 18, 1962, p. 49.

Cook reported in *Harper's* the results of interviews with or questionnaires submitted to almost 400 doctors by Dr. Paul Gemmill of the Wharton School, University of Pennsylvania. Forty-nine percent of the doctors said they were "often" occupied with treating minor ailments, while 30 percent conceded this happened "occasionally," and 21 percent said "almost never." (Is this percentage higher or lower than before NHS?) And while 79 percent were "sometimes" bothered with "frivolous" calls, 71 percent also said that prompt exams and early visits helped them deal more effectively with their patients' medical problems.[29]

As for the alleged vast increase in paper work, Dr. Gemmill's inquiries led to the finding that while 39 percent thought that paper work under NHS was "burdensome," 61 percent did not find it so. "Both sides agreed that NHS had increased certain kinds of form-filling but that it was largely offset by no longer having to make out bills and prod patients for private fees."[30] The European editor of *Look* magazine wrote, "The records that the NHS doctor is obligated to keep are more than offset by the gain of not having to send out bills."[31] Robinson calculated that doctors spent not over an hour or so per week on paper work for the NHS. Dr. Titmuss said British general practitioners had fewer certificates, forms, and accounts to handle, as well as no unpaid bills. Almont Lindsey, a history professor at the University of Virginia, states that only about one fourth of the doctors were concerned about their clerical work.[32]

Is the National Health Service swamped with bureaucratic employees? The British government stated in 1962 that it employed only 32,000 administrative and clerical personnel—or

[29] "Socialized Medicine, Ten Years Old," *Harper's Magazine,* May, 1959, p. 36.

[30] *Ibid.*, p. 36.

[31] Edward M. Korry, "Socialized Medicine: Does It Work in Britain?" *Look,* December 20, 1960.

[32] *Socialized Medicine in England and Wales: The National Health Service, 1948–1961,* Chapel Hill, University of North Carolina Press, 1962, p. 199.

roughly one for every 1,500 persons.[33] (Converted into the current United States population, this would mean about 127,000 U.S. employees, rather than 1,740,000. And most, if not all, of these would replace employees now working for private insurance companies.) Furthermore, administrative costs run to about 3 percent, a truly remarkable record.[34]

Do the bureaucrats tyrannize over doctors and infringe on their professional freedom? Dr. Eckstein declares that "There is . . . no bureaucratic tyranny over the profession . . . if anything, the opposite. . . ." Sir Guy Dain, spokesman for the British Medical Association during the original negotiations over establishing NHS, wrote that "A doctor has complete clinical freedom in the treatment of his patients."[35] Even critics of NHS in Britain do not accuse the Health Ministry of interfering with the doctor's freedom to treat and prescribe as he wishes.

The doctor-patient relationship is said to have improved rather than deteriorated under NHS because the financial barrier between them has been abolished. The doctor can now feel free to prescribe what he thinks the patient needs, without worrying about the patient's ability to pay. Robinson says, "Most doctors . . . regard the elimination of the fee for service not as a handicap but as a positive advantage to doctor-patient relations. . . ."[36] Other sources widely agree on this point.

By most accounts, British doctors are very busy—which is also true of American general practitioners. Yet, 59 percent of the doctors queried by Dr. Gemmill said it was "reasonably easy" to give adequate care to their patients, 38 percent found it difficult, and only 3 percent said it was "impossible."[37] *Look* magazine noted that "doctors are generally working fewer hours" than before 1948, probably because the proportion of doctors to population has risen.

[33] "Britain's National Health Service," New York, British Information Services, *Background to the News,* April, 1962, p. 3.

[34] Robinson, *op. cit.,* p. 49.

[35] Cook, *op. cit.,* p. 32.

[36] Robinson, *op. cit.,* p. 47.

[37] Cook, *op. cit.,* p. 36.

It is true that income levels remain a source of constant dissatisfaction with British doctors, but their salaries have improved under NHS, and they make approximately four times as much as the average British worker. (The ratio is almost the same as in the United States.) Their seemingly low salaries primarily reflect the much lower salaries for British professionals in general, compared to their American counterparts. In the words of Dr. Lindsey, "They are one of the most highly paid groups in England." Dr. Titmuss notes that doctors are better paid than accountants, lawyers, actuaries, university teachers, and architects.[38]

Doctors are not free to set up practice in overdoctored areas, but this should be counted as a reasonable, responsible regulation in the public interest. One of the major achievements of NHS, in fact, is the sharp statistical decline in the number of persons living in underdoctored areas—from 60 percent in 1948 to less than 20 percent today.

Doctor emigration? Robinson says there is no "firm evidence" that emigration patterns have changed because of NHS.[39] Dr. Titmuss says the alleged 600 emigrations yearly include doctors working for international organizations like the World Health Organization, doctors taking graduate work abroad, women doctors who marry foreigners, and others who later return to Britain.[40] Former Minister of Health Enoch Powell calls the emigration figures "nonsense," and "grotesque allegations."[41] The government also insists that emigration is a two-way street. Whereas some doctors do leave Britain, others come.

The British government takes pride in the fact that the number of general practitioners has increased since 1948 from 16,750 to over 20,000 and that the number of specialists (who earn up to three times as much as g.p.'s) has increased by one

[38] *Op. cit.*, p. 26.
[39] *Op. cit.*, p. 49.
[40] *Op. cit.*, p. 26.
[41] "British Health Services: Criticism Rebutted," New York, British Information Services, *Background to the News,* June 15, 1962.

third. Dr. Titmuss finds that the number of doctors per capita in Britain has increased 21 percent since 1949 while the percentage has declined in the United States. A recent British committee, he states, was unconvinced after 19 months of study that the British need more doctors, while it is widely acknowledged that the United States faces a growing and serious shortage of them. Finally, the government asserts that there are long waiting lists to enter every medical school in Britain. In fact, there are about 30 applicants per vacancy compared to a ratio of 3 to 1 in the United States.[42]

British health records are said to be remarkably good rather than distressingly bad. British men outlive American men, and British women outlive American women. America has poorer infant mortality rates than a dozen countries that have public health insurance programs. Cook notes that deaths from tuberculosis in Britain dropped from 23,076 in 1947 to 4,784 in 1957; infant mortality rates fell from 41 per 1,000 live births in this same period to 23.1. Death rates from rheumatic fever, gastroenteritis, whooping cough, measles, and diphtheria have also dropped very rapidly in recent years.[43]

Don Cook's study showed that "more of the population get better medical care than in any other major country on earth." Of 1,500 patients who filled out questionnaires for Dr. Gemmill, 37 percent said they thought they were getting better medical care than before 1948, while 50 percent thought it was about the same. Only 13 percent thought it had become worse.[44]

Dental care is indeed woefully deficient, but no one denies that this was true before NHS also. The bad condition of British teeth has long been known to even casual students of British life.

That medical research lags behind research in the United States is generally admitted. This, however, reflects greater

[42] Lord Taylor, "America's Medical Future," *The Nation*, September 28, 1963.

[43] Cook, *op. cit.*, p. 37. Also see Almont Lindsey, "How Socialized Medicine Works," *The New Republic*, June 4, 1962, p. 11; "The Reporter's Notes," *The Reporter*, August 7, 1958, pp. 3–4.

[44] Cook, *op. cit.*, p. 36.

American affluence and far greater public expenditures to support medical research. There is nothing about socialized medicine that prevents a British medical researcher from doing work as good as his counterpart elsewhere.

Although there has been a modest increase in private health insurance, about 97 percent of the people are still registered with NHS. Private insurance does provide a queue-jumping privilege for nonemergency hospitalizations (emergencies are always taken care of under NHS) and enables a patient to obtain a private hospital bed. Significantly, however, the number of beds paid for privately in British hospitals fell from 1951 to 1963 by about one sixth, indicating general satisfaction with NHS hospital service.

As for the over-all success of the program, it is difficult to find a sober, responsible, unemotional account that is not generally favorable. On the tenth anniversary of NHS, the *Journal of the British Medical Association* carried columns of praise for its performance. Don Cook says "opponents who would turn back the clock ten years and return to the old medical system are really nonexistent."[45] The widely respected *London Times* said, "If the AMA has any regard for the truth, they should put the record straight: the American people should know that far from being a failure the British service can be counted a qualified success."[46] Winston Churchill's personal physician declared that "If consultants were asked whether they desired to go back to the old days. I believe the overwhelming majority would prefer the conditions of today."[47] Dr. Eckstein avers that "[The Service] has made nothing appreciably worse and a number of things appreciably better."[48] Lindsey says "That the Health Service has won its way into the hearts of the British people was demonstrated in every poll taken. . . . The Social Surveys in 1956 reported that 90 percent of the people gave the NHS a favorable rating. Seven percent were undecided and only

[45] Cook, *op. cit.*, p. 32.
[46] *British Medical Association,* July 14, 1962, p. 105.
[47] Cook, *op. cit.*, p. 32. Also see *U. S. News and World Report,* April 12, 1957, p. 66, and *Business Week,* June 1, 1957, p. 109.
[48] Eckstein, *op. cit.*, p. 236.

3 percent voted negatively. . . ."[49] The European editor of *Look* declared in December, 1960, that "every independent survey" of the National Health Service has found it to be an "overwhelming success."[50] In 1962, a Gallup poll showed that 89 percent of the people were still satisfied with NHS. Perhaps most convincing of all, a four-year study by forty of Britain's leading doctors, drawn from nine British medical associations, reported in 1962 that the British system was essentially "sound."[51]

The British Medical Association, disturbed by what it regarded as the AMA's blatant misrepresentation of NHS, once stated, "We have watched with dismay the mushroom growth of the AMA's public relations activities and the colossal sums spent by it to defeat what our American colleagues call socialized medicine. The dismay is at the probably inherent weakness of American medical services if such a vast effort has to be expended on misrepresentation of what is happening in Britain. . . . The AMA still prefers to distract attention from the weaknesses of American medicine by hammering away at Britain's NHS."[52]

Critics discharge a final salvo. Improved health statistics, they say, are the product of modern medical research rather than of the peculiar merits of NHS. John and Sylvia Jewkes remind us that British health would have improved whether or not NHS had come.[53] As for two-way migration, it is the British doctors who emigrate, while more poorly trained Commonwealth physicians fill the junior physician posts in hospitals. The abuses of "free" service are proved by the government's decision to require nominal charges for prescriptions, obtaining false teeth and glasses, and for some other services, after an experiment with "free" services. And there is simply too much evidence of doctor dissatisfaction to brush it aside as insignificant.[54]

There is no reason, of course, why those Americans who are

[49] "How Socialized Medicine Works," *op. cit.*
[50] Korry, *op. cit.*
[51] Titmuss, *op. cit.*, p. 20.
[52] *Journal of the British Medical Association*, July 14, 1962, p. 105.
[53] *Op. cit.*, p. 122.
[54] "Britain's Angry Doctors," *The New Republic*, April 10, 1965.

concerned about, or hopeful of, an extension of public health insurance should be preoccupied with the British system at the expense of other national systems.[55] In France, for example, the patient pays his medical bills, but 80 percent of the cost is returned to him from an insurance fund financed by employers, employees, and the government. In Switzerland, private health insurance is dominant, but it is subsidized by the central and local governments. Denmark requires those in the lower income brackets to join privately administered "sick clubs" to which employers and employees make a contribution. The self-employed and those in the higher income brackets are eligible to join these clubs if they make appropriate contributions. More than three quarters of the population is covered by this plan, which pays for most of the patients' medical and hospital bills. In European countries with public surgical insurance, surgical fees are paid on the basis of a schedule jointly drawn up by the doctors and the government. Flagrant abuses would obviously occur if each surgeon could charge the government whatever he wished.

An excellent summary of "socialized medicine" abroad by William A. Glaser appeared in the impressive new quarterly, *The Public Interest*.[56] Mr. Glaser's study was based on research in Europe (both Communist and non-Communist countries) and in the Middle East. It involved visits to 16 countries and interviews with scores of officials concerned with medical care.

Glaser properly distinguishes between systems of national health *insurance*, by which governments simply arrange a public method of paying for medical costs, and systems involving the establishment of a national health *service*. The first type frequently covers most of the population, but commonly excludes the unemployed, those who have never worked or worked very much, businessmen, and the more affluent. Under the latter system, the government assumes responsibility for providing medical services to all citizens and sets up an administrative

[55] See "How Europe Deals With Medical Care: What's Provided, Country by Country," *U. S. News and World Report*, July 30, 1962.

[56] " 'Socialized Medicine' in Practice," *The Public Interest*, Spring, 1966.

apparatus for meeting this responsibility. National health services are most common in the more underdeveloped countries, but Britain and the U.S.S.R. also have adopted them.

Glaser's study bears out the British experience in that doctors hold the upper hand in both national health insurance and national health service plans. Where judgment must be passed on the professional ethics, activities or competence of doctors, doctors judge. ". . . In most administrative decisions made by mixed committees with lay and professional members, the doctors exercise weight beyond their numbers; and in decisions made by lay administrators in the health services, the laymen often act on professional advice."[57] Moreover, new medical systems are rarely instituted against the will of the medical profession; where this does happen (as in Belgium and Saskatchewan), adjustments are soon made in the system to meet the continuing demands of the profession.

The traditional method of paying doctors is normally followed when new systems are adopted. Doctors usually have a right to join the system or stay out; they may also have both public and private practices, with the latter catering to those who can afford to pay for special privileges and services. To insure that doctors' incomes keep pace with those of the rest of the population, arrangements are made for periodic renegotiations of doctor compensation. As a result, Glaser says, " 'Socialized medicine' often works to the benefit of the doctors" as unpaid bills disappear and a combined public-private practice proves profitable.[58] Administrators, however, frequently accuse doctors of seeking out and giving premium attention to privately paying patients while skimping on their other work (this complaint is much more common, however, in underdeveloped nations where doctors' pay is necessarily meager).

" 'Socialized medicine,' " Glaser continues, enjoys a "mixture of successes and disappointments. [It] enables the poor to get medical care more easily, since financial barriers are reduced, but the quantity and quality of care are never altered as much

[57] *Ibid.*, p. 94.
[58] *Ibid.*, p. 97.

as its creators had hoped."[59] In underdeveloped countries, tax-supported hospitals and clinics often spring up where they are most needed. The quality of work done by general practitioners changes very little. Poor persons are no longer deterred from seeing the doctor because of cost, but this does not turn out to be as important a development as was once expected.

Glaser believes that additional public expenditures which are made for health facilities and equipment in many countries which undertake "socialized medicine" would be less important to America. "American doctors are already so well equipped on the average that increased public spending will not materially improve their facilities." He says "national health insurance may ultimately come to America by evolution—not by government fiat but by the private parties themselves using government procedures and sanctions to carry out their public mission."[60]

Some form of public health insurance or service exists in every industrialized nation in the world. Although doctor dissatisfaction with salaries leads to occasional battles with the government, the *principle* of public health insurance generally becomes relatively noncontroversial among doctors and patients alike. Whatever the merits of national health insurance, indications point strongly to an intermittent effort to broaden public health insurance in the United States.

Americans can consider a variety of alternatives to the British system, then. Perhaps they will choose to extend compulsory hospitalization insurance to all citizens, as the Canadians did a few years ago; or hospitalization plus subsidized private surgical insurance for those who need it; or major medical insurance, publicly financed, to pay only abnormally heavy family medical bills. (That is, the family might be expected to meet the first $300 to $400 of medical expenses, with public insurance paying the balance.)

A 1965 amendment to the Federal Social Security Act permits Washington to establish a system of matching grants to help

[59] *Ibid.*, p. 104.
[60] *Ibid.*, p. 106.

states pay the medical expenses of families too poor to pay those bills but not poor enough to qualify for Kerr-Mills payments. The program is optional with the states, but many of them have already taken advantage of it. If coverage is spotty and standards of eligibility vary widely, pressure will grow to grant uniform benefits for all the nation's poor through an all-federal program.

A further possibility may also materialize. Administration support already exists for the passage of a "Junior Medicare" bill to extend free medical and dental care to children.

Unless the political climate changes, important extensions of national health insurance may not be long delayed. Nevertheless, the resistances are likely to be more effective here than elsewhere for a number of reason. Antagonism to "socialized medicine" may have deeper roots than in any other modern nation; the United States has perhaps the world's most advanced system of private health insurance (about 75 percent of the population is covered by some form of health insurance, and the figures gradually rise), rendering a comprehensive public system less attractive than for other countries; and the general level of American affluence also reduces the pressures for such a system.[61]

Thus, although the weight of evidence does suggest that the British Health Service has worked rather well, this does not mean that America is derelict unless it promptly gets in step. America is not Britain, American medicine is not British medicine, and American needs are not necessarily British needs. For these reasons, the nation is unlikely to rush headlong into a system of national health insurance without taking a prolonged, searching look at the full implications of such a step. Probably the first post-Medicare president of the AMA was correct in predicting that "the greatest battle of all lies ahead"[62] but the terms of settlement of that struggle cannot be foreseen. We can look forward

[61] For brief general studies of National health insurance, see Seymour Harris, "National Health Insurance," *Current History,* August, 1963; Michael M. Davis, *National Health Insurance,* League for Industrial Democracy (112 East 19th Street, New York, N.Y. 10003), 1956; and "Federal Compulsory Health Insurance," *The Congressional Digest,* March 1949.

[62] John Bird, "Your Doctor and the AMA," *Saturday Evening Post,* January 1, 1966, p. 48.

with either exhilaration or trepidation to the spectacular national brawl that seems destined to burst out some day.

Are we overly engrossed with the problem of meeting medical costs? Dr. Robert S. Morrison believes we are, suggesting that the nation might profitably divert more of its energies in the years ahead to the following: accelerating the trend toward the quality medical care provided by group medical practice; reducing the "ridiculous disparity between surgical and medical fees"; learning to operate our hospitals as efficiently as the Swedes (who use one-third fewer employees than we do); looking into the possibilities of more home baby deliveries (Holland has a majority of deliveries at home at a cost of about one-twentieth that in the United States, and with infant mortality rates far below ours).[63] Citing shocking figures on unnecessary surgery, Dr. Paul A. Lembcke thinks such abuses might be substantially reduced by more surgical postaudits, and by closer relationships between teaching hospitals and other hospitals.[64] Dr. Osler Peterson also challenges the quality of medical care frequently practiced in the United States, as indicated by spot checks of doctors' work.[65]

While health insurance plans capture the headlines, then, other and perhaps equally important medical problems receive limited public scrutiny. A reminder of these neglected problems may well be timely in the light of our political preoccupation with health insurance alternatives.

[63] Robert S. Morrison, "New U. S. Patterns," *The New Republic,* November, 9, 1963, pp. 40–41.

[64] Paul A. Lembcke, "Is This Operation Necessary?" *The New Republic,* November 9, 1963, pp. 15–17. Also see *Time,* May 13, 1966, p. 47.

[65] *Op. cit.,* p. 21.

CHAPTER

◂ 6 ▸

WHAT ABOUT THE "WELFARE STATE"?

What does the totality of our government welfare measures mean for our future? What effects will these measures, in the aggregate, have on the American national character and on the national economy? Granted that some public welfare measures may be necessary, how far can we go in protecting the individual from the rigors of life without sacrificing those qualities of personal independence, self-reliance, and responsibility that are essential to the full development of the individual and to the health of society? Have we set in motion forces that, in a context of vote-getting maneuvers by politicians eager for public office, seem almost irresistibly destined to carry government paternalism to dangerous dimensions? Has the gradualness of our evolution toward welfare-ism obscured the debilitating effects that a fully developed welfare state can have on a once-pioneer society? Do we sufficiently realize, as we move step by step toward an ever enlarging welfare state, that these steps cannot be viewed in isolation but must be judged by their cumulative impact? These questions deeply concern millions of Americans who fear for the future of their country.

The road to today's "welfare state" has been long and tortuous, passing through terrain that we recall today with a shudder. The United States version evolved in large measure along lines patterned after the British experience, aspects of which were immortalized by Charles Dickens' account of the treatment of the poor in *Oliver Twist.*

The first British statute dealing with the problem of the poor was enacted in 1349 in the presence of a severe labor shortage occasioned by the Black Death. To prevent vagrancy and insure the maximum supply of labor, the British made it a crime, punishable by branding or mutilation, for any physically fit worker to decline employment when it was offered. In 1531, the British licensed the aged and impotent poor to beg within the confines of their neighborhoods, only to prohibit all begging five years later. In its place the government established an organized system for soliciting and distributing alms to the poor. The law distinguished between those poor who were able and willing to work on public works projects and those who were not and called for the punishment of those unwilling to work. Pauper children were to be apprenticed at an early age so that they would be a minimum burden on society. The law proved inadequate, because it relied on voluntary contributions to provide the necessary poor-relief funds. In 1572, therefore, a tax was levied for the poor, with the proceeds to be distributed first to the sick, aged, and disabled paupers and their families; any surplus funds were to be used to provide work for able-bodied paupers.

The famous Elizabethan poor law, passed in 1601, carved out the principal outlines of the relief system that was to endure in both England and America for nearly three centuries. Three categories of assistance were provided by this law: (1) able-bodied adults were to be put to work within each parish on projects of a public character; (2) when possible, paupers' children were to be sent to foster homes until they were eight years old, at which time they were to become indentured servants of their masters for the next 16 years (girls were to perform domestic labor until they either married or reached the age of 21); and (3) others were to be placed in almshouses or workhouses (sometimes the two were combined). In some instances, however, "outdoor relief" was provided for persons or families living in their own homes if the need was temporary or workhouses were full.

To be eligible for aid, applicants were required to take a paupers' oath, and their names were listed in publicly displayed notices. Inasmuch as foster parents were sometimes in short supply, many children were raised amidst the aged, the disabled, the chronically ill, those with minor criminal records, the mentally defective, and the insane. Some workhouses were let on contract, with the managers granted a meager monetary allowance for each inmate. Even this pittance often shrank before reaching the poor, because workhouse operators sometimes lined their own pockets first, leaving the poor to exist as best they might on what remained. Not surprisingly, the latter were often so weakened from malnutrition that they fell easy prey to sickness and disease.

In 1697, paupers were required by law to wear a conspicuous blue or red "P" on their outer garments, a measure designed not only to punish them for their destitution but to discourage those who might be disposed to indolence.

The famous "Speenhamland system" was introduced in 1795. All workers whose wages fell below a minimum level were declared eligible for a supplementary allowance from the state, with the allowance adjusted in accordance with the fluctuating price of bread and varying with the number of children in a worker's family. This system (currently under reconsideration by some writers today—see pp. 257–260) led to a variety of abuses. Employers were naturally tempted to reduce the levels of wages, the number of persons eligible for aid grew by leaps and bounds, and the costs to the treasury reached prohibitive levels.

Dissatisfaction with the Speenhamland system was heightened by Thomas Malthus, who contended that state efforts to aid the poor were inevitably self-defeating. Malthus thought he had discovered a natural law dictating that population would normally grow more rapidly than the means of subsistence. Tragic though they might appear, famines, pestilence, and wars played a salutary role in restoring a temporary balance between food supplies and population. If the poor were aided by public grants, Malthus warned, they would only remain alive longer and reproduce more rapidly than food supplies expanded, setting the stage for even greater famine at a later date. The poor must be instructed, he said, that no one had a responsibility for their condition. They were to blame for their own hard lot, did not deserve public aid, and the sooner they faced this fact, the better.

This bleak doctrine (later reinforced by the survival-of-the-fittest theories of Social Darwinism) proved quite palatable to the more secure classes and to the economic masters of the industrial revolution. The latter were eager to shed responsibility for those who might be injured on the job, who were unable to save for their retirement, or who were unemployed through no fault of theirs. Malthus offered them a clear conscience.

In 1834, the British abolished all "outdoor relief," confining public assistance to those in almshouses or workhouses. The principle was also firmly established that no one receiving "indoor relief" was to receive the equivalent of the wages of the most poorly paid independent worker. In the words of the government, ". . . every penny bestowed that tends to render the condition of the pauper [better] than that of the independent laborer is a bounty on indolence and vice." Long considered a disgrace, poverty now became virtually a crime.

The growing spirit of humanitarianism in the nineteenth century, spurred by official investigations and literary exposés of the plight of the poor, produced a reaction against the severity of the "Poor Laws." In 1891, toys and books were permitted for the first time in workhouses; female inmates were permitted to have a cup of afternoon tea in 1894; trained nurses were permitted to care for the sick in 1897.

More basic reforms followed: school lunches were authorized for needy British children in 1906, and old-age pensions were introduced in 1908. In connection with his proposals for health insurance and unemployment compensation in 1909, Lloyd George proclaimed that his famous budget was "a war budget . . . to wage implacable war against poverty and squalidness. . . . Before this generation has passed away, we shall have advanced a great step towards that good time when poverty . . . will be as remote to the people of this country as the wolves which once infested its forests." The movement from poultices to the prevention of poverty was now launched in earnest. Several decades later, the United States followed suit.

In approaching the problem of the "welfare state," the question of definition confronts us. Just what do we mean by "welfare state"? It must be confessed that there is no consensus on the meaning of the term. Possibly no definition can be drawn that will satisfy social scientists, to say nothing of the warring factions concerned. Still, a definition or definitions must be attempted before any kind of meaningful debate can proceed.

Those who are friendly to the public welfare developments of recent decades might favor the following definition: The welfare state refers to that cluster of federal, state, and local laws that reduce individual economic insecurity and provide for a minimum standard of living for all members of society. Those who are disturbed about the recent welfare trends would doubtless prefer the following interpretation: The welfare state refers to those governmental measures that discourage the spirit of self-help by encouraging a reliance on public handouts.

More specifically, what welfare measures are thought to be embraced by the welfare state? Again, there is no consensus, but logically it would seem to include at least the following existing programs:

1. Social Security, which provides assured old-age pensions for those contributing to the system, as well as regular payments to the disabled.
2. Old-age assistance, providing pensions for the elderly who do not qualify for Social Security benefits and lack the means of subsistence.
3. Unemployment compensation, which assures cash unemployment benefits for varying periods to persons discharged through no

fault of their own and who are able to work, willing to work at a "suitable" job, and actively looking for work.

4. Workmen's compensation, which guarantees either lump-sum payments or monthly payments for a stipulated period of time for persons injured on jobs covered by workmen's compensation provisions.
5. Aid to the blind, the crippled, and to dependent children.
6. Maternity and child health services, free public health clinics, vaccination programs, school health programs, and public health measures in general.
7. Hospitalization for the aged under Medicare.
8. General welfare assistance for needy persons whose unemployment benefits expire, or who do not qualify for unemployment compensation or workmen's compensation, or who for whatever reason are unable to meet their minimum needs.
9. Programs conducted by the Veterans' Administration, including veterans' pensions, veterans' hospitals, rehabilitation programs, and other veteran benefits.
10. Tax-financed college scholarships, graduate fellowships, and other student aids.
11. Public works programs for the jobless.
12. The school lunch program, the food stamp program, and other forms of free food distribution.
13. Federal disaster-relief aid for counties of states hard hit by drought, flood, earthquakes, or other natural disasters.
14. Public housing projects.
15. The poverty program.
16. The Appalachian program.
17. Retraining programs under the Manpower and Retraining Act.
18. Assistance for depressed areas under the Area Redevelopment Administration.
19. Rental supplements.

As the list is extended beyond this point, there is less agreement concerning the propriety of including additional governmental services under the "welfare state." Many, but not all, observers include the price supports and subsidies available to American farmers. A smaller group regards our complex of governmental aids to business as part of the welfare state—tariffs; subsidies to the merchant marine and airlines; aid to the construction industry through the Federal Housing Administration and the Veterans' Administration loan guarantees; postal subsidies to the publishing industry; lending activities of the Small Business Administration; other governmental services to business. The readiness to include agricultural aid and subsidies and exclude aids to business is an inconsistency that probably reflects the greater amount of criticism leveled against the farm program. (See Chapter 3.)

Free public education could be regarded as part of the welfare state, but probably not very many persons would consider it in this light. Again, its long-established noncontroversial character is a major factor in excluding it from the welfare state. Finally, governmental efforts to promote full employment and minimize inflation are not usually regarded as welfare state activities, although a broad definition of the welfare state might well include these functions. In sum, it appears that people generally associate the welfare state with direct government aid to individuals, rather than indirect aids to industries or public measures to promote the general economic health of the nation. (Perhaps a more realistic definition would acknowledge that people opposed to the welfare state associate it with whatever public aids they dislike, whereas those in favor of the welfare state associate it with public aids they approve!)

If, then, our definition of the welfare state and the specific content associated with it is something less than clear, this reflects the lack of clarity not only among the general public, but also among professional students of public policy. Some political scientists are prone to regard "welfare state" as a term too nebulous for analysis, but because the debate swirls endlessly around the term, this chapter will attempt to shed some light on the subject, even in the absence of precise definition.

The welfare state is not regarded by most analysts as the handiwork of socialist schemers entrenched in government, nor as the outgrowth of any integrated, long-range plan. It has grown, Topsy-like, in response to particular problems and pressures in the absence of any high-level, coordinated planning reflecting a carefully thought-out philosophy of government. It has been a piecemeal development, worked out in the pragmatic fashion characteristic of American legislators, without any studied regard for the net impact of the aggregate welfare programs involved.

In large part, the welfare state has evolved as our country has evolved from a rural, individualistic economy into an urban, industrialized, interdependent economy. Under the latter, the individual feels increasingly helpless in the face of vast, inexorable, impersonal forces seemingly beyond his control but determining his economic destiny. A highly developed modern economy inevitably suffers from economic oscillations and disruptions that heighten individual insecurity and lead to demands for greater social protections. This, in turn, leads to competition between candidates advocating welfare programs that are designed to attract political support, a competition that may have accelerated the development of the welfare state.

It has also been argued that a more highly developed social conscience has emerged, giving still greater impetus to the movement. But, although some kind of a welfare state seems to be an inescapable concomitant of modern industrial society, this does not tell us how wisely America has met its problems, or how far it should go in providing security for the individual.

The Perils of Paternalism

Criticisms of the "welfare state" are divided among those who believe that extensions of welfare legislation such as Medicare have carried the welfare state as far as it should go, those who believe it has already been carried to excess, and those who would like to do away with it almost completely.

Opponents of Medicare challenged the contention that medical care for the aged had virtually become a right that should be guaranteed by federal action. If it is assumed that the essentiality of medical care for the aged demands a federal program, this raises the possibility that still other "essential services" will be regarded as requiring federal guarantees. Medical care is essential, so why not socialized medicine for the whole nation? And isn't food a necessity? And clothing? And shelter? Does the essential character of these items suggest that the federal government should insure their adequate provision? And if so, what kind of implacably benevolent totalitarianism are we moving toward?

With government—and particularly the federal government—standing by with a safety net to insure that no one will suffer economic hardship, is it any wonder that more and more Americans are developing a "gimme" attitude? Relief recipients feel that they are merely the victims of personal misfortunes, or that society has failed to provide them with fair opportunities, and therefore the state owes them a living. Theirs is not a misfortune to be overcome by personal efforts—"they cast their eyes unto Washington, from whence cometh their help." Having removed the normal penalties for irresponsibility, for indolence, for improvidence, the state should not be surprised if these qualities flourish. The "handout" state must expect the appetite for handouts to grow, because millions of people prefer the course of least resistance, the course that makes the fewest demands on their energies and initiative. Of course it is easier to accept the government's outstretched hand than to go out and hustle up a job for oneself. The result is a decline of the sense of individual responsibility and self-reliance that at bottom has been responsible for the growth of America and the greatness of its contributions. With this decline comes that erosion of self-respect that is so destructive to the human personality. When self-respect is gone, little is left from which to rebuild a useful human being. As Franklin D. Roosevelt put it in 1935, "Continued dependence upon relief induces a spiritual and moral disintegration fundamentally destructive to the national fibre. To dole out relief in this way is to administer a narcotic, a subtle destroyer of the human spirit."

Unemployment compensation, for example, although it seems to serve a noble purpose, has led to abuses and corruption on a scale that seriously disfigure the pleasant image of the welfare state its partisans like to portray. There are well-authenticated cases of workers continuing to receive unemployment compensation during their first week on a new job, demanding full payment from their employers "off the record" while they decide if they are qualified for their new job and if they like it. In seasonal industries, where work is scarce and hours short, persons drawing unemployment compensation are willing to work short hours only if they are paid off the record. Similarly, one employer noted, "We normally employ three stitchers at a wage of about $130 each or a total of $390. When business is slack, we have only an aggregate of $260 worth of stitching per week. There is a share-the-work clause in our union-management contract. But our stitchers are not willing to continue work for $86.67 each. Instead, they expect to rotate with one out of three on unemployment insurance each week. By this arrangement, a man works two weeks at $130 per week and then collects $50 unemployment insurance, which is tax free. His take for three weeks is the equivalent of about $320 in wages as compared to only $260 under a share-the-work plan."[1]

Many workers who retire on Social Security payments (and perhaps company pensions, too) also collect unemployment insurance for the maximum allowable period. Abuses are legion, suggesting not only the difficulties of protecting the taxpayers' money but also the moral erosion promoted by the temptations of "something-for-nothing" policies.

As Seth Levine (a former labor union official) concedes, "The dismal truth seems to be that no one today believes it is better to earn a dollar than to collect one. Work is only preferable if it pays twice as well." He adds, "I have been amazed by the skill of unschooled and non-English-speaking workers in calculating gross potential earnings minus taxes and traveling and other working costs as compared with available unemployment benefits. Their prowess would do credit to a junior accountant."[2] The public aid director of Cook County, Illinois, has observed, in this connection, ". . . it takes only six months of idleness for a man's work habits to start atrophying."

The Aid for Dependent Children program has produced more than its share of scandalous situations. Some examples were presented in an *Atlantic Monthly* article entitled, "Detroit's Welfare Empire."[3] The author noted that 47 percent of 68,700 children

[1] Seth Levine, "How To Play the Unemployment Insurance Game," *Harper's Magazine*, August, 1961, p. 52.

[2] *Ibid.*, p. 51.

[3] Ray Mosely, "Detroit's Welfare Empire," *The Atlantic Monthly*, April, 1960, p. 46.

on Aid to Dependent Children rolls in Michigan several years ago were illegitimate, with the figure running higher in some states. He reported that one woman was receiving monthly welfare checks of $300 a month for the support of her 14 children, 10 or 11 (she wasn't sure) of which were illegitimate. These children had four fathers, none of whom was contributing to their support. This apparently did not concern the mother, because the state was nicely taking care of her and her children. She had already received from $40,000 to $50,000 from the taxpayers to support her family, with an expected $30,000 to be added before her last child reached maturity. The author noted, however, that she "is prone to complain a little if her clothing allowance arrives late or she cannot get money for furniture." Although she may have a record number of children, her situation has plenty of parallels among other women who differ only in lesser fecundity.

The misuse of welfare funds is also a well-established and distressing fact. Some states refuse to permit relief clients to spend their money as they please, placing their allowances in the hands of social workers who spend it for necessary purposes only. But others do not, and the problems are immense in any case. Returning to the Detroit situation, the author observed, "Along Hastings Street, the heart of Detroit's worst slum area, the first day of each month has become known as Mother's Day in the bars and bottle stores. This is the day that ADC checks arrive in the mails and it is the start of a week of riotous partying. It does not take much imagination to know how these women support themselves and their children after spending the ADC checks in this fashion. Detroit police say that half of the 600 to 800 prostitutes they arrest each month are ADC clients." The article adds, "The homes of many welfare clients are nothing more than breeding grounds for crime, immorality, and severe emotional illnesses, all being subsidized with public money."[4]

The morally destructive aspects of the welfare state affect more than the human flotsam of society. Its worst impact is made on the average citizen, who gradually succumbs to the lure of

[4] *Ibid.*, p. 46.

state-guaranteed security that is held out so tantalizingly before him. Under normal conditions, he is anxious to work and is willing to set aside funds for the fiscal emergencies to which men are subject. He wants to be self-supporting and self-respecting, wants to exercise his own foresight and plan his own future. By charting his own course and making those decisions that are best adapted to his present and future needs, he demonstrates his independence, individuality, and responsibility. When government grants him this opportunity, it shows a healthy respect for those human qualities on which democracy ultimately rests—the capacity of a people to exercise the maturity and judgment and initiative that make self-government possible. When a government attributes these qualities to its people, it tends to foster their development, just as a child tends to become trustworthy when its parents exhibit confidence in his truthworthiness.

The opponents of the welfare state have more faith in their fellowmen's character and capacity than others, but they regretfully recognize that men's more responsible instincts can be gradually subverted by a government that lures them into accepting forms of collectivism that replace individual responsibility with collective paternalism. In an insecure world, the promise of guaranteed security has a potent appeal. Garbed in misleading talk about social insurance and humanitarianism and public services appropriate to an industrial society, it all too often overcomes the resistances that members of an erstwhile pioneer society and a free system had acquired.

Henry Wriston rightly warns, "With some validity it could be said that security has become the 'opium of the people' in America. You do not get boldness, or dedication to public service, or even responsible citizenship from those who choose as much idleness as possible as a way of life. They cease to be masters of the state; they become its wards. When the citizen accepts the government as his guardian, democracy is in decay."[5]

One thing should be made perfectly clear. Even though conditions are radically different from those of pioneer days, and

[5] "What's Wrong With Rugged Individualism?" *Reader's Digest,* August, 1960, p. 27. By permission of *Reader's Digest.*

even though an urban, industrial society does require different public policies than a rural, less developed society, self-reliance and initiative will never become obsolete. They are, indeed, the preconditions to a healthy and flourishing society in which freedom and maximum human development are possible. Because they are no less essential today than at any previous period in human history, governments should adopt policies that recognize their vital importance and seek to preserve and strengthen them. But this is precisely the opposite of the welfare state mentality.

Nor should we lose sight of the fact that some adversity, some hardship, and some deprivations tend to develop traits of character that are invaluable to both the individual and society. This may sound like an old-fashioned truth, but it is truth nonetheless. Only those who have had to forgo satisfactions until they have laboriously earned them, who have had to sacrifice present gratifications in order to acquire future benefits, are able to fully enjoy those benefits once they come. During the period in which hard work, sacrifice, and deprivation take place, habits of self-discipline are acquired, and a general spirit of hardihood and self-help is fostered that will serve the individual well throughout his future life.

A measure of insecurity is necessary if men and women are to feel the stimuli essential to maximum effort and optimum development. When the necessities—and some comforts—are provided by the state, some of the tensions produced by insecurity are removed. With their removal comes a tendency to relax and to forgo the kind of effort, inventiveness, and initiative that are naturally stimulated by the necessity to insure survival for oneself and security for one's family. It is only when the individual is challenged by his environment, when he must overcome that environment and the obstacles it places before him by his own efforts, that he develops his fullest potentialities. To remove the challenges is to weaken those responses indispensable to a sound and virile society.

Writing in *The Atlantic* in 1965, Irving Kristol said: "One of the unforeseen consequences of the welfare state is that it leaves so little room for personal idealism; another is that it mutes the challenge to self-definition. All this is but another way of saying that it satisfies the anxieties of the middle-aged while stifling the creative energies of the young."[6] It might be added that a society with a cradle-to-grave welfare state is a society that has deprived the individual of some of the adventure and drama of life. It has diluted the flavor with which life is invested in a more self-reliant society. With the challenges removed, the zest found in overcoming these challenges also departs, as do the satisfactions that come from the knowledge that one has personally met and mastered life's elementary requirements.

There are some uncomfortable comparisons between an America drifting ever more deeply into the philosophy and practice of a welfare state and the condition of the Roman Empire in its declining stages. There, too, was a benevolent state seeking to placate the idle multitudes with free bread and entertainment. As the state demonstrated its readiness to care for those who would not care for themselves, more and more persons flocked to Rome to avail themselves of the public largesse. As idleness enlarged and lengthened, the willingness to work decayed. To an ever increasing degree, people concluded that they were only receiving that which was their due. The clamor for increasing liberality from the government steadily grew. The moral decadence that inescapably accompanied this social development is too well known to warrant elaboration.

The motto of more and more Americans likewise seems to be, "Ask not what you can do for your government, but what your government can do for you." As Jenkin Lloyd Jones put it, "Relief is gradually becoming an honorable career in America. It is a pretty fair life, if you have neither conscience nor pride. The politicians will weep over you. The state will give a mother a bonus for her illegitimate children, and if she neglects them sufficiently she can save enough of her ADC payments to keep herself and her boy friend in wine and gin. Nothing is your fault."[7]

An often overlooked aspect of the welfare state is the coolly impersonal and mechanistic character of the relief extended to the welfare recipient. The recipient knows that he is a number,

[6] "What's Bugging the Students?" *The Atlantic Monthly,* November, 1965, p. 110.

[7] Quoted in *Human Events,* November 24, 1961, p. 794.

that the welfare department has checked him out and found that he qualifies for the aid, and that assistance is extended through laws administered by public officials with no personal concern for his welfare. They are doing a job for which they are paid from public funds, but their interest in him as a person is minimal. Thus, the recipent is denied the satisfaction of knowing that his fellowmen are personally concerned with his misfortune and willing to share their substance with him. Not only is he denied this manifestation of warm and friendly personal interest, but those who would otherwise give are denied the pleasure of having given to a fellow human in distress. There is precious little satisfaction in paying the taxes necessary to sustain the relief rolls.

Extend the welfare state further? Henry Wallich, formerly a member of President Eisenhower's Council of Economic Advisers, reminds us that the log-rolling typical of legislatures makes the expansion of government services a hazardous undertaking. "If the proponents of one kind of expenditure want to get more money for their projects, they must concede an increase also to the advocates of others. . . . Increases in good expenditures are burdened with a political discharge of less good ones." As an example, Professor Wallich cited the Area Development bill. "As originally proposed the bill sought to aid a limited number of industrial areas where new jobs were badly needed. It got nowhere in the Congress. Only when it was extended to a large number of areas with less urgent or quite different problems, were enough legislators brought aboard to pass it."[8]

As a further reminder of the caution with which we should initiate any new program, Professor Wallich wrote of "the last-ditch survival power of federal programs. . . . Old federal programs never die, they don't even fade away—they just go on."[9] Anyone familiar with Washington knows how much truth there is in the professor's complaint. Agencies have an amazing—and appalling—capacity to justify their continuance long after the need that brought them into existence has passed. Similarly,

[8] "Public Versus Private," *Harper's Magazine,* October, 1961, p. 22.
[9] *Ibid.*, p. 22.

despite the inequities widely conceded to exist in federal aid to impact-area school districts, the vested interest in these funds makes reform exceedingly difficult.

The welfare state of today involves costs of a magnitude that is not fully understood. In Britain, about 40 percent of the national budget goes for welfare state activities, without counting certain local services of a welfare nature. In the United States, spending for Social Security and other forms of welfare nearly tripled between 1954 and 1963. It now amounts to about $35 billion a year.[10] If national health insurance were added to our welfare state, this would skyrocket welfare expenditures by another $20 billion or more. The spending proposals for the "Great Society" involve more staggering financial implications than the American people realize. In 1955, federal cash spending was only about $70 billion. By 1965, this had risen to over $122 billion (including trust funds). By 1975, some economists estimate, Washington will be disbursing over $200 billion—with welfare state activities accounting for over half of this monstrous sum. Charles Stevenson of the *Reader's Digest* staff notes that state and local government spending will have to rise from over $72 billion in 1964 to nearly $180 billion in 1975 if these governments are to raise the matching funds needed to carry out their share of the "Great Society."

The total tax burden of the American citizen reached about $180 billion in 1966. Nearly 30 cents of every dollar goes to support programs administered by 2.6 million federal and 8 million state and local employees. No one begrudges governments the funds needed for national defense and necessary public services, but if expenditures were limited to these purposes, tax levels would be much lower than they are now. If we were to eliminate superfluous welfare expenditures and trim essential programs to their proper dimension, there would be a significant and welcome relief in the tax burden. We cannot expect personal incentive to reach optimum levels when taxes dig so deeply into personal

[10] Henry Hazlitt put total welfare spending at $46 billion in 1965. "Slash the Spending," *Newsweek*, March 28, 1966, p. 76. This figure, however, is out of line with most estimates.

income. Nor can we expect the American economy to perform adequately when taxes gouge the American businessman so cruelly. Welfare programs cannot be properly evaluated except as due recognition is given to the over-all impact of high taxes on the national economy. In the words of Charles Stevenson, we are "risking national ruin by inflation and taxation. And it will turn a nation of self-reliant people into a nation of individuals so dependent on government handouts that they have neither the will nor the capacity to endure."[11]

Taxes are more than economic burdens. They also represent an important diminution of freedom—30 percent of the taxpayer's dollar spent by government means 30 percent that cannot be spent at the discretion of the taxpayer himself. One of the more important facets of freedom is the right to spend one's money as one pleases—once minimum government services are provided. Every time a law is passed that spends more of the individual's money, a shrinkage of freedom takes place because the individual has lost control of a still larger portion of the fruits of his labor. Everyone recognizes that when a social worker spends a welfare client's check for certain specified purposes (because the client has demonstrated irresponsibility in spending the check himself), the latter's freedom to make decisions vitally affecting his life has been reduced. The same is true when the government takes the taxpayer's money, on the assumption that he is incapable of spending it as wisely as the nation's politicians can spend it for him. This is one of the more disquieting aspects of the steadily rising national budget—based as it is on the premise that people cannot be trusted to spend their money wisely. It bespeaks a low estimate by Washington of the people they claim to be serving.

The relationship between big government, big bureaucracy, big spending, and a steadily contracting realm of individual freedom is one of the most solemn issues facing our nation. Whenever a new law is passed, the individual has a little less freedom than he had before. Whenever an increased appropria-

[11] "What Price the Great Society?" *Reader's Digest,* March, 1966, p. 53.

tion is passed, freedom is forced to retreat a little further. When people cannot choose voluntary health insurance instead of compulsory health insurance or voluntary savings policies instead of compulsory Social Security payments, freedom is diminished. When workers between 65 and 72 cannot earn more than $1,500 a year without losing Social Security benefits, their freedom is restricted. When people are compelled to pay taxes for the support of ne'er-do-wells and shiftless persons, their freedom declines. When employers are compelled to pay unemployment compensation benefits—to which workers have made no contribution—and to fill out innumerable forms, adhere to innumerable regulations, and submit to endless inspections and investigations, their freedom has dwindled. The impact of the Leviathan state—that federal juggernaut which spreads its tentacles in every direction, seeking ever new authority over the lives of its people in the guise of serving them—has not been properly assessed.

Thomas Jefferson once noted, "The government can only do something *for* the people in proportion as it can do something *to* the people." The annual flood of new legislation and the seemingly inexorable growth of new or increased tax levies—this is a phenomenon with frightening implications for those who believe in the individual, in his right to order his life as he pleases (so long as he does not injure others), and in his capacity to solve his problems without the interference or unwelcome assistance of a growing army of bureaucrats and bureaucratic legislation. Freedom in a democratic state is not lost overnight by a dictator seizing power and crushing ancient liberties under an iron heel. It is lost little by little, almost imperceptibly, as the arm of government reaches out in an ever widening arc to supplant private decision-making with collective decision-making. But because this process is so gradual and insidious—and always under the cloak of benevolence—people do not put up the resistance they would if the cumulative impact of a series of small erosions were brought forcibly to their attention. People become accustomed to new restrictions, and it is difficult to convince them of the dangers involved until irremediable damage is done. Then it may be too late to recover the ground freedom has lost to the governmentalists, ground occupied and defended by persons who have acquired a vested interest in the government "services" that flow out to them.

Speaking of freedom, Henry Wriston has summed it up well: "Nothing in the Bill of Rights promises that the freedoms there guaranteed can be enjoyed in comfort or in a serene atmosphere. . . . Dostoyevsky lived in a land of tyranny; he knew its corrosive effect. With the wisdom that comes from a lack of liberty, he asserted that 'tragic freedom' is better than 'compulsory happiness.' It is a lesson we need to ponder."[12]

The wasting away of freedom invariably accompanies the development of a socialist state. It is frightening that Americans should almost unanimously disapprove socialism in the abstract while embracing it in the concrete. Since the early 1930s the nation has inched—or lurched—toward socialism without Americans realizing where the road they were traveling led. Pseudo-liberals, state planners, bleeding hearts, and governmentalists in general seek to mislead the people into identifying their programs with progress and social reforms. If socialism represents progress, they are right, but thoughtful students of history and the contemporary scene know better. Socialism is statism, the exaltation of the state at the expense of the individual. In their hearts Americans know this is true, but they fail to draw the necessary relation between a touted "reform" and the socialist structure it is erecting in jigsaw puzzle fashion.

Not that the Socialist party will directly attain power in the United States. As Barry Goldwater has observed, socialism as a political movement offers no real threat to the United States, because the party is tiny, weak, and moribund. Even the socialist parties of Western Europe have lost their momentum, have largely abandoned their earlier doctrinaire concepts, and have become closely akin to conventional nonsocialist democratic parties.

But Senator Goldwater sees another threat that is all the more serious because it is poorly understood:

[12] *Op. cit.*, p. 28.

The currently favored instrument of collectivization is the Welfare State. The collectivists have not abandoned their ultimate goal—to subordinate the individual to the State—but their strategy has changed. They have learned that Socialism can be achieved through Welfarism quite as well as through Nationalization. They understand that private property can be confiscated as effectively by taxation as by expropriating it. They understand that the individual can be put at the mercy of the State—not only by making the State his employer—but by divesting him of the means to provide for his personal needs and by giving the State the responsibility of caring for those needs from cradle to grave. Moreover, they have discovered—and here is the critical point—that Welfarism is much more compatible with the political processes of a democratic society. Nationalization ran into popular opposition, but the collectivists feel sure the Welfare State can be erected by the simple expedient of buying votes with promises of "free" hospitalization, "free" retirement pay and so on. . . . The correctness of this estimate can be seen from the portion of the federal budget that is now allocated to welfare, an amount second only to the cost of national defense.[13]

Senator Goldwater says he does not

welcome this shift of strategy. Socialism-through-Welfarism poses a far greater danger to freedom than Socialism-through-Nationalization precisely because it is more difficult to combat. The evils of Nationalization are self-evident and immediate. Those of Welfarism are veiled and tend to be postponed. People can understand the consequences of turning over ownership of the steel industry, say, to the State: and they can be counted on to oppose such a proposal. But let the government increase its contribution to the "Public Assistance" program and we will, at most, grumble about excessive government spending. The effect of Welfarism on freedom will be felt later on—after its beneficiaries have become its victims, after dependence on government has turned into bondage and it is too late to unlock the jail.[14]

In a final warning, Goldwater declares that ". . . the material and spiritual sides of man are intertwined; . . . it is impossible

[13] Barry Goldwater, *The Conscience of a Conservative*, Shepherdsville, Ky., Victor Publishing Co., 1960, pp. 69–71.
[14] *Ibid.*, p. 70.

for the State to assume responsibility for one without intruding on the essential nature of the other; . . . if we take from a man personal responsibility for caring for his material needs, we take from him also the will and the opportunity to be free."[15]

The Founders built wisely when they framed the Tenth Amendment, which states, "The powers not delegated to the United States by the Constitution, nor prohibited by it to the States, are reserved to the States respectively, or to the people." This amendment was designed to insure that the federal government could exercise only those powers delegated to it, rather than overlap its boundaries at the expense of the states. The founders never intended the national government to establish a welfare state. None of the delegated powers grants this authority. The reserved "police powers" of the state have historically been regarded as the powers to protect the public health, morals, safety, and welfare. Only by a misinterpretation of the spending clause has the national government been able to extend its grasp into welfare matters. By dangling welfare "benefits" before the states in return for the power to supervise the administration and expenditure of those "benefits," the government has taken a back-door approach to a form of regulation it could never justify on strict constitutional grounds.

The upshot has been federal controls over unemployment insurance, over the Aid to Dependent Children program, over a wide variety of other grants-in-aid for relief purposes. It has produced complete federal administration of the Social Security program. The federal government also controls hospital construction under the Hill-Burton Act, regulates airport construction, controls slum clearance and urban renewal programs, sits in judgment on local poverty programs, enforces its particular interpretation of nondiscrimination in the use of federal funds, and in numerous other ways has overleaped its proper boundaries to fasten its initially friendly, but gradually tightening, grip over matters that are properly reserved to the states. An example of federal dictation to the states occurred in 1951, when Washington threatened to curtail welfare funds to Indiana unless the latter

[15] *Ibid.*, p. 75.

repealed its law making public the names of those receiving welfare payments. In this case Indiana held firm, and Washington yielded. Another example, in 1966, involved the Office of Economic Opportunity, which sought to withhold funds from Chicago because that city's educational pattern did not suit OEO's standards. Again Washington yielded to local pressures, but the outcome of future clashes will not always be so favorable. In any case, federal programs cannot be assessed individually; they must be evaluated in the light of their part in gradually undermining the federal structure which is essential to the concept of limited government and which undergirds the rights of free men. It is deeply disquieting to watch legislative bodies adopt expediencies that have surface plausibility when viewed in isolation, without considering the ultimate effect of those expediencies on the structure of government and the fabric of freedom.

State and local governments, as is well known, are closer to the people than Washington. They have a better insight into local needs, a better conception of local opinion concerning the satisfaction of those needs, and a more realistic grasp of the fiscal realities than Washington. Being more responsive to the particular needs of a state or an area, they can better cut the policy cloth to fit the frame. And they can do so within the framework of truly popular control, maintaining the integrity of local self-government. It is always healthier for people to solve their own problems by their own efforts than to pass the buck to Washington. The latter can become a habit and a disease, resulting in the attenuation of the spirit of self-help and community responsibility. When our people reach the point where they habitually shirk their duties of local self-government and supinely permit a far-away centralized bureaucracy to solve problems they could solve themselves, democracy's days are numbered.

The Logic of the Welfare State

The defenders of the welfare state are convinced, according to Sidney Hook, that the only modern alternative to the welfare state is the "ill-fare" state. They believe the attack is based largely on the ringing affirmation of platitudes that are largely irrelevant to today's society or to the specific problems we face. They are convinced that their opponents take isolated abuses and generalize sweeping indictments from these. And they believe a number of *non sequiturs* can be cited that seriously weaken the detractors' case.[16]

Welfare state proponents insist that inadequate recognition is given to the factors producing poverty. These factors, they assert, do not support the rather censorious and patronizing attitude that welfare state critics often seem to hold toward the unfortunate members of society.

The causes of poverty are legion, but these are among the more important: depression or recession, which bring unemployment and economic hardship as a consequence of forces beyond the lone worker's control; automation, which makes working skills obsolete—a particularly serious disaster to those beyond 40 years of age; inflation, which robs savings of their initial purchasing power; accidents or occupational diseases—for which the individual is not personally responsible; other forms of illness, among the paramount causes of poverty; low-grade intelligence, which precludes the individual from earning enough to save for emergencies; emotional instability—the result either of genetic inheritance or of unwholesome family conditions which had a crippling effect on the growing child; loss of the family breadwinner through death, divorce, or desertion; a large family—the care of which leaves no opportunity to accumulate financial reserves; a nonwhite racial inheritance, which severely limits earning opportunities (one half of Negro families in the South made under $1,200 a year in 1964, and a Negro college graduate typically makes about the same income as a white person with an eighth-grade education); inadequate educational opportunities during one's youth, or the necessity to leave school early to help support the family; and a variety of other factors largely beyond the individual's control. Thus, the implicit (if often un-

[16] Sidney Hook, "Welfare State–A Debate That Isn't," *The New York Times Magazine*, November 27, 1960.

spoken) premise that poverty is largely a moral disease that can be cured if society is "tough enough" with its victims is a premise unsupported by a calm and rational analysis of the facts.

The critics also pass all too lightly over our change from an agrarian society to an urban, industrial society. Farmers can tighten their belts and survive even when economic conditions are desperate; they can take in their parents and in-laws, if necessary, and supply their minimum needs. But urban families cannot be so self-reliant, and their dependence on the proper functioning of the economic system cannot be overestimated. When 12 million persons were unemployed during the Depression, there was no point in exhorting them to be self-reliant and independent and to glory in the disaster that could help them build noble characters. The attempt to transplant the principles and ideals of an agrarian, pioneer society to the industrialized metropolitan complexes of today is as futile and misdirected as an attempt to apply the principles of the guild system to a modern automated factory.

Self-reliance will indeed never become obsolete, but there is ample scope for its operation in the welfare state. The individual who moves beyond the plane of mere survival into the realm of success (however that term is interpreted) will almost always be one who exercises self-reliance, initiative, and personal responsibility in disciplining himself to the effort and sacrifice success entails and in taking advantage of opportunities as they arise.

Everyone agrees that provision of some kind must be made for persons who, for whatever reason, are unable to buy the necessities of life. So the choice is not, "Shall we or shall we not have a welfare state?" but, "What kind of a welfare state shall we have?" Even Elizabethan England had its welfare state—one that established workhouses and imposed the most severe conditions on those unable to care for themselves. The choices, then, are, broadly: a system of private charity or a system of publicly provided assistance drawing on general tax revenues and administered in conjunction with means tests or a system using social insurance to the maximum feasible degree.

The private charity alternative scarcely deserves serious consideration, because it is not only psychologically unsound, but wholly unrealistic. Private charity could never meet the routine demands for help in our great cities, to say nothing of unusual emergencies. It would be spotty, uncoordinated, uncertain, and chaotic. Although it might be pleasant for the contributors to feel that they had given directly to persons in distress, their satisfaction would be at the expense of the recipients. The latter are often acutely embarrassed at being the object of personal charity. They feel uncomfortably obligated to those who have helped them, and they vastly prefer the impersonality of public relief to the alternative of a psychologically distressing scene in which their helpless and poverty-stricken status is nakedly exposed before their friends and neighbors.

For reasons made clear in an earlier chapter, most welfare state defenders prefer a system relying heavily on social insurance. They believe it (1) relates individual contributions to individual benefits, thereby preventing the growth of a something-for-nothing spirit; (2) avoids the humiliations and degradation accompanying either private charity or means-test public aid; and (3) is more soundly financed.

Does the welfare state actually encourage indolence? The examination of specific programs suggests that this fear is largely groundless. Does workmen's compensation really encourage people to injure themselves so they can collect compensation? Does aid to the blind and crippled and disabled encourage anyone to become blind or crippled or disabled? Does Medicare cause the aged to feign illness? And will the kind of woman who has a succession of illegitimate children while on relief make a rational decision to forgo illicit relations if aid to her children is reduced? Does unemployment compensation encourage idleness (except in rare instances, where cheating admittedly takes place)? If a worker is fired for cause, he does not immediately qualify for benefits. And because unemployment compensation normally returns less than 40 percent of the worker's wages, how many people—especially men with families—prefer idleness and a 60 percent income slash to working on a job which provides them not only with some of the comforts everyone wants but also with the self-respect and community respect nearly all men covet?

Granted that a few men are indifferent to community disapproval, they usually are such hopeless characters that they will not be shocked into reform by any system of charity.

The social compulsion to work is exceedingly strong in our society. Reinforced by the natural desire for greater material satisfactions and increased security (and further reinforced by the salutary nagging of wives who are outraged if their husbands won't work, and by the readiness of collection agencies to repossess TV sets), these pressures are such that only a tiny percentage of adults will deliberately choose a life of idleness when the alternative is a 150 percent increase in income. General relief payments, it should be added, are also far below the income workers can obtain through employment.

As for Social Security, it was widely predicted that the guarantee of publicly provided pensions for the aged would seriously discourage private savings and would administer a heavy blow to the private insurance industry. Insurance companies now freely concede that this was a faulty prediction, because insurance has grown at an unprecedented rate since Social Security was introduced. Furthermore, despite the growth of our many-faceted welfare state, there has been no decline in national savings in proportion to national income. This is an extremely important fact, because if the premises of those opposed to the welfare state are correct, a reduction in personal savings should have set in.

During the Depression skeptics insisted that the national relief program had sapped the will to work. When jobs became available during the war, however, virtually every able-bodied person took a job—including more and more women. Experience repeatedly confirms the premise that when jobs are plentiful, unemployed persons as well as many who had not previously listed themselves as unemployed step forward to take those jobs. The criers of alarm have not been vindicated by the objective facts.

But the most compelling evidence that the welfare state does not necessarily impair the willingness to work is provided by the experiences of Western Europe. Sweden, for instance, has long functioned with a generous "cradle-to-grave" welfare state, yet unemployment has been reduced to about 1 percent in recent years.[17] West Germany has had a highly developed welfare state longer than any other country in the world, yet the West German economy is the most productive in Europe.[18] Other Western European countries also have considerably more advanced welfare states than the United States without suffering any impairment of the willingness to work. During the 1950s, in fact, those countries made considerably more rapid economic advances than the United States, and their percentage of unemployment was generally lower. If the welfare state produced the horrendous results attributed to it, this phenomenon simply would not have occurred.

We are told that under the welfare state much of the challenge of living is removed, and that life takes on a flat and insipid flavor because of the security in which the individual is swaddled. This is an interesting charge, but one that is both superficial and wholly lacking in objective supporting evidence. Does the excitement really go out of life because the bare necessities of life are assured by the state? Does life become dull and tasteless because starvation no longer threatens? Does any reasonable person actually believe that modern life is so bereft of challenge under the welfare state that it no longer calls forth our best? The major challenges of life are still with us: attaining a high degree of competence in a chosen field, as well as broadening and deepening one's range of interests; being the best husband, wife, father, or mother one is capable of becoming; standing up for unpopular causes and beliefs; helping solve any of the manifold knotty community problems that exist; bringing one's intelligence and energies to bear on the great national and international problems. One can even hope to become a millionaire, if that is one's ambition. America has 90,000 of them, and

[17] For a defense of Sweden's way of life, see Werner Wiskari, "Rejoinder to Sweden's Critics," *The New York Times Magazine,* October 23, 1960, p. 61. But also see Gunnar Myrdal, "The Swedish Way to Happiness," *The New York Times Magazine,* January 30, 1966. Myrdal takes an ambivalent position.

[18] For a change in German working habits, however, compare Flora Lewis, "Hans Schmidt Lives to Work," *The New York Times Magazine,* May 24, 1959, p. 15, with "Men of Leisure," *Newsweek,* May 25, 1964, pp. 46, 48.

their numbers have been rapidly increasing over the past ten years.

There is no need to deny that a certain amount of hardship and deprivation can have beneficial effects on the formation of character, or that too many comforts and luxuries coming too easily may not only sap the spirit but also reduce a person's capacity to fully enjoy material advantages. But this is largely irrelevant to the question of the welfare state. We are not talking about comforts or luxuries, but only about the subsistence levels provided by social insurance or public assistance. Moreover, do not those who most vociferously proclaim the merits of hardship and adversity do everything in their power to insure that their own children have plenty of nourishing food, warm clothing, adequate shelter, the best educational opportunities, the best medical care, and as many other "advantages" as they can provide? Why is it desirable for some children to enjoy these privileges, but good for other people's children to go without? It must be borne in mind that a large part of the welfare state's benefits go to provide necessities for children. Whatever the shortcomings of their parents, children certainly deserve minimum living standards. These the welfare state is determined to furnish, and this should be a source of national pride rather than a source of reproach.

A growing number of observers think unnecessary poverty, weighing most heavily on children, could be mitigated by a system of family allowances. Canada, for example, pays mothers from $6 to $10 per child per month (up to the age of 16) to help them properly feed, clothe, and care for their offspring. Although the introduction of the program in 1944 was accompanied by predictions of disaster, it has become a highly popular and virtually noncontroversial program (as is largely true in the 30 other countries paying family allowances). Nor has it led to an increase in the birth rate, contrary to the prophecies of its critics.

It is argued that the welfare state is all right up to a point, but that we are carrying it too far. This charge, of course, has been made at *each* point along the welfare road. Whenever the state is on the verge of providing a new and needed public service, we are always assured that we are approaching the danger point.

The most recent example: for some mystic reason it was desirable to use social insurance to protect the American people against a number of unpredictable financial disasters, but it was thought alarming to use it to protect us against the greatest unpredictable economic disaster—costly illness.

If there is to be protection against illness, why shouldn't the state provide food and clothing and shelter? The answer is simple: it makes sense to protect people against heavy medical bills, but it does not make sense for the government to supply the entire population with the necessities of survival. Unemployment compensation at moderate levels can be intelligently defended, but unemployment compensation which grants the unemployed person almost as much as he would make by working cannot be defended. Aid to the blind can be defended, but not aid to those afflicted with hay fever. A good case can be made for aid to those whose resources are exhausted, but no sensible case can be made for giving these persons income returns approximating those of employed persons. So long as people maintain a modicum of common sense, the state will not undertake absurd social services or absurdly generous benefits.

Those who are most critical of the welfare state basically lack faith in the judgment of a free people to make intelligent decisions. Perhaps their skepticism will some day prove well founded, but there is scanty evidence in the realm of national economic and social legislation to sustain this skepticism. Congressional action in these fields has almost invariably stood the test of time and merited the approbation of subsequent generations. If Congress is to be faulted on this score, its weakness lies in doing too little, too late. Most economists, for instance, believe unemployment compensation should equal 50 to 60 percent of wages, not 35 to 40 percent. And most Social Security experts believe Social Security payments have generally erred on the skimpy side. Some people talk as if the life of an ADC mother were a bowl of cherries. Are they aware that the average ADC family of four received the munificent sum of $125 per month in 1965? This is living high on the hog? And do they really believe the ADC mother, before she beds down with some male friend, shrewdly calculates the cash value of the child that may result from the night? In any case, do we want to penalize children for the bad luck of being born to a poor and unfortunate mother?

A more accurate picture of ADC is the following: "The typical ADC mother in Chicago is a poor Negro—the girl left behind to raise illegitimate children. She is insecure, uneducated, unsophisticated, frightened. She lives in a hovel and has no social or recreational outlet. She craves security and is vulnerable to men."[19]

Our choices in dealing with admitted ADC abuses are various: (1) We can, as in Mississippi, make it a crime for a "welfare" mother to give birth to a second illegitimate child. But how can an ADC mother pay a fine? And who will care for her children if she goes to jail? (2) We can terminate all aid when an ADC mother has illegitimate children or misspends money on alcohol or other nonessentials. But again, should children be punished for parental sins? (3) We can authorize social workers to spend most of the ADC check on essentials, leaving only a few dollars for discretionary spending by the mother. This is humiliating, but in extreme cases may well be necessary. (It is a practice already widely followed by welfare departments.) (4) We can raise the minimum wage in order to make employment a more attractive option. (Perhaps this could be done while establishing public day-care nurseries, as in Scandinavia, to better enable mothers to work.) (5) We can devise a system that reduces ADC payments to a working mother but on a scale that maximizes the incentive to work. (6) We can provide an adequate number of psychiatric social workers and other skilled counselors to help the ADC mother with her family and emotional problems. (This is a long-range objective; there is already a grievous shortage of such personnel.)

Some of these choices have much to commend them. If the critics of the welfare state wish to concentrate on constructive recommendations, friends of the welfare state welcome their contributions.

Log-rolling is indubitably a characteristic of the American

[19] "The Mystery of Rising Relief Costs," *U. S. News and World Report*, March 8, 1965, p. 41.

legislative way, and it is an untidy, undisciplined, and sometimes wasteful way to conduct the public business. But it is the American way of forming legislative majorities in the absence of cohesive, disciplined political parties. Those who solemnly warn of its costs generally do so only when Congress is considering measures they dislike, not when Congress acts in areas in which they feel action is needed. The prospect of log-rolling cannot be logically used as an excuse for legislative inaction where urgent problems exist, or legislative paralysis would set in. The same applies to the argument concerning the future of agencies that have outlived their usefulness. Of course new programs should not be established until mature deliberation has demonstrated their need, but the prolonged nature of our legislative process normally insures that this takes place. Does any knowledgeable person really believe it is easy to persuade Congress to innovate —especially where money is involved?

Where will the welfare state end? No one can answer with certainty, but the experience of Western Europe provides a solid basis for optimism in the ultimate judgment of a free people. Most Western European nations have rounded out their welfare states with national health insurance—and then turned their attention primarily to increasing productivity. Although children's allowances are provided in some of these states and sickness compensation (in addition to medical insurance) in others, the political parties generally have not sought the continuous extension of the welfare state in pursuit of votes. It is not too difficult to convince the people that welfare programs must be paid for, and therefore they should be instituted only when a rational case can be made on their behalf. The onward march of the welfare state has been substantially halted in Europe because state services in this area have substantially fulfilled their potentially useful role. We can assume that American public opinion will be no less enlightened than its European counterpart.

Isn't the comparison with ancient Rome rather strained? The Roman Empire was supporting a swarm of permanently idle persons without making any real attempt to find work for them. No re-employment training programs were in effect, nor were there tools at hand to stimulate their economy into full production. It was not a disgrace to be idle, nor did the shops bulge with the kind of goods that make materialists out of all but the hardiest modern consumers. Rome supported its idle with grain wrested from conquered territories, whereas America engages in major foreign aid programs to help other countries. The widespread ownership of property, the work ethic, the humbler role of the military, the successful operation of a democratic system, the relative absence of graft in our national public service—in these and a hundred other characteristics America differs from those evils of ancient Rome that ultimately brought about its downfall. America may or may not be in a period of moral decline, but what reputable sociologist attributes our moral problems to the existence of the welfare state?

The welfare state is indeed costly, but if the money is well spent for necessary purposes, it is a justified cost. It is one mark of an enlightened state that it makes adequate provision to meet the needs of its people; savings achieved at the expense of human misery are indefensible. The blind, the crippled, the needy children, the jobless, the aged without necessary resources, and so on—these unfortunates surely deserve help from a society as affluent as ours. Furthermore, because everyone agrees that these groups need help through either private or public contributions, the moneys expended are a "drain" on our national and personal income however they are raised. Money spent for private insurance policies represents a reduction of the individual's total resources just as much as money deducted by a payroll income tax for public insurance. To illustrate, if a $20 billion tax were substituted to pay for a comprehensive national health insurance program, the nation would not be spending any more for health than it is now. It would simply be paying for its health costs by a different method.

Just how large is "welfare spending," anyway? The Departments of Labor and of Health, Education and Welfare spend about $7 billion per year—and an important portion of this expenditure goes for such noncontroversial items as aid for defense-impact school districts, the Mediation and Conciliation Service, enforcement of Taft-Hartley and other labor laws, the United

States Public Health Service, and statistical and educational publications.[20] The only way to expand "welfare spending" into the dimensions that cause some Americans to shudder is to add farm price support and school lunch programs (about $3 billion —the balance of the $7 billion USDA budget goes for such programs as research, extension services, grading and inspection, the Forest Service, and Food for Peace); include all pensions and benefits for veterans (more than $5 billion); add about $20 billion for Social Security payments and several billions more for unemployment compensation. (The latter programs, as well as the federal highway and federal employee retirement accounts, are budgeted in special trust funds and, hence are not included in the regular administrative budget.)

When most Americans discuss "welfare" spending, they are probably thinking of *public assistance* programs. According to the *Social Security Bulletin* for November, 1963, federal, state, and local expenditures for public assistance were slightly over $5 billion for the fiscal year 1962–1963. Outright relief payments in 1966 continued to hover around the $5 billion mark. Considering the total federal, state, and local budgets of about $180 billion, these represent a rather modest proportion of public spending. Surely they are well below the sums brandished by those who seek to persuade us that we have become an unconscionable "handout state."

It is true that federal, state, and local spending for almost all purposes is rising, but this is to be expected in a society with a rapidly growing population. The critical questions about spending are: (1) Is the volume of spending *in relation to gross national product* rising? (2) Are taxes so high that they discourage savings and investment needed to maximize economic output? (3) Are the public expenditures for justifiable purposes?

So far as Washington is concerned, the answer to the first question is "no." Federal spending unrelated to defense, international affairs, and outer space dropped from 8.1 percent of GNP in 1947

[20] Morris Udall, "Where's the Welfare State?" *The New Republic*, October 1, 1962, p. 13.

to 5.8 percent in 1961 to 5.7 percent in 1966. A nation with a rapidly rising income can and should spend more to meet its obligations—and those obligations are bound to grow as we seek to convert our fantastic abundance into improved public services and higher private living standards. By 1975, our gross national product may well be nearly $1.25 trillion—a sum that will enable us to spend far more to meet the needs of population growth and to improve the quality of our society, without imposing heavier tax burdens. (A major war effort, of course, could alter this outlook.)

The answer to the second question is that there is no evidence that savings and investment have been impaired by the Great Society's programs. On the contrary, investment is setting all-time records, business profits are doing the same, and the economy has been making the most remarkable progress in history. Each year we are adding between $40 and $50 billion to our GNP, and this figure seems destined to rise in the years ahead.

Finally, Congress is not recklessly squandering its money on useless programs, nor are the American people urging Congress to do so. Each program is carefully and exhaustively considered on its merits; many of them, as has been shown, are designed to take people off the welfare rolls. Precisely *which* programs would the critics have America abandon, and just how much would this reduce over-all spending?

Even before the tax cut in 1964, America's taxes were not as high as those of many other advanced nations. Taxation consumed 26 percent of the American GNP, while West Germany taxed 34 percent of its GNP. Only Belgium and Denmark, among the industrial states of Europe, had lower taxes than the United States. No economist, moreover, has been able to demonstrate that the tax level is so high that the savings required to finance needed private investments are at inadequate levels. If America was not growing as rapidly as it should, and if economic activity was less than satisfactory in the 1950s, that was primarily because of insufficient consumer demand. Whenever consumer demand is present, business does not fail to produce the goods that the consumer is able and willing to buy.

Big Government and Personal Freedom

If taxes reduce freedom, then the very existence of government is a challenge to freedom. No government can exist without taxes, and it is a bit difficult to establish an effective tax system on a voluntary basis! Actually, taxes do not reduce freedom in a democracy, because no tax is imposed on the people without their consent—given through their freely elected representatives.

If the people of this nation prefer that some of their money be spent for a public purpose, they are exercising their freedom in making that choice. It would be a denial of freedom if we were to forbid the government to impose taxes for purposes the people thought desirable. Hence, in the most realistic sense, the existing level of taxes in a democratic nation represents the will of the people, and such taxes are an expression of their freedom to choose, rather than an encroachment on their freedom.

As for the allegedly pernicious effect of big government on individual freedom, this can be strongly contested. Currently we have about 2.6 million federal employees, a federal budget of about $110 billion, and a host of laws and governmental agencies. Big government is indubitably upon us. But how much freedom have we really lost? All of our constitutionally guaranteed freedoms and rights—speech, press, religion, assembly, suffrage, due process of law, freedom of travel, choice of occupation—are still enjoyed by our people. In the most flagrant instance of the denial of constitutional rights—the position of the Negro—it can be argued that this has reflected an insufficiency of federal power and an excess of local power.

The major challenges to individual freedom in America have been associated with periods of insecurity rather than with big government. The Alien and Sedition Acts had no relation to the size of government; nor was big government as such responsible for the wholesale violation of individual rights associated with the abolition movement or the indefensible crackdowns on free speech during World War I and the immediate postwar period or the Japanese "concentration" camps of World War II or the inhibiting fears and pressures and timidities of the McCarthy period. These partial eclipses of individual freedom grew out of popular apprehensions, not out of big government.

In modern democracies, the extension of government power may enlarge or protect individual freedom rather than restrict it. Federal civil rights activities ranging from anti-KKK laws to federal laws insuring Negro voting rights *protect freedom* from private or state and local invasions. Antitrust laws protect the freedom of the small businessman from arbitrary economic power. The Norris-LaGuardia Act protected the right of the worker to join a labor union by outlawing yellow-dog contracts. The Wagner Act further protected that right from coercive management pressures. On the other hand, the Taft-Hartley Act shielded the worker from intimidation and coercive tactics by unions and union organizers. The "Bill of Rights" contained in the 1959 labor reform bill further guarded the worker's right to fair treatment within the union and to full participation in union decisions. Federally aided programs annually rehabilitate over 100,000 disabled persons—persons whose true freedom is far greater with a job (and its income) than it would be without this "governmentalism." Unemployment compensation enables the worker to shop around for a job best suited to his skills, instead of being obliged to take the first job he finds. His effective choices are thereby broadened. Measures that insure the worker against economic insecurities provide a freedom from fear—the fear of destitution and of being unable to take care of his family. Governmental efforts to insure full employment advance the worker's freedom—the man with a job has not only greater self-respect, but his increased income furnishes him with a much wider range of activity choices.

Many other examples could be given of governmental programs which, far from diminishing freedom, actually enlarge it. It is important to remember that whatever gives young people better education, better medical care, and better cultural surroundings, in terms of adequate libraries, parks, museums, etc., enhances the opportunity for individual self-development and, hence, widens the areas of ultimate choice for the individual. A person with inferior education or poor health or inadequate vocational skills, or who was raised in surroundings that benumb and deaden rather than encourage and inspire, has fewer doors open to him than those raised in more fortunate circumstances. Perhaps the finest work the government can do is to help provide each youngster with the best possible environment for stimulating the development of his highest potentialities. The "welfare state" helps provide the minimum essentials, while other government programs, such as educational expenditures, public health, urban renewal and redevelopment, and employment retraining, carry forward the work. The total contribution of federal, state, and local governments toward helping the individual exploit his talents is enormous and should be recognized for its fruitful character.[21]

Many critics of the welfare state aim their fire almost exclusively at activities of the national government, finding its functions to be peculiarly obnoxious and dangerous. This is an attitude that will not bear up under informed examination. In modern times, especially, the central government tends to speak for the more enlightened conscience of the nation and for the nation's long-range interests, while state and local governments all too often represent the more provincial and backward outlook. Certainly federal initiatives in the fields of conservation, education, health, housing, trade, research, and equal rights for Negroes testify to the relatively advanced thinking of the national government as contrasted with the often parochial attitudes of local governments when confronted with problems of more than local consequence.

There are grounds for challenging the consistency of those claiming to fear expanding federal power. When welfare measures are proposed, the familiar arguments against Washington are all wheeled out and placed in position, and the barrage begins. But these field generals conveniently forget all about the ominous aspects of federal power when someone suggests that labor unions should be more tightly regulated. The critics of the welfare state were most vehement in demanding the Taft-Hartley Act and the Labor Reform Act of 1959. Now they are demanding

[21] For a general discussion of this and other aspects of the welfare state, see Hook, *op. cit.*

the application of antitrust laws to labor. Thus, it appears that these groups behave like everyone else: when Washington is granted fresh power that promotes their interests or ideological preferences, they applaud; when it acts in a contrary fashion, they deplore. It's another case of whose ox is gored.

And another thing. It is easy—so very easy—to berate Washington for "grasping for power" by performing functions that should be left to the states and localities. But does not a dispassionate historical study reveal that Washington acts only when states and localities have been unable or unwilling to act? Can a single instance be found where local governments were adequately handling a social need, only to have those services thrust aside and supplanted by a power-hungry Washington? These endless attacks on Washington may provide thunderous applause from after-dinner business audiences, but only because the charges are unexamined. Even President Eisenhower, staunch opponent of centralized power that he is, once told the Conference of Governors that Washington could never have entered areas formerly reserved to the states "without the neglect, acquiescence or unthinking cooperation of the states themselves."

Unconstitutional? The Constitution specifically authorizes the national government to "spend for the general welfare." And if money is offered to the states—to be accepted or rejected at their pleasure—of course Washington can attach conditions to insure its being spent efficiently for the intended purposes. The Supreme Court largely exists for the purpose of determining the constitutionality of legislation, and it has put its seal of approval on grant-in-aid programs and on the interpretation of the spending clause that sustains federal action in these challenged areas. Do Barry Goldwater and his supporters really know more about the Constitution than does the Supreme Court?

Federalism has been indispensable to the development of our country; it will continue to guarantee local control of strictly local matters. But there is no reason why Americans should not look upon Washington as a partner of the states, assisting them where this proves necessary and upgrading their standards where this can properly be done. Elected representatives in Washington are responsive to local opinion and local needs in the same way as state representatives. They are probably closer to their constituents than state representatives, in every sense except geographically. Voters follow national policy developments much more closely than they do state legislative affairs; they send far greater volumes of mail to their national representatives. Washington congressmen are generally of a higher order of intelligence and competence than state legislators (the best state legislators frequently aspire to a seat on Capitol Hill), and they are watched, criticized, and encouraged by the nation's foremost journalists and public affairs analysts. State legislation, on the other hand, is given relatively small attention in the press. If more and more power is gravitating to Washington, this is a historic trend reproduced in every modern nation in the world. It flows from the fact that our problems are increasingly national problems in an age when national consciousness is on the rise and state loyalties and identifications are declining. As for fears that centralized power always leads to tyranny, freedom is as secure in Britain as anywhere, and political power has been highly centralized in Britain for a longer period than in any democratic nation in the world.

Is it possible for the state to assume responsibility for the material side of man without intruding on the spiritual side? Indeed it is, for a very good reason. In modern times, democratic citizens want to use the government—which is their servant, subject to their wishes—for advancing their economic security. But they do not want the government to tell them how they may worship, what they may say, what they may read, what they must believe. So long as they want the former and not the latter, legislators dependent on popular votes will seek to promote economic security while continuing to respect the Bill of Rights.

It will also be denied that the welfare state involves accumulated restrictions on freedom that, although individually small, are collectively ominous. Defenders of the welfare state insist that no genuine freedoms are lost as the result of individual welfare programs. If individual programs do not reduce fundamental freedoms, they will not do so collectively. It is illogical to argue that this program is desirable and that program is justified and another program is valuable but that collectively they menace freedom or are otherwise undesirable. One of the fundamental weaknesses in the welfare state critics' position is their tendency to (1) lambaste the welfare state as a whole without specifying which welfare programs should be eliminated; or (2) lambaste the welfare state while tacitly (or specifically, when pinned down) approving its individual components. Unless critics are specific in their indictment, their generalized attacks on the welfare state are basically meaningless.

If the critics' real grievances against the welfare state lie in its maladministration from time to time, or in ill-considered aspects of welfare programs that need improvement, the defenders will join them in efforts to eradicate those weaknesses. Of course these programs are far from perfect, and a thoroughgoing reappraisal from time to time would yield useful recommendations for strengthening them. In fact, welfare state defenders are especially anxious to eliminate "bugs" in the programs, because these tend to weaken public support for welfare programs in general. Does the entire controversy, when it is boiled down, reduce itself to the shared view that the programs should be administered as economically as possible and that chiselers should be the object of administrative crackdowns? If so, the controversy has evaporated.

Is the welfare state socialism—or a half-way station to socialism? Socialism means public ownership of the means of production, transportation, and communication, and the welfare state is wholly unrelated to public ownership. To equate socialism with an extension of government services, or even with an extension of government regulation, is to pervert the meaning of the word. When people talk of "creeping socialism" in the United States, they really mean creeping government services and creeping government regulation. But socialism has become a verbal goblin with which to scare people, to divert attention from the substantive facts, and to substitute an emotional reaction for a rational one. Socialism, as the term is used by welfare state foes, has proved to be a useful propaganda missile, but its use only confuses rather than enlightens.

Even if a program were socialistic (which defenders deny welfare programs are) this would be irrelevant to its desirability. The crucial question is never whether a program is socialistic, but whether it is good or bad. If it serves a useful public purpose, it is a good program regardless of what ugly labels are applied. If it doesn't, it is bad, regardless of what dazzling labels are applied.

It is hard to argue that socialism is always bad, in any case, because most Americans prefer to keep public education "socialized" and most of them also approve of the Tennessee Valley Authority, the Grand Coulee Dam, the Post Office, the Atomic Energy Commission, REA, public water systems, our 169 veterans' hospitals, our mental hospitals, and various other "socialistic" enterprises. Even if we call social insurance "socialistic," most Americans support it. Each program, it is reemphasized, must be examined on its own merits—and name-calling solves no controversies.

Welfare state defenders might add a few words about the "bureaucratic" aspects of big government. There can be no gainsaying the fact that serious problems arise in administering a public service the size of ours. The President's responsibility for controlling and directing millions of employees is immense, as the Hoover Commission graphically demonstrated. The resistances that big bureaucracies can create to fight off challenges to their vested interests—or their inertia—are formidable ones. Problems of coordination are staggering, and inefficiencies are obviously harder to identify and correct than in smaller organizations. An element of irresponsibility enters into operations of the magnitude of the national government, because this is inherent in the nature of things.

The conclusions that may be drawn from this, however, are sometimes ill-founded. First, only a small percentage of our big government is represented by federal welfare functions. Second, no one can seriously contend that government is so big that, regardless of what new needs arise, Washington should assume no further responsibilities. The federal government cannot stand still, any more than any other institution can.

The major problems growing out of our vast public service arise where different agencies have policy-making responsibilities that impinge on a given problem. When a variety of agencies make policy decisions that affect inflation, full employment, foreign trade, or business regulation, it is of the utmost importance that coordination be achieved so that agencies do not work at cross purposes. As government enlarges its scope in these fields, coordination becomes more difficult.

But this problem has no important relation to the establishment of a new agency to administer a new welfare program—such as Medicare. The latter agency is not making policy, but administering a program narrowly prescribed by Congress. It does not need to be coordinated with other agencies, so far as policy is concerned. It is substantially self-contained, and it can function just as efficiently as if the government were one tenth the present size. The Social Security Administration, which is one of the world's more efficient administrative agencies, is not less efficient because a hundred agencies are concerned with foreign affairs or business regulation or full employment.

And—that awful word over and over again—bureaucracy! As used, the term conjures up visions of hardhearted, ruthless officials, drunk with power (although tied up in a hundred administrative knots), and thirsting for the blood of liberty. Perhaps it is pointless to protest against the use of a word that so well serves the propaganda interests of certain groups, but in our more sober moments we all must recognize that public servants are just ordinary Americans like ourselves. They will err on occasion, of course. Some of them are inefficient, some are discourteous, and some find power disturbingly tasty, but they are a cross section of America's strengths and weaknesses. Certainly federal civil servants are not a breed apart, with singularly fearsome characteristics and a concealed hostility to basic American values.

The best studies indicate, furthermore, that the "bureaucrats" administer the welfare state with at least a tolerable degree of efficiency. Federal administrative reviews of state and national welfare programs, reviews made by state agencies themselves, and independent surveys show that only about 2 or 3 percent of the persons receiving aid in the various grant-in-aid programs are actually ineligible for such payments. This corresponds closely to studies made in Great Britain. When Joseph Mitchell, the newly appointed city manager of Newburgh, New York, made national headlines by proposing a rigorous series of "reforms" to put an end to "chiselers, loafers, and social parasites" on the relief rolls, reporters later discovered that he had found only one able-bodied man on relief who could work for the city in return for his relief check. Although his welfare commissioner found two cases of fraud, Mitchell could discover no additional ones.[22] Mitchell resorted to such extraordinary measures as requiring all relief recipients to report to the police station for their relief checks, but his best efforts completely failed to substantiate his sweeping charges that the relief rolls were loaded with persons having no legitimate claims on public assistance. Even *U. S. News,* which is quick to seize on evidence that might discredit the "welfare state," conceded in 1965 that "nationwide, relief experts say that chiseling is not a major factor."[23]

Most defenders of the welfare state would probably deny that it is a major national issue. At most, it presents vexing but primarily minor problems common to all advanced societies. The task of improving and reforming welfare laws and administration is one to which all modern governments must perpetually attend. But as for "welfare-ism" representing a spreading cancer eating at the vitals of American morality and economic health, they regard this as a part of the mythology of the American Right—a mythology which, unhappily, has been sold to a surprising proportion of the American people.

Welfare state foes, in rebuttal, insist that economic freedom is a bulwark of the entire structure of freedom. If it is undermined, we do irreparable damage to freedom's presence and freedom's prospects. The welfare state involves controls that are subversive of a free economy, even if the full effects of that subversion are not readily apparent. Similarly, a few decades are too few to permit the subtle moral corrosions of the "handout state"

[22] Meg Greenfield, "The 'Welfare Chiselers' of Newburgh, N.Y.," *The Reporter,* August 17, 1961, pp. 37–40.

[23] "The Mystery of Rising Relief Costs," *U. S. News and World Report,* March 8, 1965, p. 40.

to be fully manifest. The impact of government paternalism on a people is all the more serious because increasing moral and spiritual flaccidity come about so gradually and stealthily that the evil goes unnoticed. The perspective of history is required, but that perspective is not to be found amongst the facile defenders of the welfare state.

While it may be true that Western Europe has not yet experienced the fruition of welfare politics, the picture is hardly as rosy as it has been painted. A respected foreign correspondent recently observed,

> Austria today is in many ways the most socialized country in the western world. . . . In continual efforts to break the 18-year [political] deadlock, each of the coalition parties has tried to outbid the other in social welfare programs. Both have succeeded. The German Social Insurance Law was passed in 1956 and was amended for the eleventh time in July of this year. Each amendment has provided increased benefits. There are two new amendments in the works . . . every sixth Austrian is a pensioner. . . . The state provides every conceivable type of pension and a few all but inconceivable ones. There is, for example, a pension for orphan and double-orphan students above 24 years of age.[24]

South America provides another example of a welfare state run wild. Uruguay allows those over 40, who lose a job through no fault of their own, to retire at full pay for life. Unemployment compensation nearly equals normal pay. Women who have worked 10 years and then have a baby can retire at full pay. The official government work day is six hours, but most workers informally reduce this to about four. The upshot is inflation, increasing indolence, and a major threat to the economic welfare of the country.[25]

Writers of all political persuasions agree that Britain's low rate of man-hour output and its chronic economic crisis have

[24] George Bailey, "Is Austria Here to Stay?" *The Reporter,* October 24, 1963, pp. 45–46. Copyright 1963 by The Reporter Magazine Company. By permission.

[25] James N. Wallace, "If You Want to Know How Far Welfare Can Go," *U. S. News and World Report,* September 27, 1965, pp. 73–74.

largely grown out of widespread worker unwillingness to do a day's work for a day's pay. The brisk working pace exhibited by German workers up to 1960 has also begun to slacken.[26] (Are affluence or welfare policies to blame?)

Is it not true, moreover, that Washington liberalizes our Social Security law every election year? The phenomenon never fails, yet this trend is the sure road to ultimate disaster. (Rebuttal: The question is not, has the law been liberalized, or broadened in its coverage—but, has it been *unwisely* liberalized or broadened? Most professional students of Social Security flatly deny that the law has unduly liberal benefits and would argue that its payments are still too meager to meet demonstrated needs.)

Speaking of mythology, what mythology can compare in falsity and destructiveness with the myth that Washington is all-wise, all-knowing, and altogether beneficent? The illusion that progress and federal expansion are Siamese twins is the most insidious myth circulated in our times. Unless it is dispelled, and dispelled soon, it may be too late to regain our ebbing freedoms and the independent control of our destinies. There is always the danger that the people will become so comfortable in the cozy cocoon of the state that they will lose not only the capacity to break free, but the will as well. When men are content to be the compliant wards of the state, the ultimate destruction of human dignity has occurred.

Many middle-of-the-road observers agree that detractors of the welfare state have overblown their case and used many an argument that collapses on close scrutiny. But they insist that America needs the equivalent of a British Royal Commission to give our more controversial welfare state programs (especially ADC and unemployment compensation) the kind of unsparing national examination they have never really had. Surely a better job of administering these laws can be done than the states are now doing—even if more federal controls are required. It is hard to be unconcerned over those who accept unemployment compensation when they (1) are making little or no effort to get a

[26] "Men of Leisure," *Newsweek*, May 25, 1964, pp. 46, 48.

job; (2) reject possible employment because (under certain unusual circumstances) it offers no more, or little more, than they can get from jobless pay; (3) have already found another job; (4) are receiving Social Security or other retirement pay; (5) are on strike (as two states permit); (6) have been discharged for misconduct; or (7) have quit their jobs for personal reasons. (Most states knowingly permit workers who fall under categories 2, 6, and 7 to receive benefits after waiting periods of five to eight weeks.)

They are also disturbed by the growing propensity to take sick leave, whether sick or not, simply because the time has accumulated; by welfare checks spent on alcohol and gambling; by the failure of communities to require able-bodied relief recipients to work on useful community projects; and by the willingness of too many people to accept welfare-type benefits for which they may be technically eligible but which are ethically dubious, to say the least. For example, how many veterans receiving 10 or 20 percent disability pensions are actually sufficiently disabled to reduce their earning power?[27]

Most students of welfare administration believe that a certain amount of chiseling is inevitable—even in a system of private charity, because the capacity to feign need was not invented with the welfare state. They agree that vigilance is always necessary to keep chiseling to a bare minimum, and there is never a time when administrative officials can afford to be complacent about their performance. But much more than merely the efficient administration of funds is needed. The poor need to learn how to help themselves, so that the cycle of poverty, squalor, backwardness, hopelessness, and bitterness that is passed on from generation to generation can be broken. And this is where the "Poverty Program" comes in.

[27] John E. Booth, "Veterans: Our Biggest Privileged Class," *Harper's Magazine,* July, 1958. Also see John E. Booth, "Veteran Against Veteran," *The Atlantic Monthly,* October, 1965.

CHAPTER

◂ 7 ▸

THE WAR ON POVERTY

What are the dimensions of poverty in the United States? "Poverty" obviously is a relative term—the standard of living of most low-income Americans would be regarded as affluent in most African and Asian countries. The current definition of poverty accepted by the government includes a couple with an annual income of $2,000 or less, a family of three making less than $2,500, a family of four making less than $3,000, and so forth. It was estimated in 1965 that from 30 to 35 million persons fell into these categories, including approximately 15 million children.

Poor families tend to cluster in certain geographical areas as well as in metropolitan slums: Appalachia; southern portions of Illinois, Indiana, Ohio, and Missouri; northern portions of Michigan, Minnesota, and Wisconsin; the Spanish-American populated areas of the Southwest; and much of the rural South.

The poor also are concentrated in the following sociological categories: About 45 percent of Negro families made less than

$3,000 a year in 1964 (although 70 percent of the poor are whites); 60 percent of poor families were headed by a person having no more than an eighth-grade education; nearly half of the aged were poor; one fourth of all poor families had lost the father through death, desertion, or divorce; most Indians and migratory workers were included; also, families with five or more children were heavily represented among the poor. Interestingly, in 1965 only about 6 percent of poor families were headed by an unemployed person.[1]

The poverty program was launched as the outgrowth of a number of developments. Michael Harrington's *The Other America*[2] helped arouse the nation to the nature and dimensions of poverty in this land. President Kennedy was deeply shocked by the face and smell of poverty during his Presidential campaign in West Virginia. He was also disturbed by a report that among the 50 percent of potential military recruits found unfit for the draft, a large proportion were ineligible because of remediable physical and educational deficiencies. Finally, fears that high school dropouts and other uneducated and unskilled persons might become permanent welfare clients in our automated age spurred further support for an action program. President Kennedy allegedly gave his approval to the establishment of an antipoverty program three days before his assassination.

In 1964, Congress established the Office of Economic Opportunity (OEO), under the direction of the successful Peace Corps administrator, Sargent Shriver, with an initial budget of about $785 million (doubled the following year). The program, shaped in a "crash" atmosphere, contains the following major elements.

A Job Corps, aimed at attracting high school dropouts and other "marginal" youth aged 16 to 21, was designed to correct the educational, physical, social, and technical deficiencies of young people with unpromising futures. Volunteers (some attracted by the slogan, "Be Somebody") are sent to camps through-

[1] A Gallup poll in 1965 revealed that 46 percent of Americans attributed most poverty to circumstances; 54 percent blamed it on lack of effort.

[2] *The Other America: Poverty in the United States*, New York, Macmillan, 1962; Edgar May's *The Wasted Americans: Cost of Our Welfare Dilemma*, New York, Harper & Row, 1964, also aroused considerable interest.

out the country for a maximum period of two years. These camps, mostly run under contracts with private corporations, provide young people with medical attention, basic literacy training, counseling, and vocational education. Although sustained work experience in conservation, reforestation, care of park and tourist facilities, and so forth, is important to youth often badly in need of such discipline, the camps are heavily oriented toward job training. Students who found formal schooling a bore and a frustration show greater willingness to learn when reading, writing, and mathematics are tied in with training for a specific job skill in which they are interested. In addition to technical training, the corpsmen are often taught such elementary matters as how to shake hands, how to sit rather than slouch, how to ask an employer for a job, how to dress respectably. They are urged to tone down their earthy language in the interests of obtaining and holding a job. Emphasis is placed on punctuality, getting along with other workers, and a sense of responsibility. In some camps, misbehavior is punished by penalties imposed by peers.

Corpsmen receive $30 a month spending money and free board, room, and work clothes, plus an allowance for one good suit. They also are awarded a terminal payment of $50 for each full month in camp. The program is thus relatively costly—initially about $9–10,000 per person per year—but the government hopes the investment will pay off in reduced criminality, unemployment, welfare payments, and, above all, in the salvage of potential human wreckage. It is also hoped to reduce costs to about $6,000 a year per person, once the program becomes stabilized.

For those unable or unwilling to enter the Job Corps, OEO sponsors Neighborhood Youth Corps. These corps, operated by local governments, schools, hospitals, old-age homes, and private nonprofit agencies, provide work experience for young people. Enrollees are paid up to $1.25 an hour for working in hospitals, parks, conservation programs, or other state or municipal projects. Thus, those who need to help support their families, or who will not continue in school unless they can earn some money on the side, are encouraged to finish their education. The program initially cost about $1,000 per person annually.

A work-study program was also created to help lower-income students attend college. With the federal government again supplying most of the funds, colleges are able to provide useful work for more than 100,000 youngsters whose families are unable sufficiently to help finance their higher education. Students are permitted to work up to 15 hours per week under this program.

Operation Head Start (see p. 22) was designed to help culturally underprivileged children compete on equal terms with other children at the first-grade level.

Volunteers in Service to America (VISTA) proposed to attract thousands of young people for a year's service to their country at pay corresponding to that of the Job Corps. Largely drawn from the ranks of college students with a yen for the Peace Corps but an unwillingness to commit themselves to two years abroad, volunteers follow up six weeks of basic training with labor assignments to help the families of migratory workers, or work on Indian reservations, in mental health centers, or in classes for the mentally retarded, or render educational assistance in slum schools or in adult literacy programs. Some universities give up to nine hours' credit for a year's service in VISTA.

The major activity sponsored by OEO involved the Community Action programs. Inasmuch as scores of federal, state, and local agencies were already engaged in some form of assistance to needy persons, the OEO proposed to coordinate the educational, employment, welfare, housing, health, consumer information, credit, legal aid, and vocational training functions of these agencies (as well as of private groups doing similar work) and give financial support to selected aspects of their work. Rather than seek to establish a huge Washington bureaucracy, with overcentralized direction and administration, OEO hoped to stimulate the maximum local energy, initiative, and imagination toward eradicating or minimizing poverty. A considerable amount of money was set aside for experimental work and demonstration projects. OEO was well aware of its pioneering character and of the immense difficulties involved in achieving satisfactory results where existing social welfare agencies had so often failed.

OEO stresses local job counseling and job training programs, as well as educational improvements in schools and classes especially concerned with lower-income-group children. But it also encourages the establishment of neighborhood service centers (called "Little City Halls") in which knowledgeable people can provide the poor with advice and assistance they might not seek at City Hall. In some cities certain types of free legal aid are supplied, along with advice to persons being victimized by unscrupulous small-loan agencies or installment-purchase frauds. Persons being charged exorbitant rent by landlords who refuse to repair substandard premises are advised how to obtain redress or to find better housing; persons needing help for their physical or emotional problems are counseled. In general, these service centers seek to bring needy persons into contact with existing agencies that may help them.

One of the more controversial—and one of the most significant —facets of the Community Action Programs involves federal financing for local family planning clinics. Large families, especially those in which the husband is chronically jobless or in which there is no husband through death, desertion, or divorce, contribute heavily to the dimensions of poverty in America. Yet, polls reveal that the poor prefer families no larger than those favored by the more affluent[3] and usually welcome help in limiting their families.

The director of the Children's Bureau in Washington advocated that family planning services, financed by federal matching funds, should be available as a matter of "right" to all needy persons who want them.[4] Welfare workers usually agree that few services are more badly needed or would do more to alleviate both the welfare and the poverty problems. Equality of opportunity, to many observers, is particularly crucial in obtaining access to family planning information because few misfortunes cast a longer shadow than those of women bringing unwanted children into a world that offers them bleak opportunities for a satisfying life.

Many citizens strongly support public family planning services

[3] *Newsweek,* September 13, 1965, p. 26.
[4] "B – – th C – nt – – l," *The New Republic,* September 25, 1965, p. 6.

as a means of reducing the number of illegitimate children born to women on relief rolls. A county in North Carolina reported that every dollar spent on family planning clinics saved an estimated $25 in ultimate welfare costs. Whether or not this is a representative figure, few informed persons would question that the investment yields high dollar dividends over a period of time.

Some authorities believe that the mere existence of free clinics is not adequate. Welfare agencies may find it necessary to take the initiative and discuss family planning with welfare clients who need advice and assistance. It is difficult to forecast how rapidly municipal action in this area will take place. The Catholic Church is divided in its attitude toward public initiatives, but a potent element within the church continues to put up resistance to the use of public funds to support birth control activities long regarded as morally repugnant by it. The Gallup poll, however, shows that 63 percent of Roman Catholics approve of federal funds to support birth control clinics where these are requested by local communities.

Many Negroes suspect that some enthusiasts for family planning clinics really want to use them as a means of reducing the Negro birth rate. It may be that family planning efforts among Negroes will have to be carried out by Negroes if they are to be successful. Fortunately, many Negroes realize the urgent importance of action among their people. For example, the Chicago Urban League has observed, "to fight poverty without birth control is to fight with one hand tied behind the back." Negro membership on the national and local boards of Planned Parenthood is increasing rapidly. Moreover, it is interesting to note that middle-class Negro families are smaller than comparable white families.[5]

Should birth control information be available from local governments to all women, regardless of their marital status? Is this necessary to prevent unwanted children from entering homes

[5] Hannah Lees, "The Negro Response to Birth Control," *The Reporter*, May 19, 1966, p. 48.

sorely unprepared for their presence? Or will services to unmarried girls promote a casual attitude toward premarital relations and bring about a serious deterioration of moral values?

This is one of those harsh moral dilemmas that plagues every age, since it involves a conflict of widely shared values. An excellent case can be made for the view that premarital chastity is a sound human value, which the state should not undermine. On the other hand, birth control information could prevent personal tragedies among many whose moral values are almost nonexistent anyway.

Despite the various forms of opposition, the long-run trends suggest that the public family planning movement will pick up momentum, with the program assuming major proportions within a decade. Whether or not the results will be equally dramatic remains to be seen.

Criticisms of the poverty program have been manifold and persistent. A House Republican called the program "a national catastrophe." The House GOP leadership referred to it as "a churning Disneyland of administrative chaos." Richard Nixon said the program was "first in promises, first in politics, first in press releases—and last in performance." The administrators of the program have been accused of receiving exorbitant salaries. Negroes, and the poor in general, were said to be inadequately represented on the poverty planning boards. Various agencies, coordinated under Mr. Shriver's "single umbrella," sometimes have been more anxious to fight competitive agencies for control of the program than they were to serve the poor. Ingrained bureaucratic tendencies in local welfare agencies, such as the clinging to outmoded but traditional procedures, the multiplying of paper work, and an irritatingly patronizing attitude toward the poor, were incorporated into the program. Charles Silberman wrote of "the tragic flaw of paternalism."[6] Critics charged that political bosses often staffed the program with political hacks rather than with the best-qualified persons. The program was said to be degenerating into a huge political pork barrel, providing more muscle for existing political machines than help for

[6] "The Mixed-Up War on Poverty," *Fortune,* August, 1965, p. 226.

the poor.[7] Congressman Adam Clayton Powell, chairman of the House Committee overseeing the program, demanded the resignation of Sargent Shriver as administratively inept.

One outspoken critic of the poverty program has been Saul D. Alinsky, executive director of the Industrial Areas Foundation and one of the most refreshing—or ominous (choose one!)—figures on the American political scene. Mr. Alinsky believes the program will bog down in local politics, red tape, and welfare agency fumbling; he also is convinced that the central approach is wrong. Although the poverty program requires that the poor be represented on the Community Action program planning boards, "to the maximum extent practicable," he regards this as so much window dressing. At bottom, he believes, much of the poverty program is simply a ballooning of preexisting government attempts to help the poor, when the real need is to organize the poor to help themselves. Trained as a sociologist and criminologist, Alinsky is persuaded that the poor can solve their own problems if they can be jarred from their sense of hopelessness, if they can come to recognize their common interests and learn the ancient lessons that power is essential to the correction of injustice, that there is "no evolution without revolution," and that the time is now!

Charles Silberman's *Crisis in Black and White*[8] catapulted Alinsky's views and activities into public prominence, and much of what follows was derived from this book and from two articles in *Harper's Magazine* entitled "Conversations with Saul Alinsky."[9]

Alinsky does not commence his organizational work unless he has been invited by a significant cross section of leaders and groups in a city. When he and his staff arrive, one of their first jobs is to listen. "You do more organizing with your ears than with your tongue,"[10] Alinsky says. Thus, his men start prowling through the poverty area with instructions to listen to street-

[7] See William F. Haddad, "Mr. Shriver and the Savage Politics of Poverty," *Harper's Magazine,* December, 1965.

[8] New York, Random House, 1964.

[9] M. K. Sanders, ed., "The Professional Radical," *Harper's Magazine,* June, July, 1965.

[10] *Ibid.,* July, p. 56.

corner talk and to barroom gossip and to strike up conversations with a wide variety of persons in order to accurately identify popular grievances, worries, and fears. This process also helps identify potential local leaders, so they can be drawn together for discussions leading to an action program.

Once the groundwork has been laid, Alinsky organizes neighborhood and community meetings at which he reminds the inhabitants in vivid language of the miseries, inequities, and frustrations they endure. His tactics, as Silberman puts it, are to "rub raw the sores of discontent" and "sharpen dormant hostilities" against those believed responsible for their plight.[11] He warns them that if they want conditions improved, they must do it themselves. His job is to help them create an organization that can jolt the status quo, bring effective pressures to bear where they are most needed, and make his services unnecessary as soon as possible. The poor must write their own constitution, select their officers, plan their campaigns, and strive to become as potent a pressure group as those the middle classes take for granted as essential to the protection and advancement of their class interests.

To help instill hope and to demonstrate and dramatize the possibilities of effective action, Alinsky takes the earliest opportunity to mount campaigns such as those used by the Woodlawn Organization of Chicago. His people hung huge signs announcing "This Is a Slum" on apartment buildings whose owners resisted repairs and rehabilitation. If the landlord still refused to act, they would picket his lovely house in one of the "plush" residential areas, carrying signs lettered, "Your Neighbor Is a Slumlord." On a broader front, Alinsky organized rent strikes, with slum tenants collectively withholding rent until the landlords met their obligations. Businessmen who shortchanged their customers and loan sharks who charged exorbitant interest rates became the object of parades and other publicity campaigns challenging their abuses.

Alinsky does not trust unpaid volunteers to do the work necessary to a vital, ongoing community organization. He uses a full-time staff, but he insists that the community itself must ordinarily

[11] Silberman, *op. cit.*, p. 331.

be prepared to pay staff salaries entirely within three years of his entry into the community.

One of his most challenging jobs is to penetrate the thick layers of hopelessness that envelop the poor and convince them that "They *can* fight City Hall." This transformation is extraordinarily difficult, for no attitude is more widespread among the poor than a resigned air of "But what can anybody do about it?" Alinsky relies on spokesmen for the status quo to help his cause along. In their hatred and fear of his role, leading community figures sooner or later unlash such virulent attacks on him that the poor often conclude, "This guy must have something or the powers that be wouldn't belt him around like this." Or community leaders make stupid decisions that tend to unify and arouse the poor and bring sympathy and support from other elements of the community that might otherwise remain uninvolved.

As might be expected, Alinsky engenders passionate opposition. He does not behave like a "nice man" who seeks a consensus and operates politely through conventional channels while waiting for the city council, the mayor, the administrators, and the courts to improve the lot of the poor. He goes about stirring folks up, sharpening divisions and hostilities, stimulating and then utilizing "class conflicts" to achieve his ends. He is utterly fearless, possesses a gift for colloquial eloquence, and is caustically critical of the status quo and its defenders. He talks frankly about power politics, the fruitful role of conflict, the necessity to strip away the pious phrases about "community welfare" and "working together" that are often used by status-quo spokesmen to disguise the self-interest that lies beneath.

Alinsky recognizes the dangers associated with his movement. He concedes that "Militancy can become an end of its own and power can be misused and abused. . . ." But he observes that all movements have their dangers, and he hopes his advice and example will minimize the dangers inherent in this one. Others agree that extraordinary measures initially may be necessary to persuade City Hall, unethical merchants, and slumlords that the poor mean business and mean to win as respectful attention for their grievances as the more well-to-do have always received. But they stress the importance of working through channels wherever possible, and of punitive action at the polls when officials are resistant. Activists, they warn, should be sure of the facts and the law before mounting any campaign against a merchant or property owner. Action that remains responsible while Alinsky is on the scene may fall into the hands of vigilante mentalities when he departs.

Is Alinsky's approach sound and feasible? Probably much more experience is necessary before firm conclusions can be drawn. Some who are sympathetic with his objectives nevertheless doubt that the poor can ever be galvanized into a consistently effective political force. Political apathy and political naiveté have always been more pronounced among the poorer and less educated elements of the population. Can a sense of common purpose, resolution, and responsibility be engendered or long maintained among those whose background so seriously militates against the development of the qualities required for prolonged and effective political action? Will the indigenous leaders of the poor, if they discover their own potentialities, go on to personal successes leading them to different goals and to alienation from their "own people"? Mr. Alinsky is committed to a full-bodied democratic faith—a faith that the poor are fully capable of playing their part in effective self-government. Only time will tell whether this remarkable man is more optimistic than realistic. It is already clear others cannot readily duplicate his skills. Intensive efforts by the OEO to arouse interest in elections at which the poor could choose persons to represent them on antipoverty boards were dismal failures; participation was negligible. Thus while surveys, hearings, and the appointment of some poor persons to advisory councils may be most useful in illuminating attitudes and priorities held by the poor, local efforts to eliminate poverty may have to rest primarily in the hands of those within the existing power structure. If there were a dozen Saul Alinskys, things might be quite different. But one man can do only so much.

The OEO has responded to its critics by seeking to patch up or reform its organization and procedures where the criticism was believed to be well-founded or politically damaging. It reminded critics that the alternative to utilizing existing local organizations, for all their weaknesses, was to create parallel, overlapping, and mutually hostile agencies. To invite a knockdown, drag-out battle with mayors and their lieutenants throughout the land might well foredoom the entire program to failure. Congress wrote no provision into the law requiring that its administrators be politically naive. Admittedly, reliance on local administration meant that criticism of local corruption and bumbling would ricochet into OEO headquarters. But this was an inevitable hazard—and preferable to the even greater hazards of nationalizing an enterprise of this nature.

Of those fundamentally dubious of the program on other grounds, OEO people asked, "Should we avert our eyes from the poor, consign them to relief rolls, and let them perpetuate the poverty cycle among their children and their children's children, or should we do all in our power to rectify the conditions that produce poverty?" Because the question can only lead to one answer, most of the continued controversy over the program will doubtless revolve about "How can we do it better?" rather than "Should we do it at all?"

Scandals, inefficiency, blunders, and stupidity are bound to appear and recur in a program of this magnitude, dealing with problems rooted in centuries of neglect. Some enterprises will presumably work well and be enlarged; others will be modified, cut back, or eliminated as evaluations of effectiveness proceed. The program's frankly experimental character will, hopefully, lead to a continuous process of reformulating and improving the concepts and techniques associated with it. It may be many years before anything approaching optimum success is reached. But it does appear that the nation has begun a journey from which there can be no turning back.

Because the federal antipoverty programs directly affected only an estimated 10 percent of the poor in 1966, some writers believe a more efficient, far-reaching, and decisive effort should be made to terminate poverty in prosperous America. The most rapid way to do so would be to adopt some variation of the Speenhamland system—such as Milton Friedman's proposed Negative Income Tax.[12] (See also p. 202.) Under this system, the nation would

[12] *Capitalism and Freedom,* Chicago, University of Chicago Press, 1962, pp. 191–195.

guarantee every family an income of $3,000. Each family, regardless of its earnings, would fill out an income tax form, and those whose income fell below the "poverty line" of $3,000 would be reimbursed by the national government for the difference between the family's actual earnings and $3,000. Under Mr. Friedman's proposal, the Negative Income Tax would replace the rather bewildering array of welfare and social insurance programs now in existence, thereby wiping out poverty virtually overnight.

A Negative Income Tax would have many alleged advantages. From an administrative viewpoint, it would represent the quintessence of simplicity—the multitudinous record-keeping and costly means-test investigations could be largely discarded. In this age of electronic record-keeping, the number of civil servants necessary to administer the system would be minimal—far below the number needed to maintain the present system. Social workers, who now spend an estimated two thirds of their time establishing the fiscal eligibility of welfare clients and periodically reviewing the relevant facts, would be freed from this oppressive burden. Instead, they could apply their professional skills to the rehabilitation of poor families—helping them with problems of health, family disorganization, budgeting, birth control, job training and the identification of employment opportunities, planning the best use of family resources, and so forth. Finally, the freedom of the poor would be enhanced, because they would be able to use their income as they saw fit, instead of having their income partially provided by the state in the form of food stamps, clothing, or other "in kind" goods. As for the costs involved, these would largely be offset by the savings realized through the elimination of existing welfare programs. To the degree that costs might exceed current expenditures, this would be the price to be paid for insuring a minimum standard of living for all of our people.

The stark simplicity of the Negative Income Tax appeals to some people. So does the argument that this benefit would remove a major inequity in the current system: the more well-to-do are now able to enjoy substantial income tax savings through deductions permitted for dividend receipts, charitable contributions, and interest payments on home mortgages, while the poor are unable to take advantage of these and other forms of negative benefit.

But the plan has drawbacks, also, including some rather formidable ones. For one thing, income tax statements reflect earnings but not assets. Under-reporting of income might also be common. More important, our current welfare state system is planned to maximize work incentives by insuring that need really does exist where outright charity is involved, by contributory social insurance, by requiring beneficiaries to work (where possible), and by making work more financially rewarding than idleness. But the Negative Income Tax would often sap the willingness to work whenever employment promised to yield an annual income under or only modestly above $3,000. The deeply held conviction that a man should earn his bread by the sweat of his brow has not lost its force in America. The nation is willing to make exceptions for involuntary idleness, for income assistance for the aged, the disabled, and for children, but it appears in no mood to accept a plan that might prove irresistibly tempting to those lacking pride or ambition.

Because of the probability that the Negative Income Tax in the form advanced here would induce intolerable idleness, its costs would also go well above the $11 billion some proponents estimated would be necessary (in 1965) to elevate 33 million persons out of the statistical ranks of poverty. The national costs of work not done and of income taxes not paid on such work, plus the probability that some families with marital difficulties might find it profitable to separate—all of these would raise costs far above the initially proposed figure. If automation should (contrary to most current indications) lead to massive and irremediable unemployment, a system like this might have to be tried, but Americans seem certain to reject it in the absence of a demonstrated catastrophe of this nature.

In an effort to meet these objections, Michael D. Reagan has recommended that we guarantee only an income of $1,500 per year and offer supplements above that level on a declining basis in order to minimize the disinclination to work.[13] If an ingenious

[13] "Washington Should Pay Taxes to the Poor," *The New York Times Magazine*, February 20, 1966. Also see Eveline Burns, "Where Welfare Falls Short," *The Public Interest*, Fall, 1965, and James Tobin, "The Case for an Income Guarantee," *The Public Interest*, Summer, 1966.

system could be devised for stiumulating work incentives while insuring a minimum income level, the plan would doubtless receive serious attention in the future. Most, however, would prefer to improve and enlarge our current programs for helping all able-bodied persons obtain the education, the vocational training, and the job opportunities they need rather than focus attention on massive, generalized cash grants. The latter would doubtless be the simplest and fastest way to obliterate poverty, but the dollar costs and the human costs seem prohibitive.

(Professors Richard A. Cloward and Francis F. Piven have suggested that the most rapid way to bring about a guaranteed annual income would be for those interested in the poor to acquaint them with their legal rights and encourage them to demand those rights in full. They say that for every person currently on welfare, another is eligible but doesn't know it or doesn't insist on his rights. They contend that local relief agencies, in their eagerness to cut costs and keep relief rolls at rock-bottom levels, improperly disqualify large numbers of applicants. If a major campaign were launched to get as many people as possible *on* relief, the resulting crisis would cause a breakdown of the current ramshackle system and the establishment of a more rational system![14])

Some critics suggest that we could encourage a willingness to work by modifying those existing laws that discourage people from working. Specifically, they would abolish or amend: (1) laws that impose an earnings ceiling on those qualifying for Social Security payments; (2) laws that penalize those who prefer a poorly paying job to idleness by eliminating or sharply reducing welfare benefits whenever even meager earnings begin; (3) laws that evict persons from public housing projects when their earnings rise beyond a rather low level.[15]

Some economists are convinced that the maintenance of a

[14] "A Strategy to End Poverty," *The Nation,* May 2, 1966.

[15] A. Walinsky, "LBJ's War at Home," *The New Republic,* January 15, 1966. Also see Richard M. Elman, *The Poorhouse State: The American Way of Life on Public Assistance,* New York, Pantheon Books, 1966 (an attack on the present welfare measures as perpetuating poverty by their inadequacy).

rapidly growing economy is the soundest guarantor of the steady reduction of poverty in America. In 1965, for example, 2 million families moved out of the poverty sector because of our dynamic economy. Full employment, however, does not materially reduce poverty among migratory workers, Indians, large families, and families broken by the desertion, divorce, or death of the breadwinner. (The latter group, which includes 7 to 8 million children, usually makes less than half as much money as intact families.) To reduce poverty most rapidly among these groups, it has been proposed to liberalize and expand the existing system of social insurance. Higher Social Security payments could bring millions of aged persons above the poverty level. Improvements in unemployment compensation levels and in coverage could modestly reduce the number of poor. So could raising the minimum wage level and including most of the 20 percent of American workers excluded from its coverage. Amending the Social Security Act to provide payments for temporary disability (payments for permanent disability are already made under the act) would shrink the dimensions of poverty. A system of family allowances, such as those in Canada and many other countries, would make significant inroads into poverty. (Experience in Canada, France, and Sweden does not support the fear that family allowances raise the birth rate.) Social Security payments to the millions of "social orphans"—children living with only one parent or no parents—who are currently excluded from ADC benefits could diminish the poverty ranks. New Zealand and Australia already follow this practice.[16]

A final—although most unlikely—reform could make substantial reductions in poverty statistics. Leon Keyserling points out that the regressive character of our tax system seriously disadvantages low-income groups. He says that in 1960 those with incomes under $2,000 paid 38 percent of their income in federal, state, and local taxes; those earning from $2,000 to $5,000 paid from 38 to 41 percent; those earning from $7,500 to $10,000 paid 22.3 percent; those earning over $10,000 paid 31.6 percent.

[16] A. L. Schorr, "Program for the Social Orphans," *The New York Times Magazine*, March 13, 1966.

Keyserling adds that the tax cuts of 1964 only tended to worsen the picture.[17]

Eliminating federal tax loopholes for the well-to-do and drastically altering the sales tax-excise tax basis of state taxation systems could permit low-income families to spend considerably more on their family needs. Such a reform, however, will not take place tomorrow morning before breakfast. As Khrushchev once said about another matter, *that* will happen when shrimp learn to whistle!

Appalachia: Fair Deal or Misdeal?

Appalachia covers parts of 11 states and is inhabited by some 16 million people. Income, education, and employment are well below the national average throughout this region. Harry Caudill, whose *Night Comes to the Cumberlands*[18] dramatically brought national attention to the plight of this area, offered the following observations in a notable article in the *Atlantic*, "Misdeal in Appalachia."[19] "The bleak hillsides, the gray mining camps, the littered roadsides and the tattered, dispirited people have haunted millions. . . ." He speaks of the "incredible squalor of the typical mining community," notes that "the creeks and rivers are reeking sewers." Five hundred huge "culm heaps . . . mountains of mining wastes and low-grade coal—containing millions of tons of fuel, are forever burning. Their acrid fumes cloak countless valleys. Simultaneously, billions of gallons of sulfuric acid water drain daily from unsealed mines and open coal auger holes. These nauseous contaminants must be restrained if Appalachia is to shed its grim reputation."

Mr. Caudill's eloquent portrayal in his book of the sickness of the area helped bring about federal action to deal with the problem. In 1964, Congress appropriated a billion dollars, to be spent over a five-year period, to help rejuvenate the area. Over three fourths of the money was to be spent on highways. The plan was

[17] "Taxes from Whom, for What?" *The New Republic*, April 23, 1966.
[18] Boston, Little, Brown, 1963.
[19] *The Atlantic Monthly*, June, 1965. Copyright © 1965 by The Atlantic Monthly Company, Boston, Mass. 02116. Reprinted with permission.

to link core cities with one another, and with other areas beyond Appalachia, in an effort to make them a more attractive investment opportunity for business and industry. A special effort was to be made to upgrade about 50 counties that appear to have the greatest industrial promise. The balance of the money was to be spent on hospital construction and maintenance, vocational schools, the development of timber resources, the reclamation of strip-mined land, sewage treatment plants, and for general administration. The hope of Congress and the administration was that sufficient industry could be drawn into the area to create "growth centers" that, in turn, would attract the inhabitants of the hills and hollows into these centers to find a better life.[20]

Although Mr. Caudill could take a larger measure of credit for a major act of Congress than all but a few individuals can ever hope to take, its provisions were a bitter disappointment to him. In his *Atlantic* article he called the Appalachian Regional Development Act "a grim hoax." The billion dollars are "little more than a drop of aid in a bucket of need." Congress was sold "a bill of shoddy goods."

Several aspects of the act particularly troubled him. He contended that the root causes of the area's poverty are the absentee ownership of its resources and corporation irresponsibility in the economic raping of the region. "Absenteeism and anonymity curtain the vast domain of giant corporations which own the region's wealth." They own vast holdings of oil, coal, gas, and limestone, they drain the wealth from the area, and they dominate the local governments that meekly acquiesce in scandalously lenient tax policies. The wealth, he said, is as much under "foreign" ownership as is much of the wealth of Central America. Unless there is a basic alteration in the political structure of the area, unless control can be wrested from the despoilers, he saw little hope for the region. The end result of the highways may well be to facilitate the economic ravishing of the region. As for the "growth centers," he believed that "the accentuation of a spotty prosperity will make the rich wealthier still without al-

[20] Jerald Ter Horst, "No More Pork Barrel: The Appalachia Approach," *The Reporter*, March 11, 1965.

leviating the misery of the poor." The cycle of poor people, poor schools, poor job training, poor pay, and more poor people will be unbroken.

As an alternative, Mr. Caudill proposed a TVA-like project for the area, to exploit its vast hydroelectric potential (now specifically forbidden by the Appalachian act). Abundant and cheap energy developed by federal dams would attract industry, reduce floods, produce fertilizer, and provide funds for the rehabilitation of the region. A modest royalty per kilowatt would finance a major effort to upgrade the educational performance of Appalachia, which Caudill regards as its foremost need.

In addition, he recommended the creation at strategic locations of new towns that would "absorb much of the present dwindling population and would bring new talent into the region." He concluded with the warning that unless we become far more aroused about the fate of the area, Appalachia "can go back to sleep—the sodden sleep of the impoverished, the embittered, and the hopeless."[21]

It will be fascinating to observe, in the years to come, whether the government program proves to be soundly conceived or whether Mr. Caudill's pessimism is borne out. Should the latter be vindicated, Congress will doubtless reconsider its current plans.

The War on Poverty: Some General Notes

If the nation chose to do so, it could wage the war on poverty on a number of other fronts. Inequality before the law is an old, old story for the poor. The police are more likely to arrest the poor as criminal suspects; dragnets are carried out in humble rather than suburban districts. The poor are treated less deferen-

[21] Also see Reese Cleghorn, "Appalachia: Poverty, Beauty and Poverty," *The New York Times Magazine*, April 25, 1965. In "Paradise Is Stripped," *The New York Times Magazine*, March 13, 1966, Mr. Caudill recommended that strip mining be permitted only "where terrain and weather permit complete reclamation." The mining companies should be responsible for this reclamation, but Washington should undo the neglect of the past by restoring to health 1.75 million acres destroyed or severely damaged by strip mining (pp. 84–86).

tially by the police and the courts after they are apprehended than is the man in the gray flannel suit. The poor cannot pay bail and often must spend weeks or months in jail awaiting trial, whereas the more prosperous are not only free on bail, but are in a more advantageous position to prepare their defense.

The well-to-do can often hush up cases involving the delinquency of their children or persuade the judge to release the offender on promise of providing psychiatric care or the discipline of a military school. Middle- or upper-class defendants can afford to obtain the more expensive—that is, the more capable—lawyers. If they are convicted of a capital offense, the affluent, as former Warden Lewis E. Lawes of Sing Sing once noted, go to an asylum, while the poor go to the chair. The choice between 30 days in jail and a $100 fine is an easy one for the prosperous, but the destitute go off to jail. Whether a convict is released on probation often depends on the availability of a job—which is harder for the poor and unskilled to locate.

The poor pay higher interest rates on borrowed money, because they more frequently do business with small loan agencies. They are gypped more often by merchants taking advantage of their ignorance of the law. Typically, their children attend inferior schools (the poorer neighborhoods seldom attract the superior teachers). Welfare clients, ignorant of their rights under the law, are sometimes deprived of those rights without the procedural protections implicit in due process of law. Finally, the poor are more heavily represented in the armed forces and therefore in the casualty rolls, because they are less likely to be in college and thus be eligible for educational deferment. For example, while only 11 percent of the population is Negro, 22 percent of the armed forces (in 1966) was Negro.

Some of the inequalities endured by the poor can never be fully rectified. Others will doubtless be the object of fruitful public and private attention during the years ahead.

CHAPTER

◂ 8 ▸

A BALANCED ECONOMY IN A CHANGING WORLD

No government responsibility has had higher priority since the 1920s than providing jobs for those willing to work. Few misfortunes have more searing psychological effects than prolonged involuntary idleness. Especially for the male, inability to earn a paycheck eventually brings a sense of acute frustration, a loss of self-respect and self-confidence, and either a growing hostility toward the society that tolerates the intolerable or a turn inward toward apathy and a kind of dull hopelessness. The wounds may be so deep as never to fully heal. The growth of Nazism, fascism, and communism in the 1920s and 1930s eloquently reminds us of the political dangers posed by prolonged and extensive unemployment.

The nation's affirmative stake in full employment and a high rate of economic growth is also immense; the beneficent effects of a healthy economy are vast and far-reaching. In addition to averting psychic tragedies, full employment confers a lavish cornucopia of economic benefits. Economist Leon Keyserling estimates the nation lost $590 billion of potential output from 1953 to 1964 because of underutilization of manpower and equipment.[1] Although unemployment figures fluctuated during the late 1950s and early 1960s from 5 to 7 percent, a good deal of "hidden unemployment" was also present. The unemployed officially include only the jobless who are actively seeking work, but when jobs are scarce many women, aged persons, and teenagers abandon the search as futile.

Although no knowledgeable person would want to single out a given factor as the major cause of juvenile delinquency, joblessness among teenagers is undoubtedly significant. Jobs also are important to many over the age of 60. Because work contributes increased self-respect, a sense of usefulness, and a feeling of being "in the stream of things," it can be as important as the money earned.

Almost all students of agriculture are troubled by the nearly one and a half million farmers who earn less than $2,000 a year. The Department of Agriculture has estimated that perhaps one third of these, given sufficient technical help and credit, could attain a satisfactory livelihood on the farm, but almost a million "underemployed" farmers ought to shift over to off-farm labor. The quickest way to draw them into more profitable and socially useful labor is to achieve or maintain a high employment economy.

A vigorous economy also diminishes employee opposition to labor-saving machinery and weakens worker attachment to featherbedding practices.

Industry produces more efficiently at near capacity levels than at the 80 to 85 percent maintained in the late 1950s. Because many costs are relatively stable (wages and salaries of the managerial and clerical work force, maintenance costs, property taxes, depreciation, etc.), whatever the level of output, adding the nec-

[1] "The Great Society," *The New Republic*, June 12, 1965.

essary labor to bring about the full utilization of existing productive machinery reduces per-unit production costs.

Corporation earnings rise rapidly during good times, yielding the profits necessary for investment in new or improved plants and equipment. A full employment economy mitigates our persistent balance of payments problem, because the American economy becomes an attractive investment opportunity for American capital that might otherwise flow abroad—there to become a potential demand on our limited gold reserves. A full employment economy is a high importing economy. The more we buy abroad, the larger the benefits accruing to the underdeveloped countries that sell us raw materials. Dollars obtained through sales to American importers provide the foreign exchange these countries desperately need and are just as helpful as dollars obtained through foreign aid. An active economy facilitates government retraining programs, because retrainees are more easily recruited and take a keener interest in their work if jobs are clearly in sight. More important, business itself undertakes the training of unskilled workers when economic conditions are buoyant, thus relieving the government of a responsibility it can rarely perform as well as private enterprise. (This was dramatically demonstrated in 1965–1966, when corporations began scouring the nation for surplus labor and training the unskilled more rapidly than had once been thought possible.)

Edwin L. Dale, Jr., has commented that a 1 percent increase in our gross national product (the value of all goods and services produced) solves more problems than all the retraining programs, poverty programs, and distressed area programs put together[2] It also contributes to the reduction of abuses in welfare programs, because fewer persons remain on relief rolls. Full employment is of particular importance to the Negro. Negro unemployment rates for years have been twice as high as for whites, while teenage Negro joblessness rates triple that of white youngsters. The unskilled and semiskilled generally have the greatest difficulty obtaining employment, and Negroes fall disproportionately within this category.

[2] "The Big Gun on Poverty," *The New Republic,* August 7, 1965, p. 14.

Finally, full employment adds about $6 to $7 billion per year to federal revenues, income badly needed to finance federal programs spawned by our rapidly changing society. New programs can be financed without new taxes, old ones enlarged where necessary, and the $13 billion interest on the national debt can be more easily borne. State and local revenues also annually rise by billions when the economy functions well. Finally, America demonstrates to doubting nations that a free people and a relatively free economy, combined with intelligent governmental direction, can meet the economic challenges of our time. No wonder Gunnar Myrdal said, before the boom of the mid-1960s got underway, "I am convinced the world's greatest problem is how the hell to get America out of economic stagnation."[3] (The American economy growth rate was badly out-distanced by Western European countries in the late 1950s and early 1960s.)

A few basic economic facts should perhaps be explained at the outset. National income, production, and employment are closely related to the total volume of demand (or spending) in a nation. If there is enough public and private demand for goods and services, employers will hire idle labor. But if there is inadequate demand, the sale of goods and services will not be large enough to justify hiring all the men and women who want jobs.

Economists often divide spending into four categories: domestic consumer spending; business investment; government spending; and foreign purchases. The total spending for finished goods and services is referred to as aggregate demand, which in turn equals the gross national product (GNP).

Whenever less than full employment exists, any significant decline in over-all spending normally leads to greater unemployment. Thus, if business invests less because of uncertainty about future business prospects, or consumers spend less because of anticipated hard times, or if government reduces its spending or foreign purchases shrink, a decline in economic activity and, hence, of employment ordinarily follows unless one of the other spending components increases its spending comparably. Furthermore, the decline tends to be of an accelerating or "snowballing"

[3] "T.R.B.," *The New Republic,* June 18, 1962, p. 2.

character. For example, if the auto industry cuts back investment by 10 percent, the steel industry's sales will fall. It will be obliged to lay off men or institute a shorter working week, thereby reducing the purchasing power of steel workers. Steel workers will buy fewer goods from the retailers, who in turn will buy less from wholesalers. The latter group will then be obliged either to lay off workers or reduce their hours, while their reduced profits will shrink their spending capacity and discourage new investment. Wholesalers buy less from the manufacturers, who buy less from raw materials producers, with similar effects on hours, employment, and profits. The downward spiral picks up momentum and widens unless there are offsetting factors at work in the economy—which there often (but not always) are.

On the other hand, if one or more of the spending components increases spending, which is not canceled out by a decline in the spending of another component, an upward cycle is set in motion involving precisely the opposite economic characteristics. Just as the downward spiral can lead to recession and eventually depression, the upward cycle can also lead to full employment and, in some instances, to inflation. (Actually, total spending must normally increase, merely to maintain a given percentage of employment, because the population steadily rises and per-man-hour output increases several percent a year.)

The Road That Led to Keynes

Depressions were not always looked on as malignant developments to be exorcised by a concerned government. Rather, they were regarded by many students as inevitable and, on balance, beneficent. Inevitable, because there were bound to be occasions when businessmen would overinvest in certain areas or otherwise use poor judgment in the planning and conduct of their affairs. These accumulated business errors should reap their natural reward, painful though this might be. In a world marked by the survival of the fittest, the inefficient and ill-adapted must perish. The purging of the economy brought about by recurrent economic crises might seem harsh to the victims, but natural law insured that society as a whole would gain.

The attitude of many businessmen and bankers was well put by Secretary of the Treasury Andrew Mellon at the outset of the Great Depression. Mellon advised, "Liquidate labor, liquidate stocks, liquidate farms, liquidate real estate. . . . It will purge the rottenness out of the system. High costs of living will come down. People will work harder, live more moral lives. Values will be adjusted and enterprising people will pick up the wrecks from less competent people."[4] A view roughly similar to this also prevailed in much of Europe before 1929.

A brief review of the causes of the Great Depression and of subsequent recessions may help provide a background against which the reader can better understand the economic phenomena involved in a full-employment policy.

The roots of the Great Depression of 1929 to 1942 were not well understood during that period, nor is there unanimous agreement in identifying them today. Herbert Hoover, supported by many economists, thought America was sucked into economic disaster as the consequence of a world-wide depression. Other factors are usually cited today. Whether a germinal or merely a precipitating factor, residential construction had fallen off by about one third in the late 1920s, setting in motion important downward economic forces. The durable goods industry had also ceased growing before the recognized onset of the Depression, partly because automobile production leveled off after a rather steep climb. Some writers believe the growing concentration of income in the hands of upper-income-bracket people and of large corporations made it increasingly difficult for consumers to buy the necessary quantity of goods. Others discount this factor. There is quite general agreement, on the other hand, that the Federal Reserve Board followed an ill-advised "easy money" policy which, combined with its lack of control over the buying of stocks on margin, led to a wild speculative stock-buying spree that pushed upward the price of many major stocks from 300 to 400 percent from 1928 to 1929. When the stock market balloon burst, business confidence collapsed also. Net investment de-

[4] Carl N. Degler, "The Ordeal of Herbert Hoover," *The Yale Review*, Summer, 1963, pp. 565–566.

celerated to the point of zero. Before long more than 12 million Americans were unemployed, farms were being foreclosed at the rate of over 100,000 a year, private-home foreclosures rose to alarming levels, businesses went broke in droves, and the ultimate disaster—the near collapse of the banking system—added the final touches to the worst economic catastrophe in modern times.

President Hoover did not fully share Mr. Mellon's philosophy, but he was deeply committed to the principle of the balanced budget, and he resolutely opposed using federal funds for direct unemployment relief. He repeatedly sought to inspire confidence in the resilience and "snap-back" qualities of the American economy, but he also took a number of concrete steps to help overcome the Depression. He urged bank reforms to prevent excessive funds from being diverted to stock market speculation. He prompted an $800 million public works program that put roughly one million men to work. He gave assistance to drought-stricken farmers. He helped establish the Reconstruction Finance Corporation to lend money to near-bankrupt businesses and banks. And, with great reluctance, he finally agreed to permit the *lending* of federal funds to states whose financial resources were exhausted. Further than this Mr. Hoover would not go, except to urge employers not to cut wages and encourage states and localities to institute major public works programs.[5]

In 1964, a major tax cut received the support of a majority of Congress as a means of stimulating the economy, but in 1932, President Hoover asked and received support for a bill to *raise* taxes as a means of balancing the budget. During his 1932 campaign, Franklin D. Roosevelt repeatedly criticized both Mr. Hoover's unbalanced budget and his 50 percent increase in spending since 1927, pledging to cut the budget 25 percent if he were elected!

Although Roosevelt later reversed himself and accepted the necessity of an unbalanced budget and the desirability of "pump-priming" measures to get the economy back on its feet, deficit spending was confined to a rather modest level, in terms of most

[5] *Ibid.*, pp. 566–573.

modern economic thought. Unemployment shrank to less than 8.5 million and business and agriculture made a partial recovery, but the Depression remained severe until after Pearl Harbor. Mr. Roosevelt's critics attributed the failure of full recovery to a lack of business confidence growing out of the abandonment of the gold standard, the "harassment" of businessmen by an administration allegedly antipathetic to private enterprise, and the "drastic" social reforms of the New Deal period that created grave doubts about the future of constitutional government and capitalism in the United States. Others derided these charges, insisting the Depression persisted because deficit financing was tried on altogether too small a scale. Lack of confidence in the administration was of small consequence, they said. The real problem was lack of confidence in the ability of the consumer to buy the businessman's goods.

Business of course flourished during World War II, but fears of a postwar depression were widespread. Economic and popular journals teemed with depression analyses and recommendations for postwar economic programs. Immediately after the war, when apprehensions of renewed economic disaster were at their height, Congress vigorously debated and finally passed the Employment Act of 1946. This act declared

> It is the continuing policy and responsibility of the Federal Government to use all practicable means consistent with its needs and obligations and other essential considerations of national policy, with the assistance and cooperation of industry, agriculture, labor, and State and local governments, to coordinate and utilize all its plans, functions, and resources for the purpose of creating and maintaining, in a manner calculated to foster and promote free competitive enterprise and the general welfare, conditions under which there will be afforded useful employment, for those able, willing, and seeking to work, and to promote maximum employment, production, and purchasing power.

The Churchillian ring is absent, but the nation was finally committed to maintaining full employment and maximum production by the energetic use of federal initiative and planning.

America has experienced four postwar recessions—in 1948 to 1949, 1953 to 1954, 1957 to 1958, and 1960 to 1961. (A recession is currently defined as a downward trend in production and an upward trend in unemployment for more than six months.) Rather than describe the specific economic configurations involved in each recession, a few generalizations will be made.

Recessions were touched off by combinations of the following: a decline in residential construction; a "consumer pause" during which, for a variety of reasons, consumers reduced their normal volume of purchases while taking stock of economic developments; a major cut in defense spending; a decline in exports; excessive and premature tightening of credit by the Federal Reserve Board leading to unduly reduced borrowing and spending; a decline in private investment (following a period of overinvestment in relation to short-run demand); and excessive inventory accumulations (perhaps occasioned by rising prices or by unwarranted optimism about future sales) that reached a point at which buying temporarily fell off. Each of these (in the absence of counterbalancing factors) has helped trigger downward economic spirals.

The nation recovered from these recessions partly because of natural economic developments (such as a resumption of inventory purchases or of normal consumer spending) and partly through such governmental initiatives as tax cuts (1954 and 1964) the liberalization of housing credit, an increase in defense spending, public works, and other federal spending. Partial credit for the brevity and moderate character of the downturns is also given to the "built-in stabilizers." Unemployment compensation enables jobless workers to continue receiving about one third of their former incomes. Farm price supports prevent rapid declines in farm income that might have a dragging effect on the economy. Social Security checks help maintain income for the aged. The sheer magnitude of federal grant-in-aid programs, payments to veterans, defense spending, highway spending, and so forth, also reduces the shocks to the economy that grow out of the business cycle. Finally, regulations of the stock market tend to prevent disasters like 1929.[6]

A persistent controversy exists over the appropriate remedies

[6] Edwin L. Dale, Jr., "We Are Depression (But Not Recession) Proof," *The New York Times Magazine*, April 4, 1965.

for recessions. Where federal action is required, should taxes be cut? Or should federal spending be hiked for such items as education, hospitals, roads, urban renewal, urban transportation, and conservation? If taxes are cut, should they primarily benefit business and the more affluent groups in order to provide incentive and investment funds needed to bolster the economy? Or should the tax cuts be concentrated mainly in the middle- and lower-income groups because they provide the bulk of purchasing power needed to take the goods off the market? Or should increases in public spending be accompanied by tax cuts? If so, in what proportions? The controversial possibilities are infinite.

Since the mid-1930s, the Democratic party has tended to favor increased governmental spending as the antidote to recessions and unemployment. The Republicans, on the other hand, have placed greater emphasis on governmental economies and on measures to directly stimulate business. When President Kennedy sought to energize the economy by a whopping $11 billion tax cut—with substantial reductions for taxpayers in all brackets—this represented a sharp break with traditional party proposals and introduced considerable confusion into the popular images of the two political parties.

The administration's position rested on both political and economic premises. Whether or not increased governmental spending was a desirable stimulus, Mr. Kennedy concluded that Congress would not go along with this option. Only a tax cut was politically feasible. Furthermore, the administration accepted the contention of some economists that the existing tax take rose so rapidly during recession recovery periods (particularly from corporations) that the budget moved prematurely into a surplus position. When a budget surplus appeared, the federal government found itself willy-nilly withdrawing money from circulation rather than depositing it. Reducing the money flow tended to put a damper on the expanding economy, leading to a series of partial recoveries and preventing the kind of economic "take-off" that could fully mobilize the economy's potential.[7] If taxes could be

[7] Walter Heller, "Tax Reduction," *Vital Speeches,* July 1, 1963, p. 262. Also see Joseph Kraft, "Economics of the New Frontier," *The New Republic,* October 20, 1962, p. 12; Walter Heller, "Fear Threatens Our Prosperity," *The Saturday Evening Post,* November 9, 1963.

reduced, then, the budget would not be brought into balance until more complete recession recoveries were achieved. At that point, balancing the budget would be desirable to prevent inflation.

The administration tax cut was offered in the teeth of an $8 to $9 billion dollar federal deficit, thus prompting fears that red ink would reach startling dimensions. The administration hoped, however, that the increased spending that would accompany the tax cut would sufficiently accelerate purchasing, investment, profits, and employment so that the expanding national income would ultimately yield as much tax revenue as before, thus balancing the budget on a higher economic plane. Because unbalanced budgets at a higher tax level were becoming almost commonplace (topped by a $12.6 billion deficit under Mr. Eisenhower in 1958), why not test the judgment of many economists who believed a tax cut was the remedy for the economy's "tired blood"? Japan and various Western European nations had been acting on the "demand" theory for years, and they had achieved both a much higher rate of economic growth and a lower rate of unemployment than the United States.

The American economic performance, following a tax cut in 1964 that totaled $11.5 billion during a three-year period, brilliantly vindicated President Kennedy because it helped produce the most prolonged and lusty period of economic growth in peacetime United States history. The GNP shot up from $620 billion in 1964 to well over $700 billion in 1966. Unemployment declined from nearly 7 percent to less than 4 percent, and federal revenues rose by about $7 billion a year. For all practical purposes the success of the experiment demolished the long-held theory that it was "fiscally irresponsible" to seek to stimulate the economy by "deficit spending." Previously a highly verbal school of thought contended that deficit spending would only swell the national debt, raise doubts about national solvency, threaten inflation, and jeopardize business confidence in the government.

The tax cut also represented a smashing victory for the theories of John Maynard Keynes. Lord Keynes, a famous British economist and one of the notable figures of the twentieth century, first provided the scholarly rationale for using government tax and spending policies to balance an economy at high employment levels. His views, set forth in 1936 in *General Theory of Employment, Interest and Money,* had won wide endorsement from economists long before the United States government was prepared to act on them.

Although the propriety of tax cuts (under certain conditions) is now well established, controversy continues over another proposal of President Kennedy's. In 1961, he recommended that Congress grant him discretionary authority to raise or lower taxes within a range of 5 to 25 percent for limited periods of time. This would enable the administration to adjust tax rates rapidly either to dampen inflation or to provide a further spending stimulus. Congress rejected the request, however, regarding it as an attempted executive intrusion into a cherished congressional prerogative. Nor has Congress been more receptive to the general idea during the Johnson administration.

The Ever-Pregnant Threat: Inflation

Every modern government chronically worries about unemployment or inflation (and sometimes about both at the same time!). Insufficient spending means unemployment. Too much spending means inflation. And because the economy is dynamic, restless, ever adapting to new technologies, changing consumer tastes, developing governmental programs, and shifting patterns of business investment, adjusting total spending to achieve the right balance from month to month is never quite possible in a relatively free economy. Even if economic forecasting were a more exact science, the economists would run into a problem of values. Should we, as Edwin L. Dale, Jr., suggests, "go for broke," give the economy its head and encourage it to sop up unemployment to a 2 percent level, even at the risk of a temporary 3 to 4 percent inflation?[8] Mr. Dale says some European countries have achieved true full employment by running such risks. His faith in our economy's productivity convinces him that inflation, if it should reach the projected level, could then be brought

[8] "The Case Against a Tax Increase," *The New Republic,* April 2, 1966.

under control (the Vietnamese war, temporarily at least, will deny Dale's theory a fair trial). Or should we tolerate a modest amount of unemployment (perhaps 4 percent) as the necessary price for a more stable dollar? Liberals and conservatives generally divide on this issue, with the latter willing to trade a higher degree of unemployment for price stability than liberals are willing to accept.

Persistent and major federal deficits since 1958 (1960 excepted) have pretty conclusively demonstrated that federal deficit spending is not inflationary if prudently introduced into an economy operating with considerable slack. In these cases, federal moneys obtained by borrowing idle funds from banks or private investors tend to bring idle men and machines into production, leading to new goods and services to match the borrowed funds. Because inflation occurs, in the classic sense, only when money is injected into the economy faster than new goods and services are produced, deficit spending may be inflationary only if it takes place when the economy is already functioning at close to full capacity. Under these circumstances, increased spending is unable to generate new goods and services; instead, it only serves to bid up prices. (In recent decades, wage increases in excess of worker productivity, or price increases introduced by business for a variety of reasons unrelated to the money supply, may also have contributed to inflation.)

Those who stress the dangers of inflation warn that even a 2 percent annual rise in the cost of living over 25 years can cut the purchasing power of those on fixed incomes by half. They add that inflation discourages savings and, hence, reduces the prospects for sustained economic growth. Inventory speculation (prompted by the prospect of rising costs), and the subsequent slow-down in purchases during the liquidation of those inventories, can lead to recession. Or, in the government's efforts to check inflation, it may institute stringent credit controls that over-control, thus precipitating a recession. Inflation can gravely damage our precarious "balance of payments," because rising prices handicap exporters, reduce overseas sales, and leave more dollars in foreign hands—dollars that can be converted into demands on our shrinking gold reserves. Finally, prolonged "creeping inflation" can degenerate into "galloping inflation," if people eventually seek economic security through accumulating goods rather than saving money.

Although liberals and conservatives make different assessments of the dangers of moderate inflation, both are prepared to take corrective action if prices start rising by more than 2 percent a year. Four major steps can be taken, singly or in combination. The Federal Reserve Board can pinch off part of the money supply by its control of the lending resources available to the nation's commercial banks. By requiring member banks to carry greater reserves, or by raising its rediscount rate, or by selling government bonds on the open market, the Board can reduce the amount of money that banks can lend and, therefore, the amount that borrowers can spend.

While the Board's control over credit is one of our most valuable checks against inflation, this device has its limitations and disadvantages. The Federal Reserve Board has no control over the investment of internal savings by business enterprise, and big business in particular finances most of its expansion through this means. Nor can the Board control the lending power of insurance companies, savings and loan associations, pension fund custodians, and retail concerns (that is, installment buying). Thus, a substantial part of the nation's credit machinery lies beyond its reach. Its credit pinch bears down unevenly, also, because small business feels the restraints far more severely than big business.

A second method for checking inflation could be to reduce federal spending. This would also diminish inflationary pressures on goods and services, if the Congress had the wisdom and will to do the job. As indicated previously, however, Congress has never demonstrated any notable talents in this area, and realists discount this as an effective means of inflationary control.

A third technique would involve the imposition of higher taxes, without higher federal spending. This, too, would reduce the total amount of spending in the economy. But Congress is always resistant to higher taxes, except when defense emergencies force its hand.

Whether Congress is sufficiently impressed with the triumphs of the "New Economics" to act with dispatch on the not-so-new prescription of higher taxes for a feverish economy, is conjectural. The leopard's spots are very durable—but these *are* changing times. We shall see.

Another method of controlling inflation is the so-called "jawbone" approach: the President seeks to convince labor unions that the public welfare demands restraint in wage requests while seeking to convince major industries that price increases unjustified by cost increases are equally inimical to the nation. Presidents Truman, Eisenhower, Kennedy, and Johnson have all, in one fashion or other, attempted to influence potentially inflationary economic decisions in this manner. In addition to generalized appeals, the President may single out particular industries or wage contracts for concentrated attention. An effort may be made to shame the parties concerned or an appeal to their patriotism may be made. The "jawbone" approach may be supplemented by the actual or threatened diversion of defense contracts from offending companies or by the actual or threatened release upon the market of government-stockpiled materials in an effort to keep prices down.

Presidential intervention in the economy to prevent price rises currently appears to have limited usefulness. For example, pressures cannot effectively be applied to wage contracts (as in construction) that are made on a highly decentralized basis. It cannot be applied successfully to the price of services, or of most consumer goods. Where price increases crop up at a number of points, in amounts ranging from slight to significant, where should presidential pressure be brought to bear and where should it be withheld? If the President spreads himself too thin, he is bound to reduce his effectiveness and increasingly exhibit an embarrassing impotence. If he singles out particular industries as culprits while omitting others, he appears to be acting in an arbitrary and capricious manner. If he cracks down on business, the latter will naturally demand that he crack down on excessive union wage demands. Again the question arises: which contracts should he challenge and which should he ignore? The situation, alas, is never black and white.

Recent administrations have set "guidelines" to discourage unions from seeking wage rises in excess of productivity increases per man-hour. These guidelines have run between 3 and 3.5 percent. The decision to challenge price increases, on the other hand, must be based on an analysis of the total economic factors involved in the industry concerned. Sometimes this analysis has been made hastily, on the basis of inadequate study and consultation. Columnist Joseph Kraft has argued that the government should establish an executive agency with the responsibility to regularize, extend, and deepen consultations between the White House and industry so that the government will act only after ample fact-finding and an exchange of views have taken place.[9]

Perhaps the most the government can hope to do here is focus on certain key industries and unions, seek to restrain flagrant price and wage increases involving them, emphasize its determination to maintain a stable dollar, and possibly prevent the development of an "inflation psychology." When public opinion supports the President and inflationary pressures are moderate, he can have a measure of success. But when basic inflationary forces are strong, the government's efforts at persuasion cannot succeed for long.

Other possible means for controlling inflation include tax schedules that can be adjusted to discourage excessive business investment in new plants and equipment; selective credit controls; selective wage and price controls; and general wage and price controls. Formal, mandatory wage and price controls are a last resort in our economy. Business and labor violently oppose them, except in wartime, and the American people are most reluctant to approve this kind of governmental intervention. At best, such controls lack the flexibility needed, are difficult to enforce, lead to black-market operations, and hamper the adjustments necessary in a dynamic modern economy.

Whenever the economy moves from "low pressure" (marked by considerable unemployment and excess production capacity) to "high pressure" (marked by low levels of unemployment and little excess productive capacity), the dangers of inflation multiply. This seems to be the condition that will most commonly prevail in the years ahead. English economist A. W. Phillips,

[9] "Price and Prejudice," *Washington Post,* January 8, 1966.

studying the correlation between unemployment and inflation in England during the past century, discovered that whenever joblessness fell below 2.5 percent, prices rose.[10] Many economists think roughly the same correlation ("the Phillips effect") may exist in this country and warn against efforts to overstimulate the economy in an effort to reduce unemployment.

It is probable that governmental pressures in the wage and price fields will be increasingly felt in the years ahead, but no one knows what techniques can most effectively and most appropriately represent the public's interest in price stability. Public opinion is highly ambivalent concerning the proper role of government in this area. On the one hand, it tends to hold a President strictly responsible for inflation occurring during his administration. On the other hand, it tends to disapprove strong executive (or congressional) action, feeling that this unduly interferes with essentially private economic decisions in our "free economy." But how private are decisions that materially affect the public interest in stable prices?

The optimists hope that the immensely productive powers of the American economy, combined with the sharpening of international competition, will act as an adequate brake on price rises. The pessimists think we must either use old tools much more resolutely than in the past or fashion new and more feasible ones. And both groups know full well that war spending, because it cannot be nicely adjusted to the needs of a balanced economy, can play hob with all antiinflationary plans. In wartime, federal spending increases dramatically, but this is not matched by an equivalent increase in consumer goods and services. With so much manpower diverted into war production and military service, the civilian labor force cannot grind out consumer goods and services in the quantity needed to counterbalance the increase in total spending.

Congress, of course, is always more willing to raise taxes for financing a war than for controlling peacetime inflation. But even in wartime, Congress is reluctant to raise taxes rapidly

[10] Neil W. Chamberlain, "The Art of Unbalancing the Budget," *The Atlantic Monthly*, January, 1966.

enough and in sufficient volume to adequately check inflation. Nor are Federal Reserve Board credit controls normally equal to the task—even though they are helpful. If hostilities reach a certain scale, therefore, and inflationary pressures intensify, the nation usually has no choice but to consider highly distasteful wage and price controls. As previously indicated, these seldom halt inflation entirely, but they can somewhat bring about greater price stability.

Automation: Can We Ride the Tiger?

Contributing heavily to the uncertainties attending *any* full employment strategy are the unanswered questions concerning automation. Is automation a "curse," as the AFL-CIO president George Meany, proclaimed in 1963, or a blessing that promises untold benefits for mankind?

Automation has been well defined by economist Jack C. Rothwell as applying to the "development and linkage of three different technical processes: (1) the integration of conventionally separate manufacturing processes into continuous production lines; (2) the use of . . . 'feed-back' control devices which, with electronically sensitive 'fingers,' are able to compare the way work is actually being done with the way it is supposed to be done and then make any adjustments needed in the work process; (3) the application of computers which, through programmed instructions, are able to direct the entire production process."[11]

There is no doubt that automation has dramatically reduced the number of employees required to meet certain national needs. It has played a large part in diminishing railroad employment in the last 40 years from 2 million to less than 800,000 workers. Soft-coal mining, which used to employ 700,000 workers, now calls for about 100,000. (One coal machine operator can dig as much coal as 1,000 men working in the pits!) In 1953, 917,000 auto workers produced 7.3 million trucks, cars, and buses, whereas in 1963, 723,000 produced about 8.5 million.

[11] "The Shorter Work Week," *The Nation,* December 7, 1963, pp. 383–384.

Some authorities believe picking machines will largely eliminate the need for migratory farm labor in a few more years. Automatic typewriters, voice-controlled, could conceivably cost 1.5 million stenographers their jobs in the near future (although the personal satisfactions to be derived from flesh-and-blood stenographers may slow down the replacement process). It has been said that technology first revolutionized the farm, then the factory, and that now the office must take its turn. One economist contends that the 100,000 office girls annually displaced by computers "will be a spit in the ocean" compared to the clerks who will be replaced in the 1970s.[12] The number of computers increased from 400 in 1954 to more than 30,000 in 1966, with the demand continuing to increase. Computers are performing a variety of amazing tasks these days: translating Russian documents for the CIA; directing traffic on Sunset Boulevard; paying horse bets; carrying out market and route research for airlines. They are also displacing an increasingly large number of supervisory and managerial personnel. Automated grocery and department stores are said to be on the way. Mail sorting and inventory control is vastly facilitated by computers.

One possible effect of automation that has bred grave fears is its alleged tendency to reduce drastically the number of unskilled or relatively unskilled jobs. Noting that 22 of every 100 Americans have IQs of 89 or below, John Fischer says, "From the beginning of history until fairly recently—say a couple of generations ago—every society in the world had plenty of jobs for low-IQ people. They could herd sheep, pick cotton, dig ditches (even the Erie Canal was made with spades), hoist that bale and tote that load. Indeed, nearly all of the earth's work called for strong backs and weak minds—for drawers of water and hewers of wood. . . . Jobs that demanded real intelligence, on the other hand, were strictly limited. . . ." But with our modern mechanized and specialized society, only about 5 percent of American employment is available for unskilled workers. Have we the ingenuity, Mr. Fischer inquires, and the will to find socially valuable ways to put these

[12] Thomas O'Toole, "White Collar Automation," *The Reporter,* December 5, 1963, p. 27.

people to work, or must they be condemned to a lifetime of subsidized idleness and misery?[13] The Fischer analysis coincided closely with the so-called "structural unemployment" school, which argued that certain fundamental changes were taking place in our economy that bode ill for the unskilled and semiskilled job-seeker. This group of economists believed a long-term trend from a blue-collar to a white-collar economy had been accelerating in recent years, producing the phenomenon of widespread and persistent unemployment in the late 1950s and early 1960s alongside a chronic shortage of highly skilled labor. They drew upon the fact that, up to the early 1960s, the percentage of jobs for white-collar workers had increased twice as rapidly as all jobs since 1950, while professional and technical jobs increased five times as fast.[14] They also noted that per-man-hour output rose only about 2 percent annually from 1909 to 1940, 3 percent after World War II, and nearly 3.5 percent in the mid-1960s, suggesting that automation was accelerating productivity and, hence, replacing labor ever more rapidly.[15] Michael Harrington wrote in 1965 that "For . . . perhaps a third of a generation, the advance of American ingenuity is a catastrophe. Given their lack of skill and training, they are systematically misfitted for the economy which they are entering. Their future holds out chronic unemployment at worst, or at best laboring at tasks that are so menial they are beneath the dignity and education of machines."[16]

With about 3.5 million young persons entering the job market every year, the number of new jobs that needs to be created annually constitutes an imposing figure. How can the economy generate the employment opportunities our rapidly expanding population demands? Eric Hoffer notes that whereas it took $12,000 to create a new job in 1955, it requires $30,000 of in-

[13] "The Stupidity Problem," *Harper's Magazine*, September, 1962, pp. 15–16.

[14] Charles Silberman, "Comeback of the Blue Collar Worker," *Fortune*, February, 1965, p. 210.

[15] Ben Bagdikian, "I'm Out of a Job–I'm All Through," *The Saturday Evening Post*, December 18, 1965, p. 46.

[16] Michael Harrington, *The Accidental Century*, New York, Macmillan, 1965, p. 250.

creased national product to do this in 1965, and it will take $75,000 in 1975. He adds, "Our economy would have to grow at an astronomical rate to absorb the millions of unemployed . . . we shall wake up one day to find 20 million or so unemployed in our midst, and a full-blown crisis on our hands." Mr. Hoffer then goes on to say,

What worries me is the prospect of a skilled and highly competent population living off the fat of the land without a sense of usefulness and worth. There is nothing more explosive than a skilled population condemned to inaction. Such a population is likely to become a hotbed of extremism and intolerance, and be receptive to any proselytizing ideology, however absurd and vicious, which promises vast action. In pre-Hitlerian Germany a population that knew itself admirably equipped for action was rusting away in idleness and gave its allegiance to a Nazi party which offered unlimited opportunities for that action.[17]

But although many writers are pessimistic about the effects of automation on jobs, many prominent economists dissent. Victor Fuchs, for example, speaks for some of them when he declares that the evidence does not confirm the widespread belief that automation is displacing labor more rapidly than have technological advances in the past.[18]

Economist Robert Heilbroner says, "I do question whether dollar for dollar this new factory equipment is any more labor-displacing than 'old-fashioned' equipment such as fork-lift trucks, overhead conveyors, high-speed machinery, and so on. I must confess that I can neither see any reason *a priori* why a dollar's worth of 'automation' equipment should replace any more labor than a dollar's worth of less fancy mechanical equipment. . . ."[19]

The President's Automation Commission put it thus: "It is be-

[17] "Automation Is Here to Liberate Us," *The New York Times Magazine*, October 24, 1965, p. 48. Copyright © 1965 by The New York Times Company. Reprinted by permission.

[18] "Fallacies and Facts About Automation," *The New York Times Magazine*, April 7, 1963, p. 176.

[19] "Men and Machines in Perspective," *The Public Interest*, Fall, 1965, p. 330.

yond our power to know whether the computer, nuclear power, and molecular biology are quantitatively or qualitatively more 'revolutionary' than the telephone, electric power, and bacteriology."[20]

Economist Peter Drucker agrees that between 1.5 and 2 million jobs are destroyed annually, but insists automation is only one of many factors responsible for this. The totals include jobs lost because men die and their businesses fold, jobs lost through government contract cancellation, and jobs lost because normal business competition causes declines in certain products and industries. He then notes that the economy has recently been generating between 2.5 and 3 million new jobs per year. Drucker adds that although banks and insurance companies use more computers than any industry, employment has risen 50 percent in insurance and 100 percent in banking since 1946. He says roughly the same employment trends are in evidence in the air line, trucking, plastics, electronics, and pharmaceutical industries, despite their widespread use of automation.[21]

Charles Silberman argues that the structural theory of unemployment looked plausible only because the economy was limping along from 1957 to 1964, and because shifts in defense production to more missiles and electronic equipment, plus increased spending for outer space, led to an abnormal but somewhat temporary bulge in the demand for highly skilled labor. With this bulge flattening out and the economy shifting into high gear, his optimisim was succinctly expressed in a *Fortune* article, "The Comeback of the Blue Collar Worker."[22]

Mr. Drucker further observed, in 1965, that blue-collar jobs were increasing twice as fast as other jobs, while the percentage of factory production workers in relation to nonproduction workers had remained steady since 1955. From 1964 to 1965, in fact, unskilled jobs increased by 11 percent while all jobs increased by only 2.4 percent. The trend continued in 1965. From 1963 to

[20] Robert Theobald, "Should Men Compete with Machines?" *The Nation*, May 9, 1966, p. 545.

[21] "Automation Is Not the Villain," *The New York Times Magazine*, January 10, 1965.

[22] *Fortune*, February, 1965, p. 212.

1965, moreover, the largest growth in jobs occurred among Negroes, teenagers, and the unskilled, in general. Teen-age employment increased more in 1965 than in the 10 preceding years. Secretary of Labor Willard Wirtz declared unequivocally that "automation creates more jobs than it destroys." Otherwise, he said, we should be having massive unemployment already. Instead, unemployment has dropped from nearly 7 percent in 1961 to less than 4 percent in 1966. Finally, an economist with a remarkable record of prescience, Edwin L. Dale, Jr., flatly predicted in 1964 that "two or three years from now the huzzah over automation and structural unemployment will be over and forgotten. . . ."[23]

So far as the full impact of automation on jobs is concerned, several leading economists doubt that we know very much about it. Heilbroner thinks we are at about the same stage in our effort to interpret the impact of automation that we were in 1935 in seeking to understand how to cope with the business cycle.[24] Robert Solow says we simply do not know what the effect is of automation on jobs. "No one can possibly know," he states, "so no one has the right to speak confidently." Solow goes on to say that "the Great Automation Question . . . is not only unanswerable, it is the wrong question. The important point is that . . . the total volume of employment in the United States today is simply not determined by the rate of technological progress." Instead, it is determined by governmental policies. We can, Solow believes, "have full employment for any plausible rate of technological change within a range that is easily wide enough to cover the American experience."[25]

If Disarmament Should *Break Out . . .*

Could we maintain full employment if disarmament should come? Although the prospects of relatively complete disarmament in the foreseeable future are virtually nil, the possibilities

[23] "The Great Unemployment Fallacy," *The New Republic,* September 5, 1964, p. 10.

[24] Heilbroner, *op. cit.,* p. 28.

[25] "Technology and Unemployment," *The Public Interest,* Fall, 1965, p. 19.

of a substantial reduction in peacetime defense expenditures are rated good by some knowledgeable persons. For example, Gerard Piel, former editor of *Scientific American,* has observed that we now have an atomic and hydrogen stockpile with explosive power equal to that of 10 tons of TNT for every man, woman, and child on earth. There is not much point in continuing to add to this stockpile, he says. The Defense Department apparently agrees, because there is already a tapering-off in the production of atomic explosives, with further reductions scheduled. Mr. Piel adds, "With the miniaturization of violence in the step from A-bombs to H-bombs, from manned aircraft to missiles, expenditure on armaments has begun to yield a diminishing economic stimulus."[26]

If Mr. Piel's assessment is correct (unfortunately there is no assurance that arms developments will not take a new turn calling for as great or greater expenditures), the nation may have to make some important policy adjustments, after the war in Vietnam has ended, to avert an economic slump. Piel declares, "The oscillations of the business cycle since the Korean War can be traced, every one of them, to variation in the rate of government expenditure for arms."[27] Arms spending, he observes, has been playing the economic role that public works played in the first two Roosevelt administrations. But if the need for arms expenditure dwindles, the nation cannot rely indefinitely on the economic stimulus it supplies.[28]

There is no doubt that many Americans fear the economic impact of disarmament, a fear that would intensify were disarmament prospects to brighten. There is widespread doubt that the economy could absorb the amount of goods and services that could be supplied by a labor force devoting itself almost exclusively to civilian purposes. Those who believe an important measure of disarmament is a realistic possibility (and perhaps an imperative necessity!) believe that unless these fears are dispelled the public will not be sufficiently receptive to disarma-

[26] "Can Our Economy Stand Disarmament?" *The Atlantic Monthly,* September, 1962, p. 40.

[27] *Ibid.*

[28] For a supporting view, see Robert Heilbroner, "The Price of Growth," *The Reporter,* January 7, 1960, pp. 31–32.

ment agreements that might be fully justified by changes in the international atmosphere. They are convinced that planning and education must take place in order to provide the fearful with the assurances they seek that disarmament will not create serious economic hardship for defense workers and for others who might be victimized by major defense cutbacks.

In an article for *The New York Times Magazine*, economist Emile Benoit, chairman of a committee of experts that studied the economic impact of disarmament, stated that about one tenth of our peacetime economy was engaged in defense work, as well as about one twelfth of our workers. About 2.5 million worked in defense industries, 3 million in the armed forces, and over 1 million had civilian jobs with the Defense Department and related agencies.[29] (This was before the increases resulting from the war in Vietnam.)

An important aspect of disarmament apprehension, however, grows out of the heavy concentration of defense industries in certain areas. Mr. Benoit declares that from 20 to 30 percent of the employed work in defense industries in five states. But in Seattle, 53 percent of the labor force does defense work, and the figure rises to 72 percent in Wichita and 82 percent in San Diego.[30] Obviously, workers in these areas would be deeply concerned with the elimination of their jobs unless they were satisfield that alternative employment possibiilties would open up if disarmament came.

Mr. Benoit reassures us that disarmament will not come overnight. He doubts that defense expenditures would be reduced by more than $5 billion in a given year, which is less than 1 percent of our gross national product. In comparison, the defense cutback in 1954 amounted to 3 percent of our GNP, and in 1946 to 30 percent.

So far as this writer is aware, no reputable economist doubts that the nation could find useful employment for its people even

[29] "Would Disarmament Mean Depression?" *The New York Times Magazine*, April 28, 1963, p. 16. Also see Ben Seligman, "Disarmament and the Economy," *Commentary*, May, 1963; Seymour Harris, "Can We Prosper Without Arms?" *The New York Times Magazine*, November 8, 1959.

[30] Benoit, *op. cit.*, p. 16.

if major disarmament plans were adopted. Some point to the remarkable economic achievements of disarmed Germany and Japan to support their contention that modern economies can thrive without huge arms expenditures. But they also agree that cushioning the economic impact of disarmament would require some thoughtful—and bold—national planning.

As with the current employment problem, the choices with which to combat unemployment induced by disarmament are mainly stepped-up federal spending or lowered federal taxes (or some combination thereof). The "spenders" strongly support the point of view expressed in a memorandum the Kennedy administration sent to the secretary-general of the United Nations on the economic and social impact of disarmament. The memorandum stated that the United States has "a backlog of demand for public services comparable in many ways to the backlog of demand for consumer durable goods and housing and producers' plant and equipment at the end of World War II."[31]

Among the nation's urgent unmet public needs to which adequate attention might be addressed if disarmament occurred is education, which the administration declared suffers an annual shortage of some $10 to $15 billion. These billions—possibly directed to meeting building shortages on all levels; to providing special training and equipment for retarded children; to improving the education of slum children; to providing better vocational training for potential and actual high school dropouts; to offering more college loans and scholarships; to improving teacher salaries; and to enlarging adult education programs—would take up a considerable measure of slack. The memorandum also indicated that billions needed to be spent for research development and the application of adequate programs to clear up the stench, corruption, and pollution of our streams and to purify the increasingly contaminated atmosphere. (Later estimates put the cost of cleaning up our polluted rivers as high as $40 billion!) The study also foresaw the possibility of usefully spending $12 billion per year for conservation and natural resource development.

[31] Piel, *op. cit.*, p. 39.

But this is far from exhausting the list of public expenditures many regard as important. The expenditures needed to eliminate American slums and otherwise reconstruct our cities have been estimated at close to $100 billion. The improvement of deteriorated or inadequate highways could take many more billions.

Additional billions are needed for up-to-date municipal transportation systems to deal with the seemingly hopeless urban congestion that chokes so many cities. The steady drop in the nation's water tables has alarmed many experts, who say that we must make a far greater national effort to analyze the problem and provide for its correction. The use of enormous amounts of water for industrial purposes, for air conditioning, and for our increasingly urbanized population in general is making demands on our water reserves that require compensatory efforts of imposing magnitude. David Lilienthal predicts that we may have to spend hundreds of billions of dollars to assure ourselves an adequate water supply.[32]

More research needs to be devoted to the possibilities of developing solar energy to compensate for the gradual depletion of other energy sources—and to atomic and hydrogen energy as well. Large sums could fruitfully be spent on local and national beautification projects. America, some believe, can well afford to spend more for foreign aid than the two-thirds of 1 percent of the GNP now expended for that purpose. The Disarmament Agency estimates that an additional $9 billion could profitably go into space research—an area obviously offering vastly expanding possibilities for the utilization of human intelligence and energy if the nation is disposed to push rapidly toward that frontier.

Gerard Piel puts it thus: "The consensus is clear; we can offset the reduction in the arms budget by worthwhile and overdue investment in the upgrading of our human and material resources and the enhancement of our domestic existence. The possibilities inherent in the expenditure of Pentagon-size sums on these objectives stagger the imagination."[33]

[32] "300 Million Americans Would Be Wrong," *The New York Times Magazine*, January 9, 1966, p. 86.
[33] *Op. cit.*

Is our affluent society reaching such a level of satiety that the demand for the products of a work force devoted to civilian production will simply not be great enough to take the goods off the market? Is it safe to assume that we can perpetually produce more and more consumer goods without reaching the point at which consumers lose interest in simply accumulating goods with ever-declining marginal value?

Perpetually, it will be answered, is a long while. But for the plannable future, some would answer, "yes." First, human wants are basically insatiable. As living standards rise, people may want to spend their money in different ways, but considering the restlessness of man and his unceasing desire for novelty, variety, and change, it is most unlikely that he will reach a stage where more money no longer interests him. At any rate, such a prospect is so far distant that it need not concern us now.

Ask any typical American audience: how many families present would be at a loss to know how to spend their income if it were to rise by one third? The answer is predictable! Spending patterns may change drastically, but the urge to spend will remain. For example, more and more families are spending increasing amounts of money on higher education, with costs scheduled to rise much higher before this decade ends. The willingness to travel also intensifies as the means to finance this adventure appear. Millions of untraveled Americans would be delighted to spend untold billions exploring the delights of Paris, Rome, Berlin, Tokyo, Buenos Aires, Stockholm, Cairo, and the Taj Mahal, as well as traversing the less well-known portions of the globe. And as they travel, showering American dollars as they go, this in turn creates a growing market for the American goods to be exported when the dollars return. This market, it may be confidently predicted, will keep an increasing percentage of the United States work force occupied.

The desire for more private swimming pools, for more artistic furnishings, for the gratification of more cultural interests and creative desires, and for the development and enjoyment of simpler methods of individual air-borne travel (now in a rudimentary stage, but awaiting the breakthrough that is sure to come)—the human desires to be met are indeed endless. Vannevar Bush, disputing the claim that automation will lead to increasing jobless-ness, boldly declares, "There will always be enough work to do in America and everywhere else. . . ."[34]

The continued existence of widespread poverty in the United States is adduced as a further reason for the nation to press forward on the production front for many years to come. Fifty million Americans have family incomes under $4000 per year, and about 30 million of these have family incomes below $3,000. It is clear that families with incomes in this area are chronically scrabbling for little more than the bare means of existence. There can be no possibility of their helping their children through col-lege and little opportunity for them to escape a dwarfed human existence and share some of the privileges and opportunities most Americans take for granted.[35]

It is true that poverty is relative, that America's poor live well compared to that large proportion of the world's population that subsists on a per capita annual income of $100 or less. Even if incomes rose sharply, a lower strata could always be regarded as "poor," in a comparative sense. Granting this, the need to provide economic opportunities to enable these 50 million to rise to a higher plateau than they now occupy can hardly be disputed. Because it is out of the question politically (and undesirable as well) to eliminate poverty by treasury handouts, the best way to elevate many of the poor to better circumstances is for the nation to steadily increase its gross national product, enlarge its educational and employment opportunities, improve vocational training, and gradually pull the lower income groups upward along with the rest of the population.

At some point, however, the urgency of increasing our indi-

[34] "Automation's Awkward Age," *The Saturday Review*, August 11, 1962, p. 11.

[35] Dwight Macdonald, "Our Invisible Poor," *The New Yorker*, January 19, 1963; and Michael Harrington, "Our 50 Million Poor," *Commentary*, July, 1959. For a somewhat different perspective, see Herman Miller, "New Definition of Our Poor," *The New York Times Magazine*, April 24, 1963. Sharply contrasting views are seen in Robert Dwyer, "I *Know* About the Negroes and the Poor," *The National Review*, December 17, 1963, and "The War on Poverty," *The New Republic*, December 28, 1963. J. K. Galbraith's "The War on Poverty," *Harper's Magazine*, March, 1964, provides a memorable treatment of the subject.

vidual and national income will of course decline. People will prefer the option of more leisure to more income. When that point is reached, shorter working hours will be instituted, and man will face perhaps the most critical test of his existence: can he use steadily increasing leisure wisely, or will it enfeeble, enervate, and corrupt him. Already, different answers are given to the question of how wisely he is using the increased leisure *now* available.

Alfred North Whitehead once said that the vast sufferings of the Industrial Revolution grew out of a long step forward in technical innovation with no parallel steps in social, political, or economic innovation. Will our generation, faced with an economic revolution of an equally momentous order, make the same mistakes man made before?

BIBLIOGRAPHY

1. Race and Rights: Yesterday, Today, and Tomorrow

Abrams, Charles, *Forbidden Neighbors: A Study of Prejudice in Housing,* New York, Harper & Row, 1955.

Baldwin, James, *The Fire Next Time,* New York, Dial Press, 1963.

Carr, Robert C., *Federal Protection of Civil Rights: Quest For A Sword,* Ithaca, Cornell University Press, 1947.

Clark, K. B., *Dark Ghetto: Dilemmas of Social Power,* New York, Harper & Row, 1965.

Dabbs, James M., *The Southern Heritage,* New York, Knopf, 1958.

Daedalus, "The Negro American," Cambridge, The American Academy of Arts and Sciences, Fall, 1965.

Handlin, Oscar, *Fire-Bell in the Night,* Boston, Little, Brown, 1964.

Kilpatrick, James, *The Southern Case for School Segregation,* New York, Crowell-Collier, 1962.

Miller, Loren, *The Petitioners: The Story of the Supreme Court and the American Negro,* New York, Pantheon Books, 1966.

Myrdal, Gunnar, *An American Dilemma,* New York, Harper & Row, 1944.

Myrdal, Gunnar, *et. al., The Negro in America,* Gloucester, Mass., P. Smith, 1964.

Silberman, Charles E., *Crisis in Black and White,* New York, Random House, 1964.

Westin, A. F., ed., *Freedom Now,* New York, Basic Books, 1964.

Woodward, C. V., *The Strange Career of Jim Crow,* 2nd ed., New York, Oxford University Press, 1966.

2. Labor Legislation: Which Road Is the Road Ahead?

American Academy of Political and Social Science, *The Crisis in the American Trade-Union Movement,* Philadelphia, American Academy, 1963.

Beirne, J. A., *New Horizons for American Labor,* Washington, Public Affairs Press, 1963.

Brooks, T. R., *Toil and Trouble,* New York, Dial Press, 1964.

Evans, R., *Public Policy Toward Labor,* New York, Harper & Row, 1965.

Jacobs, Paul, *The State of the Unions,* New York, Atheneum, 1963.

Lens, S., *The Crisis of American Labor,* New York, Sagamore Press, 1959.

Lester, R. A., *As Unions Mature: An Analysis of the Evaluation of American Unionism,* Princeton, Princeton University Press, 1958.

Lester, R. A., ed., *Labor: Readings on Major Issues,* New York, Random House, 1965.

Millis, H. A., and E. C. Brown, *From the Wagner Act to Taft-Hartley,* Chicago, University of Chicago Press, 1950.

Reynolds, Lloyd G., *Labor Economics and Labor Relations,* 4th ed., Englewood Cliffs, N.J., Prentice-Hall, 1964.

Sultan, P. E., *The Disenchanted Unionist,* New York, Harper & Row, 1963.

Sultan, P. E., *Right-to-Work Laws: A Study of Conflict,* Los Angeles, Institute of Industrial Relations, University of California Press, 1958.

Tyler, Gus, *A New Philosophy For Labor,* New York, Fund for the Republic, 1959.

3. Billions for the Farmer?

Benedict, Murray R., *Farm Policies of the United States, 1790–1950,* New York, Twentieth Century Fund, 1953.

Benson, Ezra, *The Freedom to Farm,* Garden City, N.Y., Doubleday, 1960.

Christenson, Reo M., *The Brannan Plan: A Study in Farm Politics and Policy,* Ann Arbor, University of Michigan Press, 1959.

Cochrane, Willard, *The City Man's Guide to the Farm Problem,* Minneapolis, University of Minnesota Press, 1965.

Cochrane, Willard, *Farm Prices: Myth and Reality,* Minneapolis, University of Minnesota Press, 1958.

Duscha, Julius, *Taxpayers' Hayride,* Boston, Little, Brown, 1964.

Hathaway, D. E., *Government and Agriculture: Public Policy in a Democratic Society,* New York, Macmillan, 1963.

Higbee, Edward, *Farms and Farmers in an Urban Age,* New York, Twentieth Century Fund, 1963.

Keyserling, L. H., *Agriculture and the Public Interest,* Washington, Conference on Economic Progress, 1965.

Laloutas, T., and J. D. Hicks, *Twentieth Century Populism,* Gloucester, Mass., P. Smith, 1964.

Paarlberg, D., *American Farm Policy,* New York, Wiley, 1964.

Peterson, William H., *The Great Farm Problem,* Chicago, Regnery, 1959.

Shepherd, G. S., *Farm Policy: New Directions,* Ames, Iowa State University Press, 1964.

4. Education: What Role for Washington?

Freeman, Roger, *Financing the Public Schools,* Washington, Institute for Social Science Research, 1958, 1960 (2 vols.).

Harvard Graduate School of Education, ed., *Education and the Public Good,* Cambridge, Harvard University Press, 1964.

Kerber, A., and W. Smith, eds., *Educational Issues in a Changing Society,* Detroit, Wayne State University Press, 1962.

McCluskey, Neil, *Catholic Viewpoint on Education,* Garden City, N.Y., Hanover House, 1959.

Rockefeller Brothers Fund, *The Pursuit of Excellence: Education and the Future of America,* Garden City, N.Y., Doubleday, 1961.

Ulich, Robert, *Education of Nations: A Comparison in Historical Perspective,* Cambridge, Harvard University Press, 1961.

Ward, L. R., *Federal Aid to Private Schools*, Westminster, Md., Newman Press, 1964.

5. Medicare Now: Socialized Medicine Next?

Eckstein, Harry, *The English Health Service*, Cambridge, Harvard University Press, 1958.

Feingold, Eugene, *Medicare: Policy and Politics*, San Francisco, Chandler Publishing Co., 1966.

Gemmill, Paul F., *Britain's Search for Health*, Philadelphia, University of Pennsylvania, 1961.

Harris, Richard, *A Sacred Trust*, New York, New American Library, 1966.

Harris, Seymour, *National Health Insurance and Alternative Plans for Financing Health*, New York, League for Industrial Democracy, 1953.

Jewkes, J., and S. Jewkes, *The Genesis of the National Health Service*, Oxford, Basil Blackwell, 1961.

Johnson, Donald M., *The British National Health Service*, London, Johnson Publications, 1962.

Lindsey, Almont, *Socialized Medicine in England and Wales, 1948–61*, Chapel Hill, University of North Carolina Press, 1962.

Palyi, Melchior, *Compulsory Medical Care and the Welfare State*, Chicago, National Institute of Professional Services, 1950.

Schoeck, H., *Financing Medical Care*, Caldwell, Idaho, Caxton Printers, 1963.

Sommers, H. M., and A. R. Sommers, *Doctors, Patients, and Health Insurance*, Washington, Brookings Institution, 1961.

Thompson, W. P., *Medical Care: Programs and Issues*, Toronto, Clarke, Irwin, 1964.

6. What About the "Welfare State"?

Fox, V. J., *The Welfare Staters*, New York, Freedom Press, 1963.

Galbraith, John K., *The Affluent Society*, Boston, Houghton Mifflin, 1958.

Girvetz, H. K., *From Wealth to Welfare*, Stanford, Stanford University Press, 1950.

Goldwater, Barry, *Conscience of a Conservative*, Shepherdsville, Ky., Victor Publishing Co., 1960.

Myrdal, Gunnar, *Beyond the Welfare State*, New Haven, Yale University Press, 1963.

Reagan, M. D., *Politics, Economics, and the General Welfare*, Chicago, Scott, Foresman, 1965.

Riesman, D., *Abundance For What? And Other Essays*, Garden City, N.Y., Doubleday, 1965.

Roepke, W., *Welfare, Freedom and Inflation*, University, University of Alabama Press, 1964.

7. The War on Poverty

Bagdikian, Ben H., *In the Midst of Plenty: The Poor in America*, Boston, Beacon, 1964.

Caudill, Harry, *Night Comes to the Cumberlands*, Boston, Little, Brown, 1963.

Elman, Richard M., *The Poorhouse State: The American Way of Life on Public Assistance*, New York, Pantheon Books, 1966.

Fishman, Leo, ed., *Poverty Amid Affluence*, New Haven, Yale University Press, 1966.

Gordon, Margaret S., ed., *Poverty in America*, San Francisco, Chandler Publishing Co., 1965.

Harrington, Michael, *The Other America: Poverty in the United States*, New York, Macmillan, 1962.

May, Edgar, *The Wasted Americans*, New York, Harper & Row, 1964.

8. A Balanced Economy in a Changing World

Bator, Francis, *The Question of Public Spending*, New York, Harper & Row, 1960.

Boulding, Kenneth, and Émile Benoit, *Disarmament and the Economy*, New York, Harper & Row, 1963.

Burns, Arthur, *Prosperity Without Inflation*, New York, Fordham University Press, 1958.

Conrad, Joseph W., *Inflation, Growth and Employment*, Englewood Cliffs, N.J., Prentice-Hall, 1964.

Duscha, J., *Arms, Money and Politics*, New York, Washburn, 1965.

Hazlitt, Henry, *The Failure of the "New Economics": An Analysis of the Keynesian Fallacies*, Princeton, Van Nostrand, 1959.

Heilbroner, Robert, *The Making of Economic Society*, Englewood Cliffs, N.J., Prentice-Hall, 1962.

Heilbroner, Robert, *A Primer of Government Spending*, New York, Crowell-Collier, 1962.

Myrdal, Gunnar, *Challenge to Affluence*, New York, Pantheon, 1963.

Okun, A. M., ed., *The Battle Against Unemployment,* New York, Norton, 1965.

Ross, A. M., ed., *Unemployment and the United States,* New York, Wiley, 1964.

Seldin, J., *Automation,* New York, Coward-McCann, 1965.

Steele, G., and P. Kircher, *The Crisis We Face,* New York, McGraw-Hill, 1963.

Stern, Philip M., *The Great Treasury Raid,* New York, Random House, 1964.

Wolfbein, S. L., *Employment, Unemployment, and Public Policy,* New York, Random House, 1965.

INDEX

68 69 70 7 6 5 4